M000092964

THE GREEN VELVET MISSIONARY

God Stories
from a Jewish Believer

Steven Barry Kaplan

Copyright © 2020 by Steven Barry Kaplan

All rights reserved. No part of
this book may be reproduced
or used in any manner without
written permission of the
copyright owner except for
the use of quotations in a
book review.

For more information,

go to https://SavetheJews.org

First paperback edition June 2020

Published by:

Legacy Lane Publishing

Legacy Lane Publishing

www.LegacyLanePublishing.com

ISBN: 978-1-7352596-0-4 (paperback)
978-1-7352596-1-1 (digital)

Access
Free Witnessing Resources

Download: InSpire U App
and unlock free resources

Available July 2020
Access your tools Anywhere, Anytime
(Available on both Google Play and Apple Store)

Sign in and
Input Tracking Code: <u>800000</u>
Let us know you've read this book

What you'll find:

Witnessing Pamphlets
Workshop Training Guidebook
Daily Inspirationals
and more...

This book is dedicated to

Eddie and Lura Beckford

Your devotion to God, love for people and perseverance in light of all your persecution is most admirable. You are an inspiration to me and countless others around the world

WHAT READER'S ARE SAYING:

"I love God stories! Steven will take you on a journey of God's activity in sharing the Good News of his Messiah. Read and you will be inspired, instructed, and blessed."

Dr. Johnny Hunt, President, Southern Baptist Convention, 2008 to 2010, Senior Pastor, First Baptist Church of Woodstock, 1986 to 2019

This book was amazing! I loved reading how God faithfully walked Steve through the baby steps of his faith. How Steve humbly stayed on his face before the Lord relying on Him for every detail of his day. What an example of living a prayerful life. This book also solidified in my mind that God has an incredibly relentless love for the Jewish people. What a wonderful testimony to that! I was convicted that I need to be more intentional in my witnessing. Thanks Steve! There's something for every reader. *Lara Sparkman* (Amazon Review)

"Steven Kaplan is one of the most fiery lovers of Yeshua [Jesus] that 21st century Messianic Judaism has ever seen. His zest for seeing souls changed for eternity through a living vibrant relationship with Yeshua fuels his passion of service. We have had the honor of having Steven speak several times and he always energizes and enlivens the participants. You will love reading about his journey and the exciting walk with God that he has in sharing this love of Yeshua with the world."

Barri Cae Seif, Ph.D., Board of Directors, Jewish Outreach International (2008-2019)

"Steve Kaplan is a good friend of mine. I was just getting into ministry at First Baptist Atlanta, and Steve volunteered for me on many occasions. One could tell that Steve had a heart for ministry and a desire to share the Gospel. Because I come from a Jewish background, I had so many people come up to me and say, 'There's this guy I met out on the streets and he is Jewish and he said he knew you.' I echo the words of God that I know he will hear one day, 'Well done, good and faithful servant!'"

Pastor Paul Diamond, Assistant to Dr. Charles Stanley and Director of Local Missions, First Baptist Atlanta, GA

ACKNOWLEDGMENTS

Above everyone and over all my treasured relationships, I would like to thank God for making Himself known to me and filling my life with love, joy and peace. This book tells the story of how He came into my life in a very personal way, changed me forever and led me into ministry.

Thank you Diane K. Bell, and Legacy Lane Publishing for taking on this project and for sharing your publishing and book marketing expertise! I would like to thank my family for their love and support. God bless former co-workers Sheila Brandon and Denise Hawkins for your boldness, love and persistence to tell me about Jesus for seven months! Reverend Glenn and Mrs. Judy Harlin, thank you for your incredible support over the years. There were numerous times I wanted to quit, and God used you to keep me going!

Lee Veal, thank you for serving as the Chairman of the Board of Directors of Jewish Outreach International. You have been a valued friend, prayer warrior and Bible teacher!

Thank you to all of the Board of Directors of Jewish Outreach International past and present: Lura Beckford, Georgiana Brannan, John and Carolyn Cunningham, Dennis Kozakoff, Sharon Pollock, Moishe Rosen, Barri Cae Seif, Bill and Eleanor Tuszynski and Anna Wlasiuk. I appreciate your past and/or ongoing support, prayers and guidance. Cyril and Rhonda Gordon, I love and appreciate you both so much!

Thanks too, to all my friends at Jewish Voice Ministries. Jonathan Bernis, not only have your Messianic Leadership Roundtables and Festival Outreaches been a great blessing in my life and others, but your television program was a complete blessing in my father's life. I credit your program with discipling my father as he constantly told me he watched you on television! Thank you for all you do!

Thank you to the numerous other people who have prayed for, financially supported or contributed to our ministry in some other way. I couldn't possibly list all of you, but you are very special and greatly appreciated. This book could not have been all it is without you!

TABLE OF CONTENTS

A NOTE FROM THE AUTHOR

If first you don't succeed, try, try and try again! Writing and promoting a book has been most challenging. I have never done this before and procrastinated for many years. Thankfully, my friend Lee Veal, who serves as chairman of our Board of Directors at Jewish Outreach International, pushed me to get this done. I used to sit next to Lee and his wife when we all attended First Baptist Atlanta in 1992.

This book was originally released as "*Schlepping for Jesus*", and was launched on my father's birthday at the Christian Booksellers Convention in Orlando, Florida. My father had prayed with me to receive Jesus and was extremely proud that I had written a book! My family drove over from Tampa to celebrate. and my father took seven copies of the book, and sent them to his Jewish friends!

Later that week, we promoted the book at the Messiah Conference near Harrisburg, Pennsylvania. Since this was a Messianic Group, they preferred the book was called "*Schlepping for Yeshua*". I love my Messianic brothers and sisters and fully understand and respect their reasoning. Most Jewish believers loved the title, but most Gentiles would ask me what Schlepping meant? Since the title was causing issues and the publisher wouldn't give me a signed contract, I had no choice but to seek another publisher.

While at a conference, there was a man across from our table selling books who turned out to be a publisher. He agreed to publish my book! He renamed it, "*God Stories **f**rom the Jewish Mission Field*", and we had a signed contract.

When the new book, which was predominately the old book re-titled less the last publisher's additions, was finally finished,

I was so excited. I try to meet with Lee once a week and was so happy to finally give him a copy of the book!

Lee had been pushing me for years to get this book finished ...along with my friend Elaine Meder in Sunday School who was praying it would finally get done.   When I met Lee for lunch, he handed me a large check for the ministry which was a tithe from the severance pay he had just received from his previous job. Of all the days for me to be able to turn around and give him a copy of a book of some 25 years of our ministry!

I launched the new book on Facebook. Caren Oshen, one of my friends who I went to Hebrew School and High School with some forty years ago, congratulated me on the book, said she was going to buy a copy and couldn't wait to read it?   You could have knocked me over with a feather!

I was invited to do a "Witnessing to Jewish People" workshop in the Dallas/Ft. Worth area and was trying to get a table at a very pro-Israel conference in Dallas around the same time. I e-mailed the conference and called many times, but for some reason no one would respond to me about getting a table at their conference?

It turns out my Friends in New York were having a wedding for their daughter the same weekend as the pro-Israel Conference. I really wanted to go to the wedding, but I wasn't invited, but the last thing I wanted to do was drive up to New York before driving out to Dallas?

My two friends Steve and Patty met each other at my going away party when I went to college. He was my best friend and I even went on a family vacation to Hawaii with him and his family.   She lived four houses away and our mothers were business partners.

Not only would I know almost everyone from the bride's side of the wedding, but their daughter was marrying a pastor with a church three miles from where my friends Dean and Elaine Mabry started a church in Ilion, New York and Elaine's cousin actually worked at the Groom's church!

Pat's sister Carolyn and I were good friends growing up. Carolyn has Cerebral Palsy and told me she was allowed to have someone to assist her and invited me to the wedding to assist her! Patty said it was ok, so I was now invited to the wedding I wasn't really invited to!

I had an extra weekend before the wedding and looked for events I could attend beforehand on the way to break up the long drive. As fate would have it, the Baltimore Book Festival was taking place the week before the wedding. Baltimore has one of the largest Orthodox Jewish communities in the United States, and Jewish people like to read. I had no doubt God was leading me to get a table at the book festival. The festival table rental and hotel cost was about $1,000.

I really didn't have an extra $1,000 to spend, but I knew God was leading me to step out in faith. The day before I drove up to Baltimore, I received a check in the mail from a new supporter in the amount of $1,000! I just stood there and cried.

Thousands of people walked by our booth during this three day event and were challenged! Many Jewish people and others stopped at our booth. Some looked, some took Gospel tracts, some asked questions and some walked away angry. We sold six God Stories, 13 evangelistic t-shirts and supplied several with Gospel tracts!

I stayed with my brother on Long Island. I called up Caren and made arrangements to have lunch. I met with her and asked, "Ok, what's going on?" She said her mother had just become a believer in Jesus, and has been insisting she read certain things. Caren said she didn't want to read something her mother suggested. She said we grew up the same way, and then saw my book on line and wanted to hear what I had to say. She was going on vacation right after the book was launched on Facebook, so she bought a copy and read the whole thing on vacation.

I shared the Gospel with Caren. I said there were so many coincidences in my book that it would be hard not to believe Jesus is the real thing! She agreed. I asked her what was stopping her from believing and she said she needed a sign? I just looked at her and said, "Its all your fault! My life has been miserable for the last few months. I wanted to go to a conference in Dallas, but they wouldn't respond to me? I didn't want to drive up to a wedding I wasn't invited to but then got invited to before driving to Dallas. God wanted me up in New York just to talk with you and that is your sign!" Caren agreed and then prayed with me to receive Jesus and has been reading the Bible ever since!

I tried to contact my publisher to order more books, but couldn't get through? I had to go through his wife on Facebook to get his new contact information. Apparently, he changed his name? When I finally did get in touch with him, I ordered more books. He sent me a bill for books I never received and he was unable to locate? It got to the point where I knew something wasn't kosher. I googled the publisher and found a "less than positive" letter from one of his other authors? This left me no choice but to terminate my contract!

I was at the Messianic conference in California. A woman named Angela had stopped by my table the year before and then came back this year to help. She told me her sister is the Jewish Outreach Leader at her nephew's church in Dallas, and that I should meet them. Angela asked if I would be going to Dallas anytime soon? As fate would have it, I was on my way to Texas and would be going through Dallas.

While in Dallas, I met with Angela's sister Jeanine who turned out to be an author and highly recommended I use her publisher, Diane K. Bell with Legacy Lane Publishing.

Diane is now my new publisher, and was instrumental in publishing and marketing this new edition of my book...I've added new stories, give-a-ways and a new brand new title. My book and I will now be known as, "The Green Velvet Missionary!"...Thanks in part, to Diane!

JEWS FOR JESUS

In the early 1970s, Moishe Rosen left his position with what is now known as Chosen People Ministries based in New York City. Moishe started a new ministry known as Jews for Jesus in San Francisco, California. Jews for Jesus became a worldwide outreach to Jewish people with hundreds of missionaries on staff. Their street evangelism campaigns challenged millions of people worldwide. Many Jewish people have come to faith in Jesus through the ministry of Jews for Jesus. I am highly blessed and honored to be endorsed by Moishe Rosen!

In Memoriam

Moishe Rosen

April 12, 1932, to May 19, 2010
Founder of Jews for Jesus

From an undated open letter from 2009:

Dear Friend,

If you know the Lord Jesus Christ, if you love Him, and those He loves, then you'll be concerned to see that the Gospel is brought to the lost sheep of the house of Israel and you are surely my friend.

I was delighted to be able to meet Steven Kaplan. In these days, hundreds of energetic young Jews—talented, and committed—have been coming to faith in Y'shua (that's the Jewish way to say Jesus). Steven Kaplan is certainly one of the more impressive of these people, and I feel privileged to be able to endorse his ministry.

Steven Kaplan would qualify for service with our Jews for Jesus staff, but I think he's chosen a better path. We've had no less benefit of him in our ministry. He's been on most of our campaigns, and has had as much experience witnessing to Jews as our regular staff members. I think that he has chosen well to be independent of, yet cooperative with all other Jewish missions. When he serves with us on a campaign, he looks to his friends to support his ministry, and thus he's been able to be more available for direct, face-to-face type of witnessing than many of our regular staff.

Steven has a humble spirit. He's able to rejoice in the works and the achievements of others. But at the same time, he zealously and diligently serves on his own. Steve is a person who can manage himself quite well. No mission leader would ask more of him than he asks of himself. I've found him to be a person of integrity and honesty—one who does not boast, but truthfully tells the message of the Messiah. I personally support him because I want to have part in the good work he's doing. I feel that I can share a little of his achievement. Please take this letter as my unqualified endorsement of Steven Kaplan and his ministry.

Most sincerely,

Moishe Rosen

From a letter to the Board of Directors of Jewish Outreach
International, dated March 16, 2009:

Dear Friends:

Thank you for your invitation to serve with you in advancing the cause of Y'shua through the ministry of Jewish Outreach International. Because of where I'm at in my life, I can't attend board meetings, but I do want to be known as being part of Steven Kaplan's team. I will try to uphold his ministry by praying, by providing some of the finances, and by promoting the ministry to all those who love Y'shua.

I want you to know that I solicited this position from Steven, because I want to be part of what God is doing through him and other dynamic young people.

Most sincerely,

Moishe Rosen

LIFE OR DEATH?

Bell & Howell

When my Bell & Howell co-worker said, "If you don't believe in Jesus, you're gonna burn in hell!" I was absolutely shocked! I thought, *How dare she say that to me? Didn't she know I'm Jewish? Didn't she know my grandfather barely escaped the pogroms in Eastern Europe?* I was so mad that she had the audacity to say that to me! But then I thought, *What if she was right, and I didn't listen? What if there really is a hell, and she's the one God sent to warn me?*

So for seven months, I listened! She and another co-worker told me, "There's only one God, the God of Abraham, Isaac and Jacob." They told me, "God is holy and man is sinful, and we are separated from God by our sin." They told me, "God came to earth in the body of Jesus, the Jewish Messiah, laid down His life on the cross to atone for our sin and rose from the dead just like the Hebrew Scriptures said He would."

They told me, "By putting your trust in Messiah your sins are forgiven and you can have a personal relationship with God who wants to fill your life with love, peace and joy." Honestly, I didn't know I was waiting for a Messiah. I went to Hebrew schools for five years but only remember learning the alphabet and some prayers and watching Ku Klux Klan movies illustrating anti-Semitism.

I do know I am a sinner because I used to fast on Yom Kippur every year to atone for my sin. I remember missing classes at college one year to go to services, but thought, *what's the point? I'm only going to get drunk and act stupid again the next day.*

I asked my co-workers questions most Jewish people ask: "Will I still be Jewish if I believe in Jesus? If Jesus is the Messiah, why don't the Rabbis believe in Him? I believe in One God; why do you have three?" My co-workers were very loving and patient with me and sincerely answered all my questions. They quoted verses from the Hebrew Scriptures I sometimes didn't understand, but it made me curious to keep asking questions.

My co-workers told me they had a personal relationship with God. They believed when they prayed to God He answered them directly. I asked them how they could know God speaks to them. They told me, "You will just know." Out of everything they told me, this was the hardest thing for me to believe. They really think God talks to them? While in Hebrew school I learned how to pray to God, but I never expected God to answer back. Only nuts think God talks to them, or so I thought...

Even with working this job from midnight to 8 AM and all the other part-time jobs during the day, I couldn't even pay the interest on the $92,000 that I owed from my failed business and college loans.

Bankruptcy Court

I eventually filed for bankruptcy. I decided to ask my cousin to be my bankruptcy lawyer. When her father, my accountant, gave me her phone number, I couldn't believe it. The last four digits of our phone numbers were identical. Her number started with 666 and my phone number started with 822. This was very strange because most people, even Jewish people, know 666 is supposed to represent the devil, but was there any significance to the 822? I didn't know why, but I just knew there was!

In July 1992 I filed for bankruptcy. My $67,000 in credit card debt was gone, but I still had to pay the $25,000 in college loans.

Muttontown, New York

I came home from bankruptcy court and felt like such a failure. I lay on my bed and looked at the ceiling, questioning life. I thought about many dark times in my life. I quit law school before I even started. It had taken me seven years to graduate from college after flunking out of the first one I attended. My excessive drinking landed me in jail one night. I tried for six months to get a job with AT&T, had many interviews, but never got hired. My failed business landed me in bankruptcy court. It seemed everything I tried to do was meaningless. I thought, *Do I just work and give my parents the money? I give up! What is life all about?*

Breakfast

The next day, Denise took me out to breakfast and said, "If you don't read your Bible, you're gonna burn in hell!"

I said, "Yeah, yeah, yeah. I heard all that already!" When she challenged me to read Isaiah 53, I put my hand up and said, "I'm not reading any of that Christian stuff!"

She said, "Isaiah 53 is in the Old Testament." I must admit that although I learned how to read Hebrew for my Bar Mitzvah portion, I had never really studied the Bible before.

Muttontown, New York

I went home and looked for the books I was given at my Bar Mitzvah. They were buried in the front hall closet. I found my Chumash (the Torah and Haftorah portions from the Tanakh or Old Testament) that I read at my Bar Mitzvah service. To my surprise, Isaiah 53 was not in my Chumash. I thought, *Why were Christians telling me to read something my Jewish brethren left out?* I borrowed a Bible and read:

"We all like sheep have gone astray.
Each of us turned to his own way.So ADONAI [THE LORD] has laid on
Him the iniquity of us all."

-Isaiah 53:6

I couldn't believe it. There it was in the Old Testament, and it sure sounded a lot like Jesus! I began to question everything. *Did I believe in God?* I thought about it. *Was there a "Big Bang" that put the earth into orbit? Did single cell amoebas crawl out of the ocean and form into human beings? Maybe, but it seemed highly unlikely. So how did the materials that caused the Big Bang come into being? The only answer I could come up with was God, an all-knowing, Supreme Being, who put everything into motion.*

I thought about the Orthodox Jews who don't accept Jesus as the Messiah. *Why didn't they?* They are supposed to be the keepers of Judaism. I also thought about the Orthodox Jews I had done business with. *They sometimes lied to me and cheated me then went to the back room to put on phylacteries and pray.* (Phylacteries or tefillin are religious gear containing Scripture verses placed on the arm and head by devout Jews).

I knew that this kind of contradictory practice was not what Judaism was supposed to be about. I also thought there was no way I was going to wear those black suits, black hats and grow long sideburns, especially in summer. I just knew that wasn't what it was about! I knew there had to be some other way…

SALVATION

Muttontown, New York

On August 5, 1992, I cried out to God and asked, *God, if everything my co-workers told me is true, then You tell me and You show me!*

"For Jewish people ask for signs and Greek people seek after wisdom, but we proclaim Messiah crucified—a stumbling block to Jewish people and foolishness to Gentile people, but to those who are called (both Jewish and Greek people), Messiah [is], the power of God and the wisdom of God. For the foolishness of God is wiser than men, and the weakness of God is stronger than men."

-1 Corinthians 1:22-24

I looked up at the sand paint on my ceiling and saw a vision of two faces. I couldn't believe what I was seeing. The faces looked like two versions of an Orthodox Rabbi that I took to be Jesus. I believe God was telling me Jesus had already been here, and He would be coming back!

I remembered a time when I ran away from home, started reading the Bible, saw a cross in the sky and just ignored it. So I pushed away my sliding shutters, cleared away the cobwebs and looked out my window to see if there was another cross in the sky. There wasn't, but there was a praying mantis in my window pointing to the vision on my ceiling.

I went into the kitchen and told my mother I saw Jesus on the ceiling. She just looked at me kind of funny, rolled her eyes and said, "That's nice." I went back into my room. I thought, *God, I'm Jewish. Give me the belief level that I need to have.* I felt this incredible sense of love, peace and joy I had never known before. I knew God was real, and He had just spoken to me personally! I knew everything they told me about Jesus was true. My life had just changed, and I knew it would never be the same. I started crying. I picked up my Bible, and I started reading Matthew. I quickly switched to Revelation because I wanted to know what was going to happen in the future!

Later that night, I spoke to my brother on the phone. I told him what had happened. He said, "So big deal, there was a praying mantis in your window. There are always praying mantises in the window." I had never seen a praying mantis in my window before.

The next day, I was thinking about what had happened. I looked out the window and to my astonishment, there was another praying mantis. This time it was all scrunched up, and I knew God was telling me I saw what I saw the day before. That was the last time I ever saw a praying mantis in my window!

I started thinking, and I knew it was time to leave New York. I was 29 at the time, and I did not want to turn 30 and still be living at home. I was about to finish my computer degree and thought about where I could move to get work. I had always wanted to be a Blackjack dealer, so I thought about Las Vegas! Yeah, Las Vegas was booming, and there were probably a lot of computer jobs there as well as the opportunity to deal Blackjack. Yes, I would go to Las Vegas.

I opened a road atlas to a map of the United States. I started planning my trip to Las Vegas and looked at all the states I could drive through. All of a sudden my eyes were drawn to Georgia on the map. I just shook it off and started planning my route from New York to Las Vegas, but again my eyes were drawn to Georgia. More specifically, I saw Atlanta on the map. A third time, I started planning my route from New York to Las Vegas, but my eyes were supernaturally drawn to Atlanta for some reason?

I sat up and thought to myself, *I'm supposed to go to Atlanta?* Then Coca-Cola popped into my head. I thought, *I'm supposed to go to Atlanta and work at Coca-Cola?* God flashed a woman's blank face with curly hair parted to the side. *I asked God who I was going to marry? I fell asleep, and when I woke up, the name of a woman was on my lips.*

Bell & Howell

I went back to work and told my co-workers what had happened. They were so excited. They told me there were many people in that office praying for my salvation! Sheila told me something profound. She said, "God knows everything that has happened, is happening and will happen. Why don't you line your life up with God's plan for you?"

Muttontown, New York

I started reading the Bible (Basic Instructions Before Leaving Earth) from cover to cover and forced myself to read at least one page every day. I visited some churches as well as some Messianic congregations (groups where Jewish and non-Jewish believers in Jesus worship together in a Jewish way).

I ordered an Atlanta apartment guide which came in the mail two weeks later. I opened it up and doubtingly thought, *Ok, God, You want me to move to Atlanta. Which apartment should I live in?* As I was thumbing through the pages of the apartment guide, it was as if a light shined on the page for the Scandinavian House in downtown Atlanta. I knew that was where God was telling me to live. I thought it was ugly and didn't want to live there. I sent away for four apartment brochures.

I started sending my resume to The Coca-Cola Company. I was hoping to get a job there before moving to Atlanta to make things easier. I must have sent my resume eight times and had eight rejection letters.

My co-worker suggested a book for me to buy at a Christian bookstore which happened to be near where my family used to live on the south shore of Long Island. I called information for the number of the store. As they recited the number, I dropped the phone in shock! This number was only too familiar to me. The Christian bookstore had actually gotten my family's old telephone number!

About a month later, I had a profound experience with God. It wasn't an audible voice or anything like that, but I just knew in my Spirit God was telling me He had forgiven me, and I had to forgive someone. I thought, *I don't want to.* A second time, God told me He had forgiven me, and I had to forgive this person. Again, *I didn't want to!* A third time, God told me He had forgiven me, and I had to be ready to forgive.

I saw this person as an unforgiven sinner without Jesus. Suddenly, I just forgave this person and was released from years of bitterness, anger and hate! Jesus gave me the grace and freedom to forgive and love this person.

"But if you do not forgive others, neither will your Father forgive your transgressions.

-Matthew 6:15

Bell & Howell

I eventually got three of the four apartment brochures I had sent for, but I really didn't like any of them. I was having doubts about moving to Atlanta. My co-workers insisted God had spoken to me, and I must follow him to Atlanta.

That night I was driving home from work listening to Christian music on the radio. As soon as I switched the channel, my car started shaking. I looked out the car window to see if the ground was shaking, because I thought I was in an earthquake. I found out later my struts were no good. I had just spent a lot of money to have the car fixed and really didn't want to throw any more money into the car. I knew God was telling me to move to downtown Atlanta where I could use public transportation.

Muttontown, New York

My brother was getting married on October 25, and my mother's birthday is October 26. I decided I would take a leap of faith and follow Jesus to Atlanta on October 27. Two weeks before I was to move to Atlanta, I received a brochure in the mail from the Scandinavian House, and I just knew that was where God was telling me to live. The apartment building was on the street directly across from the phone company. I thought *it would be nice to live there and work at the phone company.*

Bell & Howell

I asked my co-workers where I should go to church in Atlanta. They told me there was a really famous pastor there with the biggest church in Atlanta, and I should go there. They gave me a going away party and a mug with the name of the woman I thought God had told me I would be marrying.

Muttontown, New York

My mother hosted a bridal shower for my future sister-in-law. Although it was just for women, I was asked to film the shower on video. One of my cousins asked me why I was moving to Atlanta. I took a deep breath, told her I had become a Christian and Jesus told me to. She grabbed my arm and thanked me for sharing that with her. She told me she was almost paralyzed, but Jesus came to her and told her she would not be paralyzed!

As I filmed the bridal shower, I was drawn to my sister's "gag-gift", which was a miniature bridal party made of trolls wearing little tuxedos and dresses made from the same material as the bridesmaid's outfits. The dresses were made out of green velvet! I was mesmerized by the trolls and just filmed them over and over and over. *What was God up to? Atlanta, Coca-Cola, 822 and green velvet?*

My Brother's Wedding

I was the best man at my brother's wedding. The Rabbi asked me to sign the Ketubah (Jewish marriage contract) which is supposed to be signed by Jews. I was rather nervous because I didn't know if I was still Jewish. *Was I?* Of course I was! The term "Jew" comes from the name "Judah" and actually means someone who worships or acknowledges God! The most Jewish thing you can do is believe in the Jewish God who came to earth by indwelling the body of the Jewish Messiah!

I made the toast at the wedding but didn't finish my drink. Jesus supernaturally took the desire of alcohol away from me. It was October 25, 1992, and that was the last alcoholic drink I ever had.

Muttontown, New York

My favorite movie is *The Sound of Music*. I decided to give my mother a *Sound of Music* video for her birthday before I left for Atlanta.

Newark, New Jersey

On October 27, 1992, at Newark International Airport in New Jersey, I hugged my family good-bye, turned and preceded down the long gateway to my plane. My family thought this was just another crazy phase in my crazy life.

I paused for a few seconds, became teary-eyed and thought about what I was doing. *I was leaving my family, my friends, my job and all my familiar surroundings. I was leaving everyone and everything I knew. I had given away all my possessions except for a one-way plane ticket to Atlanta, the*

33

items I could carry in two suitcases, $1,100 in cash, the clothes on my back and a debt for $25,000 worth of college loans I still had to pay back.

In that moment, I literally died to my old life and walked onto a plane that would take me to my new life. You could say I was born again! As I sat waiting for the plane to take off, I thought about *all the twists and turns my life had taken during my 29 years as well as the events that led up to this leap of faith into uncertainty.*

THE PROMISED LAND

Atlanta, Georgia

I woke up as the plane landed in Atlanta, lifted the shutter and looked out the window. I had so many emotions. *I was leaving everything—my family, my friends and my job—to follow this Jesus I barely knew!*

Whoever heard of a Jew believing in Jesus? I couldn't believe I was doing this. What if someone were to ask me why I moved to Atlanta? Would I have the courage to tell them? Did God really tell me to move to Atlanta? Did God really tell me to work at Coca-Cola? What significance did 822 and green velvet have?

Butler Street YMCA

I got my luggage and took a cab downtown. I really didn't know that much about Atlanta. I had made reservations at the YMCA on Butler Street. It was only $64 a week, and I didn't want to spend a lot of money. My cab driver stopped in front of the YMCA and asked, "Do you really want to get out here?" I asked, "Why not?" I had no idea it was one of the less desirable neighborhoods of Atlanta. I went inside to check in, and the desk clerk, a Black man, raised his eyebrows when he saw me. He too asked, "Do you really want to stay here?"

I brought my stuff up to my room. It was definitely not what I was used to. The room was small and dirty. The washcloth in my room looked as though someone had checked their car oil with it. I had to share a communal bathroom on my floor. It definitely wasn't the six-bedroom, four-bathroom house with a built-in swimming pool on the North Shore of Long Island I had grown accustomed to.

There was no phone, so I had to walk around the corner to use a pay phone. People were looking at me kind of funny, maybe because I was the only white person in the area. I called my mother to tell her I had made it ok.

As I hung up the phone, I asked God what I was doing there. I told *Him how anxious I was and how clueless I was about living in Atlanta. Just as I asked God, Why am I here? I turned the corner and saw a church with a*

35

big sign that said, Jesus Saves! Yes, Jesus saves us from eternal separation from God.

The Scandinavian House

I applied for an apartment in the Scandinavian House, the apartment building I believed God wanted me to live in. I wasn't able to qualify on my own, but they were willing to allow my parents to co-sign for the apartment. I ate breakfast near the apartment building and was served some white stuff called grits, whatever that was. For years, I would look up at the sky in disbelief that I was living in Atlanta, the deep South, far from the familiar ocean location I had called home.

First Baptist Atlanta

There were five different churches all around the Scandinavian House. On November 1, 1992, I walked into the big one on the next street for the very first time. The greeter at the door asked if I was single and sent me to the Singles building. They asked if I was there for Dr. Stanley, and I asked, "Who's that?" They told me he was a world famous pastor on television and that their church, First Baptist Atlanta, was probably the largest in the city. Needless to say I was speechless because I realized that was where my co-worker had told me to go to church!

Some of the singles befriended me, and took me to the church service after Sunday School. Before the service started, I asked them how much it cost to join the church, and they laughed at me. (You have to pay to join a synagogue.) They told me it didn't cost anything to join the church. My new friends, actually brothers and sisters in Messiah, started bringing me to the Tuesday night Singles' Bible Study. They picked me up and took me home.

The Scandinavian House

I moved into my new apartment. I had no furniture, but I had a blanket and pillow and slept on the carpeted floor in my bedroom. I ate my meals on a cardboard box in the dining area. Again, it was not the North Shore of Long Island, but I was thrilled to be there because I had a new life on so many different levels.

I used a pay phone in the lobby of my apartment building and signed up for a telephone number with voicemail from the phone company so I could look for a job. I found out which temporary agency The Coca-Cola Company used and called them.

Atlanta, Georgia

The agency had me come in for testing and an interview. I passed with flying colors. I told the agency I wanted to work at The Coca-Cola Company, and they told me I should have gone to their onsite agency to apply. I asked if I could do that and they said yes.

The Coca-Cola Company

I went to The Coca-Cola Company and called the agency from the lobby, to get an interview. They told me I should not have come down there without an appointment (even though the other office had sent me), and that I must leave. I tried getting an appointment, but couldn't. I was devastated.

The Scandinavian House

I asked God where I should work. I went to the pay phone and opened the phone book to the temporary agencies. To my astonishment, I opened right to an agency I had worked for in New York but didn't like. I didn't want to work for that agency again, but I knew God was leading me to it.

Secretary of State

I started accepting one-day and two-day assignments. My very first job in Atlanta was shredding documents at the Secretary of State's office.

Phipps Plaza

They sent me to an assignment setting up a new store at Phipps Plaza, and the job lasted a few days, ending on Sunday, November 8. I thought to myself, *I just started going to church, and I'm already missing a Sunday.*

There were 30 people who came to work that Sunday, and the supervisor said they needed two people to volunteer not to work that day. He looked right at me when **he said that, and I knew God was saying to go to church.**

First Baptist Atlanta

I wanted to join the church that day and get baptized, but I got there late and got lost going from the balcony to the downstairs. The church was rather large and the layout was somewhat confusing.

Bobby McCoy's House

My friend took me to Bible study the following Tuesday night, and I met Jeff Jordan. Jeff worked at The Coca-Cola Company and offered to pass my resume around! While we were at the Bible study, I saw a vision. This time it was John the Baptist. I couldn't believe it. I looked around the room to see if anyone else saw it, but no one seemed to. I don't know how I knew it was John the Baptist; I just knew, and I knew I needed to be baptized.

First Baptist Atlanta

I stopped by the church to ask questions about joining and such. To my surprise they sent me to the counseling center to meet a counselor, Paul Diamond, who just happened to be a Jewish believer in Jesus, also. It was great to meet him. He spent almost four hours explaining to me the basis of our faith in both the Old and New Testaments.

On November 15, 1992, I went to Sunday School and gave my resume to Jeff Jordan. After Sunday School I went to church and made sure to sit right in the front row so I could go up and join the church after the service. They were having a new members and Baptism class before the evening service, with a Baptism service at the evening service. What a very special blessing it was to be baptized on November 15, as it was actually the anniversary of my Bar Mitzvah.

As I went to change for my baptism, I paused before walking into one of the changing rooms. I could have picked any one of several but walked into the one God would have me to walk into. The deacons put your name on a sticker and put it on your robe so they can say your name when the pastor is baptizing you.

Someone had pulled their sticker off and put it on the wall of the changing room I walked into. I pulled the sticker off the wall and was in total shock because it was Jeff Jordan's sticker! It was a sign from God, and I thought to myself: *What can I do? How can I serve?* I was baptized in the "Jordan" River (actually, the First Baptist Atlanta baptismal pool) and was crossing into the Promised Land with Jesus!

GOD PROVIDES

The Scandinavian House

I was out of money. I had no phone in my apartment and would check for job assignments on my voice mail by using a pay phone. I was really upset. I feared I was on the verge of becoming homeless. I was more than ready, willing and able to work, but I had no easy way to check and see if I had gotten an interview or been offered a job.

Upset, I lay down on my blanket on the floor and started to fall asleep. All of a sudden one of the songs we sang in Sunday School started going through my head: *Lord, You are, more precious, than silver. Lord, You are, more costly, than gold. I thought to myself, gold, gold! I can pawn my gold college ring!* I jumped up, grabbed the ring, went to a pawn shop and used the money to buy a telephone.

Two hours later the phone rang with a three-month assignment at AT&T! I couldn't believe it. I tried and tried and tried for six months to get a job at AT&T up North, but I couldn't, but God can!

AT&T Abernathy Road

It was so exciting to be starting as the receptionist in the AT&T Health Affairs Department at their Sandy Springs location on Roswell Road and Abernathy. I met with the head Health Administrator, who was a doctor, and he asked me why I came to Atlanta. I told him I had become a Christian and God told me to move to Atlanta. He quickly changed the subject...

As part of my new job at AT&T working at the front desk, I catalogued boxes of medical records that had been transcribed onto microfiche. They explained my receptionist duties, and I asked what I was supposed to do if someone called with a drug problem? They said that never happens, but the very first phone call was from an employee on drugs wanting help! I worked with several nurses. One nurse, Hazel, had a daughter in the Singles' group at First Baptist Atlanta and her other daughter worked for The Coca-Cola Company!

The Scandinavian House

It was such a blessing to have a steady paycheck. I called my family to wish them a happy Thanksgiving. My brother asked if I had a bed, and I told him I couldn't afford one. He kept questioning me? Another family member got on the phone and asked why Jesus didn't give me a bed? I said, "If Jesus wants me to have a bed, I'll have a bed."

The Salvation Army

The next day I walked into a Salvation Army Thrift Store and saw a bunch of beautiful leather couches. I asked the Lord if I could buy one so people could come over after church, sit around and talk about Him. I looked at the $450 price tag, and I knew it wasn't the Lord's will for me to buy a couch at that time. I asked if they had any dining room tables, and the sales clerk said, "No, they're always the first thing to go." He looked around quickly, scratched his head and said, "Oh, you're lucky. There's one!"

I looked at the price tag, and it was only $39! I couldn't believe it was so cheap! I asked the clerk if that was the right price, and he said it wasn't. Since it was the day after Thanksgiving, it was considered a holiday and everything was 25% off. It was only $29, and they had someone deliver it for $10.

The Scandinavian House

When the delivery man brought my dining room table over, he looked into my bedroom and noticed I had no bedroom set. That night, he brought me a mattress and box spring with a headboard and footboard and a dresser for only $100! Jesus wanted me to have a bed!

I was so poor in those days. I'd go to singles' functions at church and take home leftover pizza and freeze it. I'd buy five cans of tomato sauce for $1 and boxes of spaghetti and cans of green beans on sale. I'd wash my clothes in the kitchen sink and hang them to dry in the front hall closet and in the bathroom to save on the coin laundry downstairs. I couldn't be happier because I had a new life with Jesus filled with love, peace and joy!

My supervisor at AT&T had given me three months to catalog all the medical records at the office in Sandy Springs, but I finished them all in one week. Apparently the guy who had the job before me would talk on the phone all day.

AT&T Peachtree Street

They didn't want to let me go and were able to send me to organize the records at the Health Affairs office at the AT&T building that was on Peachtree Street downtown. This was great for me because I was able to walk to work and save on public transportation costs.

AT&T Fulton Industrial Boulevard

It only took a short time to organize the records at the AT&T office on Peachtree Street, so they sent me to a third office in South Atlanta on Fulton Industrial Boulevard. I had to take two trains and a bus to the last stop on the route in order to be at work at 7:00 AM. every morning. This was rough, especially since I was making little more than minimum wage.

As I rode the bus to work early in the morning, I struggled. Here I was getting up at the crack of dawn, taking two trains and a bus to be at work by 7 AM for just above minimum wage. I asked the Lord why. He told me I was to be there for Hattie, my supervisor. One morning I arrived to find a lot of activity. Apparently Hattie had been in a car accident the night before. They had to get a nurse from the other location to fill in for her.

As the day progressed, we received updates about the emergency surgery Hattie had undergone. Finally, we received word that she had passed away. There were over 400 employees at this location, and she was the nurse everyone knew and loved. They had to be very careful about announcing her passing as they were afraid pandemonium would break out. I ministered to scores of grieving employees who came to the office to talk about her and the afterlife. Then I knew why God had me endure the travel to that job and had placed me there as an office receptionist while cleaning up records.

AT&T Abernathy Road

After my three-month assignment ended, I was offered a one-year job in another department at AT&T back on Roswell Road in Sandy Springs. It paid $8 an hour, and I had to work in a room without any windows in very

43

close quarters. I worked one day and told the agency I didn't want to continue there. They didn't look favorably upon this and wouldn't place me afterwards. I felt bad and obviously didn't learn my lesson (trust God) from the last assignment. Even though I left, I prayed that if it was God's will for me to work there that He would return me to AT&T.

> *"Trust in ADONAI with all your heart,*
> *lean not on your own understanding.*
> *In all your ways acknowledge Him,*
> *and He will make your paths straight."*

> *-Proverbs 3:5-6*

The Coca-Cola Company

Now that I had messed up with the temp (temporary employment) agency, I was unemployed again and struggling financially. I tried the temp agency at Coke and they finally brought me in to register. I called and called and called, but they wouldn't place me in any assignments?

The Scandinavian House

I had no income to pay the rent. Then one day the phone rang, and I was so excited! I thought it might be my agency with a job, but it was one of the singles from church. She told me I should ask the church to pay my rent. I just laughed and thought, *There's no way the church would be interested in paying my rent.*

First Baptist Atlanta

Nevertheless, I went to my church and they did pay my rent that month. I couldn't believe it, and I praise God for it! My friend also told me our church had a Thursday night ministry to homeless people, and they fed them and the volunteers. I started volunteering. Initially I started volunteering for the free food; but for five years, I continued to minister to the homeless.

One night as I came to volunteer with the homeless, the manager told me they were shorthanded and I had a choice. I could either lead music or share my testimony. It was a no brainer, I shared my testimony. I told them about my sleeping on the floor and eating meals on a cardboard box, and they stood up **and applauded! God often brings us through things to benefit others.**

AT&T Peachtree Street

I registered with other temp agencies until I could get a job. Ironically, one of the new agencies gave me a short-term assignment on the 8th floor back at the AT&T office on Peachtree Street.

Heery International

Another agency gave me a two-month assignment at an architectural firm at 999 Peachtree Street, only a few blocks from my apartment. It only paid $5.50 an hour, but I was glad to have steady income.

As I walked into work one morning, I reached into my pocket and happened to find 45 cents! I immediately ran to the coffee shop, bought some candy and shoved it in my mouth so fast I almost choked on it!

Later that day I walked into the break room and noticed a vending machine. The machine sold various types of cheese and cracker snacks for 45 cents! I stood there and thought *how foolish I was to squander that little bit of money on something stupid like candy when I could have had something a little more nutritious. I just looked at the machine and thought about which one of the eight different types I could have bought!*

The Scandinavian House

My friend Jan called to say she wanted to bring me something. This wonderful sister from church came over with a big hunk of sandwich meat! What a blessing she was, and how generous of her to do that! As she left and I started closing the door, she stopped me and said she had almost forgotten. Although I hadn't mentioned it to her, she reached into her purse and pulled out the exact cheese and crackers I had wanted from the vending machine!

> *"My God will fulfill every need of yours*
> *according to the riches of His glory in Messiah."*
> *-Philippians 4:19*

ECHAD = THREE IN ONE

The Scandinavian House

It was kind of lonely living by myself downtown with no television. I would often stare out the window at the BellSouth Tower directly across the street and think how nice it would be to work there. I volunteered at church and was there whenever the doors were open. I also volunteered at the Fox Theatre, which was on the next block from my apartment, so I could see shows for free.

I would actually spend a lot of time looking at the mailbox stuffers rather than automatically throwing them out. At least *someone* was writing to me. I would see an advertisement for a sectional couch, with an ottoman and throw-cushions, for $499. I would ask the Lord if I could get that so people could come over after church, and we could sit around and talk about Him.

My apartment building was having a door decorating competition for Christmas. First place was $100 off the rent for January! I knew putting gift wrap and fancy packages on the door would win, but the Lord led me to decorate it His way.

I covered the door with bright red wrapping paper because Jesus' blood was shed for our sins. I made a tree out of cotton balls to represent the Holy Spirit and Jesus being the Tree of Life. I put nine presents under the tree. The presents were addressed to mankind from Jesus and included the fruits of the Spirit found in the Brit Chadashah (New Testament).

"But the fruit of the Ruach is love, joy, peace, patience, kindness, goodness, faithfulness, gentleness, and self-control—against such things there is no law. Now those who belong to Messiah[d] have crucified the flesh with its passions and desires."

-Galatians 5:22-24

I didn't win the contest, but I won for doing the will of God. On Christmas Day, Dale, a friend from church called. I knew this friend from Sunday School, and he worked in maintenance at an apartment complex. People often left furniture behind when they moved out, and Dale had a truck. That night he brought over four dining room chairs, two lamps and my first couch, an act which truly represented the Spirit of Christmas.

I taped my door decoration to the wall in my apartment. It shared the message of Jesus to friends, family members, building maintenance workers and many others for years afterwards.

Bobby McCoy's House

We had been studying about the blood and the cross in our Bible study. Dale called and said he had another couch and asked if I wanted it.

I said, "Yes."

Dale said, "It's kind of funky."

I asked, "Why?"

Dale said, "It's green."

I said, "If it's from the Lord, I want it."

Dale laughed and said, "Ok, but its green velvet. I'll bring it to Bible study and then drive you home afterwards."

Dale thought it was hysterical that he was giving me a green velvet couch. What Dale didn't know was that when I was 12 years old, my father took me into New York City to have a suit made for my Bar Mitzvah. My father took me up to his tailor friend who gave me a choice of two swatches. One swatch was maroon velvet, and the other swatch was green velvet. I thought *I would like to have my Bar Mitzvah suit made out of maroon velvet*, but for some strange reason, I said, "I want the green velvet?" I actually had my Bar Mitzvah in a green velvet suit!

The Green Velvet Couch

After the study, we pulled up to the back of my building and unloaded the couch. I noticed a man inside the garbage dumpster looking for things. I thought *this was strange*. Other people considered these items garbage and threw them away, but this man thought they were treasures and saved them.

We got the couch upstairs and into my apartment. Dale went home. I just stood there and stared at the couch. I thought *God, why did You give me a green velvet couch?*

God answered me. He used the green velvet couch to teach me about Him! This couch represented Jesus. It was a love seat, and you find love and rest in Jesus. It was green, and green represents life, and Jesus is life. It was found near a garbage dump at my friend's apartment complex, and Jesus was crucified near a garbage dump. Just as the man was saving treasures out of the garbage dumpster at my apartment building, Jesus saves us from our sins.

My green velvet Bar Mitzvah suit was tailor made to fit my body just as God's Torah was tailor made to fit the Jewish people. It fit me perfectly. The suit had matching pockets, a vest and pants all cut from the same cloth. It even had a matching kippah (Jewish head covering worn to show reverence to God) made from the same green velvet material. It was a picture of perfection just like the Torah was a reflection of God's perfection!

Years ago, after my Bar Mitzvah, I took off the suit and hung it in a closet. I found it later in the closet and tried it on. I had outgrown it by then, and by putting it on I ripped it to shreds. I jumped on the suit, kicked the suit and my two brothers and I played tug-o-war with it. What represented God's perfection was mutilated and destroyed.

My sister had wanted to make a gag-gift for our brother's fiancée's wedding shower. Coincidently my sister-in-law had chosen green velvet for her bridesmaids' dresses. This was when my sister made a miniature bridal party out of the trolls. She wanted to dress the male trolls in little tuxedos and have the female trolls wear the same dresses as the bridesmaids. My sister had asked my mother if she knew where my Bar Mitzvah suit was because she needed green velvet material. My mother didn't know where the suit was, but she told my sister that she had saved a remnant!

My sister took the remnant and cut it, just like Jesus was pierced. She tore the remnant, just as the Temple curtain was torn, when Jesus was crucified, giving us access to God. My sister covered the trolls, those "sinful creatures," with the green velvet material just as sinners are covered with the blood of Jesus for forgiveness of sin. Then my sister placed the trolls in a miniature bridal party just as we are placed in the family of God and betrothed to Jesus when He saves us. God gave me a green velvet couch to teach me about the blood of His lamb, Messiah Jesus!

The Scandinavian House

I noticed a sign in the mailbox area of my apartment building advertising a couch for sale with an ottoman for $100. I prayed, "Lord, a couch and an ottoman would be really nice-looking in my apartment. Could you provide the money for it?" A week later, I noticed the sign had a new price: $75. A week after that, the sign said $50. A week after that the sign said $25. Then the sign said, "Make me an offer!" Faith without works is dead, so I went up to the apartment to look at the couch. It was kind of used looking, but I was thankful for anything the Lord might provide. I only had $18 in my wallet, but that was all it took to get my couch and ottoman! My once empty apartment was now full of furniture.

One Tuesday, I was in my kitchen warming up frozen mashed potatoes on the stove. The bottom burned and the top was still frozen. I thought, *Lord, I sure would love a microwave oven.*

I kept calling the temp agency at Coke, but they still didn't have a job for me. Thankfully, my new agency was able to get me a three-month assignment in another department back on the 8th floor at AT&T, and I could start on the following Monday. That Saturday, my friend asked me to help move his mother, who just happened to work on the 8th floor at AT&T. After we moved everything, she asked me if I wanted her old microwave oven, and she gave me a bunch of throw cushions.

I put the throw cushions on my couches and realized I had everything I prayed for after looking at the mailbox stuffer with the sectional couches, the ottoman and the throw cushions a few months back.

The first couch I had received was given in the spirit of Christmas, and to me it represented the Holy Spirit. The green velvet couch represented Jesus. The big couch with the ottoman represented God to me, as my earthly father often sat on our family's couch with his feet on an ottoman.

I had one larger couch with three sections, and it reminded me that I had a God with three aspects God the Father, God the Ruach (Holy Spirit) and

God the Light (Jesus is known as the Light of the world). The term "echad" signifies a plural unity, three in one, just as God is three in One.

"In the beginning God created the heavens and the earth. Now the earth was chaos and waste, darkness was on the surface of the deep, and the Ruach Elohim was hovering upon the surface of the water. Then God said, "Let there be light!" and there was light."
–Genesis 1

GOD'S PROMISE

The Can Opener

Our First Baptist Singles' group was having a fellowship at the home of our class directors, Joe and Susan Clamon. I volunteered to cook a broccoli casserole because it was inexpensive and one of the only things I knew how to cook. The ladies at work had given me a recipe. The recipe called for a can of soup, so I started to open the can of soup with my hand-held can opener. As I began twisting the can opener, it broke. I struggled and struggled and struggled, but it was broken.

I went into the other room and looked at a mailbox stuffer. I saw an advertisement for an electric can opener for $8.95. I asked the Lord if I could buy it. When you have little money to spend, you tend to ask the Lord how to spend every penny.

> *"His master said to him, 'Well done, good and faithful servant! You were faithful with a little, so I'll put you in charge of much. Enter into your master's joy!"*
> *-Mathew 25:21*

I went back into the kitchen and picked up the can opener and the can of soup and tried it again. As I twisted in vain, there was a knock at the door. I put down the can opener and the can of soup and answered the door. A UPS man was standing there holding a box. I said to him, "If there's a can opener in there, I'll die!

I took the box into the living room and began to open it with the gusto of a small child on Christmas morning. I moved away some of the packaging peanuts to find a gift-wrapped box. I pulled out the gift-wrapped box and took a deep breath! I ripped the wrapping paper right off, and there it was: my electric frying pan?

How disappointed I was. I thought, *Lord, what a testimony this would have been if only You had sent me an electric can opener.* I took the frying pan and tossed it aside and went back into the kitchen to try and open the can. I turned the opener, but it was broken, so I gave up and went back to the living room.

I just sat there and stared at the frying pan. I didn't want an electric frying pan; I wanted an electric can opener. I just sat there and stared. Finally, I just had to laugh. Some kind-hearted souls had sent me an expensive frying pan, and I just tossed it away like it was garbage. I knew there was a reason the Lord wanted me to have this free gift, and I should be thankful; and when I got over the disappointment, I was thankful.

I started to collect all the gift wrap; and as I put it back into the UPS box, I noticed something under the packaging peanuts. I reached in and there was another gift-wrapped package, too small to be an electric can opener, but nevertheless another gift. Did I dare open it? Could it possibly be? I began to unwrap it ever so slowly. I felt like Charlie Bucket unwrapping his Wonka bar to find Willy Wonka's last golden ticket! I took another deep breath and unwrapped some more of the paper...and there it was, a hand-held can opener!!!

I fell to my knees and wept. How fortunate we are to have such a loving Lord and Savior who shows Himself to us in such miraculous ways. I thought, *God, what are You trying to teach me?* I grabbed my Bible and randomly opened right to this verse:

"The stone the builders rejected has become the capstone!"
-Psalm 118:22

You see, two thousand years ago when the Jewish people were waiting for their Messiah, He didn't come the way they were expecting. They were expecting Moshiach ben David, a conquering hero Messiah to deliver them from the Romans. When Jesus came the first time as a frying pan to burn off all their sin, they rejected Him! If they had humbled themselves, they would have received Jesus the can opener who opens all the knowledge and goodness of everything!

Joe and Susan Clamon's House

I took my broccoli casserole to the Singles' Fellowship, which was a home group from First Baptist Atlanta. My friend Lance was there and offered to drive me home because he lived on the south side of town and would be passing by my apartment.

The Scandinavian House

Lance had a bad back and was in a lot of pain. He didn't think he would be able to drive all the way home so he just stayed at my place overnight. He asked where I was working, and I told him about my different temporary jobs. I told him God had told me I was supposed to work at The Coca-Cola Company, but I couldn't get a job there.

Lance said he used to work there. I couldn't believe it, as he never mentioned it before. Lance told me to call the director of the temp agency. He said to tell the director I wanted to take a free computer class with him, to improve my computer skills, to be more marketable.

The Coca-Cola Company

I tried calling the director at The Coca-Cola temp agency to schedule a computer class, but it took a while to get through. I finally did get through and was able to schedule a class!

When I showed up to take the class, the receptionist said she knew me.

I said, "You do?"

She asked if I went to First Baptist.

I said, "Yes."

She asked if I was from New York.

I said, "Yes."

Then she said, "You're the guy with all the furniture!"

As I sat down to wait for the class, I saw a woman's reflection in the glass door. Her hair was like the woman's hair in my vision when God told me to work at Coke. It was a sign from God that I was headed in the right direction!

I took the class and scored well on their test.

The director asked me where I was working at Coke.

I told him I wasn't working at Coke, but took the class so I'd get placed at Coke.

The director said, "This class is only for people already working at Coke, and you shouldn't have taken it!

I said, "I'm sorry, I didn't know?"

The director said, "I admire your tenacity, and I'll make sure you get placed at Coke!"

The Scandinavian House

I thought I was supposed to meet my "wife" at Beth Hallel (House of Praise) the Messianic Congregation I had been visiting. It was located in Roswell, a northern suburb of Atlanta. I thought I was supposed to meet my wife on a certain Friday night, but I wasn't really sure. A friend from church told me to decorate the mug (my co-workers in NY gave me for her) in a green velvet bow. I thought that was silly, but my friend insisted I do it. I told her I didn't have a green velvet bow, and she said to pray for one! I said, "That was so silly?" She insisted I pray for a green velvet bow, so I did.

Cumberland Mall

I was supposed to meet Dale at the mall. I took a train and a bus to get there. His truck broke down, and he never made it to the mall that day. Since I was there, I decided to look for a green velvet bow. I couldn't find one anywhere, until I walked into a card store and something caught my eye. Actually, it was green eyes. These green eyes just mesmerized me. I just stared at these green eyes. Then I noticed the whole picture. The eyes belonged to Scarlett O'Hara, and she was on a poster. Then I realized she was wearing a dress with green velvet bows on it!

I couldn't believe it. Someone had me pray for a green velvet bow and the only one I could find in the entire mall was on Scarlett O'Hara's dress. I thought, *God, did you want me to buy a poster of Scarlett O'Hara?* I threw out a fleece and thought if it was under a certain price, I would buy it. It was, and I bought it, brought it home and taped it to the wall right above my green velvet couch. *But why?*

Heery International

Later on, I was walking out of the 999 Peachtree Street building after work, and noticed several things. First of all, if you look at the 999 address carved into the ground in front of the building as you exit the building, its 666! We know what 666 represents, but what was God showing me?

Across the street was the offsite Coke building Jeff Jordan worked in. It was only five blocks from my apartment, which was significant because I had no car. Coke represented God's promise to me and 666 represented the devil and sin. Sin keeps us from God's promises.

As the Lord would have it, do you know what was in between my office building and Jeff Jordan's Coke building? Several things. One was a branch of my bank. How often do we sin by idolizing money, which keeps us from trusting in God's promises? There was also a police station in between Coke and my building. The police station represents the Law. How often do we get caught up in legalistic traditions rather than allowing God's grace to abound?

There was a phone company building, too, which represented communications. How often do we get into trouble by saying the wrong thing or not saying anything at all? And the most incredible building in between Coke and my building was the Margaret Mitchell House, where she wrote *Gone with the Wind!* What was God showing me now?

The Scandinavian House

I ran home to get my Bible and see what else God was teaching me with all this. I randomly opened the Bible to this verse:

> *"And I saw that all toil and all skill that is done*
> *come from man's envy of his neighbor;*
> *this too is fleeting and striving after the wind."*
> *-Ecclesiastes 4:4*

Labor and envy are like chasing after the wind. In other words, they are *"Gone with the Wind."* How God moves heaven and earth to make our lives exciting and fun when we seek to serve Him!

Beth Hallel

When it was time to go to Beth Hallel and look for my "wife," I decided to gift wrap the mug with brown paper packaging and tie it up with a string. Corny, yes, but *The Sound of Music* is one of my favorite movies. Several of my friends went with me that night in faith. No, I didn't meet my wife, but I did give the mug to a friend with a similar name. There were two Scriptures quoted that night, and both had profound meaning to me in this situation:

"Come now, let us reason together," says ADONAI [THE LORD].
"Though your sins be like scarlet, they will be as white as snow."
-Isaiah 1:18

I realized this passage contained the word *scarlet*. Scarlett O'Hara might be considered somewhat sinful, but the significance of the color scarlet in this verse relates to Yom Kippur, the highest holy day of Judaism. On Yom Kippur, the High Priest of Israel went into the Holy of Holies of the Temple to atone for Israel. Yes, we are supposed to have a high priest serve as mediator between man and God.

On Yom Kippur, a scarlet thread would be strewn across the Temple courts. According to the Talmud (Rabbinic Interpretation). If the High Priest's sacrifices were acceptable to God, the scarlet thread would turn white. As recorded in the Talmud (Talmud, Tractate Yoma 39b), guess what year the scarlet thread stopped turning white? The year Jesus was crucified! Jesus had become the sacrifice for sins.

The other Scripture that touched me that night was the following verse:

"The arrogance of your heart has deceived you."
-Obadiah 1:3a

I had been going around telling everyone I was going to meet my wife in a certain place at a certain time, but I really wasn't sure and really didn't know. If God really promises us something, it will come to pass. Trust Him! EXPERIENCE HIM!

To some degree, I felt that I should keep my eyes open, looking for God's hand at work. Yet at the same time, I had to be on guard against my own pride. I had to accept that the timing would be God's and not mine.

EXPERIENCING GOD

Branches Drama Troupe

First Baptist Atlanta has a Drama Troupe Ministry called *Branches*. The name comes from the Bible verse:

"I am the vine; you are the branches.
The one who abides in Me, and I in him, bears much fruit;
for apart from Me you can do nothing."
-John 15:5

I believed God was leading me to join. I interviewed with the Director. She asked why I wanted to be in *Branches*, and I told her I thought God was telling me to. I wasn't chosen, but she suggested I audition for the Summer Dinner Theatre which just happened to be *The Sound of Music*.

I went to the audition and one of the assistant directors, Linda, was a Jewish believer in Jesus who just happened to work at Coke. I was given a couple of small parts including dancing at the party. I was still struggling financially at that time. They served chopped up chicken salad sandwiches during the party scene, and I had that for dinner every night.

After the play was finished, we had a cast party and watched it on video. It turns out Kathy, the woman playing the housekeeper, fumbled her lines. She said, "Would you like some windows for your curtains?" Even though she said the line wrong, the implication is correct. Curtains are for darkness, and windows are for light. Light allows you to see things more clearly. God is referred to as light in the Bible.

"The people walking in darkness will see a great light,
Upon those dwelling in the land of the shadow of death,
light will shine."
-Isaiah 9:1

God can be represented by a window because windows give light and allow you to see things more clearly. We sometimes can't see the light of

God because we cover our "windows" with curtains of darkness (disbelief, sin, doubt, addictions, idols, and so on).

Experiencing God

While I was attending a Singles' Bible Study and going through the book, *Experiencing God* by Henry Blackaby (Nashville, TN: B&H Books, 1997), it finally happened. Coke wanted me for a two-day assignment. I told my supervisor at AT&T that I had wanted to work at Coke and this was my opportunity. They let me work at Coke with the understanding I would come back to finish the three-month assignment at AT&T, and I did.

It was so exciting to finally work at Coke. There is a fountain out front and a giant atrium in the front lobby made out of marble floors and walls. And you don't need money for the Coke machines; everything is free! It's almost like going to heaven! I was so excited about working there, and I just knew God was going to do something special. Sure enough, I was assigned to the same department as Linda, the Jewish believer from church whom I had just met at *The Sound of Music* audition. I went up to her and said, "I knew God was going to do something special, and you're it!"

Lenox Mall

After my assignment at AT&T ended, I was out of work again. I put in an application at Bennigan's, a restaurant/bar, to be a server. They told me to come back in a few days when the hiring manager would be there.

I took the train to the mall and then started across the parking lot to Bennigan's. As I got closer I noticed a big banner on the side of Bennigan's saying, "Three drafts for $1." I stopped dead in my tracts. I was so desperate for a job; I'd be willing to do most anything, but how could I be around alcohol and serve it to people knowing how I struggled with it?

I cried out to God, *What should I do? You know I need a job!* I looked down at the car next to me. The bumper sticker said, "If you're headed in the wrong direction, God allows U-turns!" I smiled, turned around and went home.

The Coca-Cola Company

I kept trying everywhere to find a job, even still at Coke. Finally, I cried out to God, *If You want me at Coke, put me at Coke!* The next day, the temp agency at Coke called. They had a one-day assignment at The Coca-Cola Foundation (Corporate Contributions Department, which is the philanthropic arm of Coke), in the same building where Jeff Jordan worked. There were several people at my church who worked for Coke, but Jeff was the only one who worked in the offsite Coke building by the Margaret Mitchell House.

How exciting it was. Absolutely nothing at all, then all of a sudden I'm back at Coke, working in a charitable area, in Jeff Jordan's building! I went to that assignment practically shaking with anticipation because not only was it a foot back in at Coke, but it was in Jeff Jordan's building! I thought, *Could this finally be it?*

My supervisor met me at the door and took me to her office. She sat me down and started to explain what she wanted me to do. I just looked at her and my mouth fell open. I was absolutely shocked because I knew she was the woman I had seen in my vision right after God told me to work at Coca-Cola! She looked at me and asked what was wrong with me? I just shook it off and said there was nothing wrong. I could barely contain myself. Her name was Angela, and I began to work for her. She was happy with my work. She told the agency I did a good job, and they started placing me again.

First Baptist Atlanta

I had auditioned for the First Baptist Atlanta Sanctuary Choir. The first time I tried out, I didn't make it. I took some voice lessons and auditioned with someone really good and was able to sing along with him. I'm not a singer nor do I strive to be one. My motives for joining the choir were primarily evangelistic as well as being able to praise the Lord. *In Touch Ministries* with Dr. Stanley and the Choir was televised, and I wanted to be on television so my family would watch and hear the Gospel. I knew they would watch at least the first time, and Dr. Stanley's sermon was all about Moses!

My sister would visit various relatives, ask if they wanted to see me on TV and then turn on *In Touch*. My grandmother would watch her little "boychik" on TV every Sunday morning from her apartment in Brighton Beach, Brooklyn.

The Coca-Cola Company

The Coca-Cola Company had a booth at the *NFL Experience* at the Superbowl when it was in Atlanta. They needed temporary help to staff their booth. I had 20 years of retail experience and was most qualified for this one-week position. The temp agency practically begged me to take this assignment. It was over a Sunday so I said no. They begged me and begged me and begged me. I've learned from my walk with God if someone is that insistent I do something, it usually means it is from God. I prayed about it and decided to interview for the assignment.

The booth was a major event for Coke employees to earn volunteer hours to qualify for Olympic volunteer assignments. The Coca-Cola Company volunteer program is called *Reaching Out*. They were gearing up for their volunteer force at the Olympics and had leaders from all over The Coca-Cola Company serve on a steering committee for the Olympic volunteer program. They organized various activities to give employees the opportunity to earn hours towards being selected as a company volunteer at the Olympics. Official company volunteers received their salary while volunteering at the Olympics. Needless to say, this process was competitive!

I had to interview with a couple of the company leaders to make sure I was the right fit for this assignment, and I was. They told me all about the Coke volunteer program, which just happened to be managed by Angela, the woman (in my vision) I had worked for! I felt completely comfortable working at the Booth. I was responsible for orienting volunteers, supplying them with merchandise, making sure the booth was fully stocked and also selling merchandise myself.

Joe Clamon, my Sunday School Director and his son just happened to come by and make a purchase. I couldn't go to church that day so God brought church to me! I worked with some of the company leaders and met volunteer employees from all over Coke.

Coke was extremely happy with my work at the booth, and the temp agency named me as "Temp of the Month." I asked for my next assignment, but there wasn't one. It was so frustrating to wait around.

Finally, they had another assignment for me. I would be reporting to Angela's administrative assistant for a two-day assignment. They liked my work so the two-day assignment was extended for over a week. Angela left a note on my desk asking if I knew how to use Paradox for Windows, a computer database program. I grabbed the note and ran as fast as I could to the elevator to go and talk with Jeff Jordan, who was a computer programmer. I asked Jeff what Paradox was. He had a box of Paradox Database software and leant it to me. I left the box and note with Angela, saying I didn't know how to use Paradox, but I would be most willing to learn it.

The Coca-Cola Company had decided to create a three-year position to support the Olympic Volunteer Program by hiring a volunteer coordinator for the program who would work directly for Angela as well as the steering committee of various company leaders. The coordinator would be responsible for maintaining Paradox for Windows databases for volunteers, coordinating community service projects and staffing volunteers for various events. The funding for this position was approved the week I was temping in the department. Since several of the employees already knew me from the *NFL Experience* Booth, my name was suggested to Angela. She interviewed me, and since I had a computer degree she was willing to let me learn the Paradox program.

She put me in the same seat as when I worked for her before, right after I said, *God if You want me at Coke, put me at Coke.* Not only was the job in Jeff Jordan's building, but my window had a view of my church! I knew that I knew that I knew that I knew this was the job that God had sent me to! The mystery of the telephone numbers (666-#### and 822-####) was revealed because it turned out The Coca-Cola **Company was responsible for having 822 volunteers at the Olympics! God's promise to me was being fulfilled!**

The Scandinavian House

The Coca-Cola Company volunteer program community service projects were newsworthy and some of them had been on television. Angela gave me a video to watch with a news program about one of the Coke service projects. When I came home, I noticed the poster of Scarlett O'Hara had fallen off my wall. I knew God was saying to me it is finished. His promise to me regarding work at The Coca-Cola Company had been fulfilled!

I watched the news program that featured the Coke service project. As I reached over to turn it off, something else came on the screen. Apparently Angela had taped over "*Gone with the Wind*" because Scarlett O'Hara was on the screen wearing the dress with the green velvet bows on it!

FORGIVENESS

Atlanta, Georgia

I auditioned for and received a part in the Atlanta Passion Play that the church does every year at the Atlanta Civic Center. Not only was I going to be on television, but I was appearing in a play at a major venue.

I had to buy make-up materials for the Passion Play. I took the train to Lindbergh Plaza and walked around. I was really frustrated as I was totally clueless about make-up?   I prayed, *Lord, I don't know what to buy! I believe You want me to be in this play, so please show me what I need to buy.*

As I looked out the window of the store I was in, the sun began to shine brighter and brighter. It was as if God was smiling at me. Then, the Holy Spirit said to me:

> *"Be still, and know that I am God."*
> *–Psalm 46:10a*

I stood there looking out the store window and thought about this message from above. Then I walked out of the store and down the street. I noticed a Cub Food super market and thought I might as well go food shopping while I was out. I proceeded to Cub Food, but passed by Marshall's Clothing Store. I had never been in a Marshall's before and had no desire to go in, but the Holy Spirit told me to.

I questioned, *God, do you really want me to go into this store?* I knew He did, but I couldn't see any earthly reason to do so. I figured I could go in and look at some clothes or something and humor God. I walked over to the men's section and looked around. I really didn't see anything I wanted or needed. I said, *OK God, I went in the store. Are you happy now? Can I leave now?* Still frustrated and disappointed, I began to walk out of the store. Just then, I noticed someone round the corner.

It was Jean, the Chairperson of the Passion Play's Make-Up Committee. She told me exactly what kind of make-up materials to buy and where to buy them. God answered my prayer! My frustration and disappointment turned to worship and thankfulness because God reminded me that He is God!

Serving the Lord in the Atlanta Passion Play was a great blessing. Hundreds of us from all different walks of life and ministry got together to act out the Bible for the tens of thousands who come and see it every year. It is so wonderful.

First Baptist Atlanta

John Glover, our Music Minister announced some of the Sanctuary Choir and Orchestra members would be going on a mission trip. I had never been on a mission trip, and I was so excited. As time went on, it was announced the mission trip would be to somewhere in Europe. I thought, *Wow!* I had never been to Europe. This is going to be great!

When it was later announced the mission trip would be to Germany, I was absolutely shocked, dumbfounded and horrified! I immediately thought of the horrors of World War II. I thought, *God, of all the places in the world, why Germany? I'm Jewish and I don't want to go to Germany! I'd rather go to Iran!*

Not only didn't I want to go to Germany, but I found out *The Sound of Music* was coming to the Fox Theatre the same week I was supposed to be in Germany. I had been waiting two years for the Sound of Music to come to the Fox.   And Marie Osmond, who I absolutely adored, was playing Maria!

I was in a weekly men's discipleship Bible study. It was the Navigators study with Scripture memorization. David, the leader, would pick me up and drive me to the study. We also got together for a half day of prayer. After praying for several hours, I knew it was God's will for me to go to Germany, but I still didn't want to go.

During choir rehearsal prayer time on the last night we could sign up for the Germany Mission trip, my friend and I asked God to make it perfectly clear to me if it was God's will for me to go to Germany. (I knew it was, but I just didn't want to go and was dragging my feet.) Later that night, my friend Chris joined choir, said he was going to Germany, and he wanted me to be his roommate on the trip! I was shocked. I told Chris I didn't have the $100 deposit to sign-up, and he told me he would lend it to me. There were no more excuses; I was going to Germany.

About a month later, the second $100 deposit was due. I thought, *God, You know I don't have any money. Where am I supposed to get $100 from?* A few days later I received a letter in the mail, and inside the letter was a check for $100! I was really shocked this time! Grandma, I asked, "Why did you send me $100?" She said, "I can send my grandson money if I want to!" She had never mailed me a check before, and I hadn't told her I needed the money.

"So also faith, if it does not have works, is dead by itself"
-James 2:17

I asked the Lord to help me write a support letter to raise funds for the Germany Mission Trip. I spent a week in prayer and wrote an evangelistic support letter that I put on green paper because green represents life. The Lord had me distribute 1,000 copies of this green letter anyplace I could, such as the march for Jesus, around church, through the mail, etc.

I was walking down Peachtree Street on my way to the super market. Robbie, one of the leaders from The Coca-Cola Company I had worked with at the Volunteer Booth, drove by and gave me a ride. I prayed for an opportunity to share with him, and he asked me what the green letter was, and I gave him a copy. I had the choir pray for him, and he actually sent in a donation dated the day after the choir prayed for him.

Needless to say, all my financial support came in. I was on my way to Germany whether I liked it or not (and I didn't like it). I realized it doesn't matter what I like; it only matters that I am obedient to whatever God calls me to do.

Germany Mission Trip

About 80 of us left for the Germany Mission on November 10, 1994, (the one-year anniversary of my joining the Sanctuary Choir). It was also the anniversary of Kristallnacht (the night of broken glass), when Jewish store and synagogue windows were destroyed during an unforgettable night of anti-Semitic terror in Nazi Germany.

In all we gave 10 German concerts with thousands of people attending. They were so happy to have us there. Several people said there was more of the Gospel Message of Jesus Christ in our music then most Germans heard in an entire year! At a lot of the concerts we would sing a song called *It Is Well with My Soul,* and then one of our choir members would give a testimony and ask people, through a translator, if it was well with their souls. Then she would sing a song called *Do You Remember?* and ask people if they remembered the day they met the Lord? I remembered the day I met the Lord and cried every time she asked.

One night we were in Rothenburg shopping. It had gotten really cold, and I needed to buy a hat. I went into a store and found a hat but couldn't afford it. I went to another store and found a ski cap that I could afford. I couldn't believe what it said on the hat. I stood there for 30 minutes trying to decide if I should buy a hat that said, "I love Germany!" I thought, *Could I really wear this hat? Could I forgive the Nazis for what they did? Could I really love Germany?* Apart from Christ, I could not wear that hat. But, I am a Christian, and I am to love and forgive everyone and everything as Christ loves and forgives me no matter what. Yes, I needed to buy and wear that hat because God was speaking to me, LOUD AND CLEAR!!!"

"For with You there is forgiveness, so You may be revered."
-Psalm 130:4

One night we had finished a concert and arrived at the hotel around midnight. We had to wait on the bus until they gave us our room keys which were pre-assigned hours before we got them. I was really tired that night, my throat hurt, my nose was running and I just wanted to go to sleep. When we got inside the hotel, we had to wait on line for the elevator. There was an elevator operator who ran the extremely small elevator. While we were standing there, I noticed the person standing next to me was the only person in the lobby that was not part of our group. I was sick, tired and barely able to stand. I started to think about the man standing next to me and thought, *What if God wanted me to share Jesus with him and I didn't and then he died?* I thought, *We are now deep into the middle of Germany, and he probably doesn't speak English. Lord, I am so tired, but if You want me to tell him about You, then please do something.* I had a real burden to pray for this man, but didn't want to witness to him in the flesh.

The elevator finally arrived. Nancy from our group was in front of me, so we put all her stuff on first and then realized she was on the third floor and I was on the fourth floor and would have to take her stuff off and put mine on first so she could get out first. This must have appeared very comical to the German businessman. We let her out on the third floor, closed the door and the elevator operator turned the key to take me up to the fourth floor. He kept turning the key and pressing buttons, but nothing would happen. We were stuck! I couldn't believe this was happening. I thought, *God, I am so sick and tired, I just want to go to bed. Why is this happening? I'm sure You know, but I don't.* The elevator finally started moving again, but we went back down to the lobby?

When we got to the lobby, the elevator door opened. The German businessman just looked at me and started laughing. He spoke English and asked what happened. (I had no clue, except for the clue named Jesus). It turns out he was a salesman for an American company and was on a business trip. When the elevator finally reached the fourth floor, the German businessman got out too. We started walking down the long hallway and both stopped at the same place. His room was directly across from mine (you should have seen the look on his face). He asked me why I was in Germany, and I told him. I reached into my pocket, and, Praise the Lord, I found one of the German Gospel Tracts that Rob had given to me earlier. I handed the tract to the German businessman, and he looked at the cover and handed it back. I said, "No, this is for you." He shrugged his shoulders took the tract, and that was the last time I ever saw him.

Before we left for Germany, I had so much apprehension. A Jew going to Germany, not being able to afford the trip, missing work and pay while I was on the trip, not being in town when *The Sound of Music* finally came to the Fox Theatre, possibly not having a job when I returned, going to Europe for the first time, singing in a smaller choir where my not-so-great voice would stand out more, etc. I thought, *Lord, how else are You going to stretch me?* Later, they asked if people would like to share a short testimony during one of the concerts, and I knew God was calling!

I felt led to share my testimony and believed God told me to share on my birthday, November 17. We gave 10 concerts with nine at churches and one at a school. The concert at the school was to be the most evangelistic. It was November 17. When we got to the school, I became extremely nervous. God was giving me an awesome responsibility, and I wanted to be obedient to his call. While we were rehearsing, we were informed that the concert would be broadcast live on radio (that information didn't quite settle my nerves). At dinner, I couldn't eat. Everyone sang "Happy Birthday," and then they handed me my present, a bag they had passed around on our buses. It was full of money they had collected for me! I was so overwhelmed from the love and generosity of the group!

Before we performed that night, my tuxedo was in disarray. John Gage, the Orchestra Director, straightened my bow tie, and Pat sewed on a loose button. Seeing the love of Christ in these two people right before I went on stage strengthened me enormously! When I actually gave my testimony, I wasn't nervous. There were 80 spirit-filled Christians standing behind me and praying over every word that came out of my mouth for the Glory of God!

I shared my testimony and ended by saying, "Just as August 5, 1992, is my spiritual birthday and today is my physical birthday, today can be your spiritual birthday!" Afterwards, two women who came there together, came up to me all excited because one was born on November 17 and the other on August 5! A sign from God!

The next day we visited the site of the Buchenwald Concentration Camp. It was nothing but empty lots and museums, and I praise God for that! The ugly prisons and gas chambers of the Holocaust era had been wiped away, but the museum stood there to make sure they were not forgotten.

The Scandinavian House

While distributing my support letter for the 1994 Germany Mission Trip, I gave a copy to Sal, the owner of the Italian restaurant in my building. He showed the support letter to Demitria, a young woman who also lived in our building. Demitria called me and said she liked my letter, and asked if I could give her a copy.

Demitria was out of work and somewhat depressed. I ran into her in the laundry room and mail area several times. I had an opportunity to share the message of love with her, and tried so much to help her with her struggles. She said she believed in Jesus. One day I ran into her at the supermarket. She told me she had seen me on television being interviewed by a news reporter. I told her, "Anything is possible when you give your life to Jesus Christ!"

I later learned that Demitria committed suicide. Only the Lord knows where she will spend eternity. I praise God for giving me the opportunity to share with her. On behalf of Demitria I want to thank anyone who had anything to do with the 1994 Germany Mission Trip because that trip indirectly gave her the opportunity to hear the message of love and forgiveness.

STRAIGHT PATHS

Branches Drama Troupe

I tried out for *Branches* again, and this time I made it! We performed drama sketches all around the Southeast at churches, college campuses, senior adult homes, and other venues. We were driving back from Myrtle Beach, South Carolina, one weekend and stopped at a Waffle House. There was a woman sitting by herself at the counter. She moved over so we could all sit together at the counter next to her. We ordered our food right before midnight. When it turned midnight, Kathy from our group reminded us that it was her birthday so we sang to her.

The woman sitting at the counter had been somewhat depressed but perked up after we sang. She asked us what we were doing there, and we told her we were a Christian Drama Troupe and had just performed at a church. She was in shock and put her head down and just about started crying. We asked her what was wrong and she told us. Her husband was dying of cancer, and she drove him down from Virginia to make sure he got to see his relatives before he died. She didn't believe in God, but right before we walked in, she asked God to show her if He was real. She immediately knew God had used us to answer her prayer! God is real!

The Coca-Cola Company

I absolutely loved my job at Coke. I developed many computer skills, talked on the phone, met people from all over the Company, organized community service projects and attended various events. I would often take the shuttle bus from our office location to the main complex. I'd take large checks or volunteer reports to the executive floors at the top of the main Coke building and interact with the top executives of The Coca-Cola Company. Other times I would go down to the basement and count t-shirts. It didn't matter what I did, whether seemingly trivial or outright fascinating, God had sent me there to be a light and a witness, and I was thrilled to have that job.

I'd pray for everyone and share with people wherever I could. I even prayed with a couple of people to receive Jesus. I pretty much was able to witness whenever or wherever I wanted. People thought I had something to do with their Olympic assignments (which I really didn't) and wouldn't dare take a chance complaining about me!

I remember one time taking the shuttle bus and feeling led to pray for the woman sitting across from me. I looked at her name tag but didn't know who she was. I just prayed for her. A month later she was killed in a plane crash in South America. It turned out my coworker used to work with her and was very upset by her passing. It gave me an opportunity to minister to my coworker.

I helped organize clean-ups and landscaping at parks and schools as part of my work with Coke, and I sometimes rubbed shoulders with Atlanta's leaders. One week I worked at the Carter Center and met both President and Mrs. Carter as well as Governor Miller. Another time I represented Coke at an event and accepted an award from Mayor Campbell on behalf of Coke.

First Baptist Atlanta

As the Coke job neared its end, I started getting anxious about having a permanent job. I saw a job posting in the Coke staffing department that I was interested in. On one hand I wanted to stay and finish my three-year temp commitment, but on the other hand I wanted to have a permanent job with benefits. I decided to go into work one Saturday and apply for the posted job. I really had mixed feelings about it.

As I walked past my church towards the Coke building, I stopped in the church parking lot to pray about it. I looked at the Coke building, and knew I was where I was supposed to be for that time. I thought, *God, if my applying for this job is not Your will, then please stop me.* Within seconds, I heard a voice call, "Steve, Steve!"

It was my friend Donna who had come to church to rehearse for the summer dinner theatre. I went over, and my friend told me someone had just dropped out of the play. They asked me if I wanted the part. I stayed for the audition and didn't apply for that job.

The Coca-Cola Company

Months later, another job in Coke staffing became available, and I applied for it. The hiring manager just happened to be reporting to another friend of mine from church. My friend Al had gotten hired into his position at Coke after I had indirectly made him aware of the job opening. Needless to say, I made it through the first round of interviews. When I went to the second interview, I told the receptionist who I was. She unhappily said, "I know who you are! I know all about you! I saw you singing in your choir."

She was a temp also and had applied for the same job. Apparently she visited my church and saw me in the choir. By that time, she was aware I had applied for the job she wanted. I'm sure she was thinking about me taking the position she wanted, which would have been a distraction to her while visiting my church. God had already given me the job I was supposed to have, but I wasn't trusting him. Instead, I was trying to get a job in staffing. My disobedience may have been a stumbling block for someone else?

Coke ended up filling the position with a permanent employee who was already working in staffing. They did offer me another temp position, but I didn't want to leave a temp job for another temp job and ended up turning it down.

Atlanta Summer Olympics

During the Olympics I was responsible for answering Coke's Olympic Volunteer Hotline with two other people taking turns for two weeks. Ironically, no one called while I was on duty, and I was able to spend all my free time witnessing around Atlanta near the Olympic venues and attend practices for our next Germany Choir Mission Trip. While I was at choir practice, I checked my voice mail. There was a message from Coke inviting me to The Coca-Cola Company Hospitality suite at a downtown hotel and the Olympic Games Closing Ceremonies! My friend in Staffing was also at the hospitality suite and told me while he used the bathroom; he got to meet Arnold Schwarzenegger. While we were at the Closing Ceremonies, my first nephew was born! How cool was that!

Germany Mission Trip

We went on a second mission trip to Germany. What a glorious, glorious mission. There is no way we could possibly know every circumstance God orchestrated by sending 77 spirit-filled Christians on a mission trip to Germany. Our two missionaries told us that Germany is 95 percent atheist and our concerts give credibility to the churches that are over there, not to mention encouragement to their members and evangelism for the unsaved.

Our first concert was in Potsdam. We gave the concert in a huge cathedral in the center of town. Tour buses stopped for tourists to come and see the cathedral (and get witnessed to). The concert was the first one listed on a program that was used for their entire concert season. Our upbeat concert listing would be a witness for months to come. The concert was publicized in the local newspaper, and several hundred people were in attendance. This concert was the beginning, or birth, of our concert tour, and it resembled the birth of our savior. As the local German pastor introduced us, the cathedral filled with sunlight, and it was as if God was smiling on us, and He was! God had called us to proclaim Him and this message to the Germans.

He brought this Bible verse (The Aaronic Benediction) to my mind:

"ADONAI bless you and keep you!
ADONAI make His face to shine on you
and be gracious to you!
ADONAI turn His face toward you
and grant you shalom."
-Numbers 6:24-26

Later we got to sing in the worship service of a Berlin church. There was one woman in particular who smiled and clapped and was noticed by all. After the concert, she got up in front of the congregation and thanked us for coming. She called us "Living Stones." She had been taken to Siberia 50 years ago and recently was allowed to come back to Germany. She had been freed by Christ 40 years ago, and she is a blessing.

We went back to the Baptist Church in Zeitz where we had sung the last time. This is the church that has a ceiling made out of ammunition boxes from World War II. They had asked me to give my testimony at this concert. What came out of my mouth was not what I had planned.

There were four American Mormons at the concert. One of the Mormons came up to me after the concert and told me he had never heard anyone speak like me. He had told someone else he had never heard anyone sing like us. The pastor told us that my testimony was perfect for the congregation. I can't even remember half the things that came out of my mouth. (I'm glad God is in control!) Barbara, one of the women in our choir, spoke with one of the Mormon boys. She had worked in Idaho a while back helping families find housing, and realized she had actually placed this boy's family in a house!

When we went to Germany the last time, *The Sound of Music* was at the Fox Theatre, and I had to miss it. I had waited a long time for it to come to the Fox, and needless to say I was disappointed. God comes first! On this trip God made up for it because we went to Salzburg, Austria, and went on *The Sound of Music* Tour. God really knows how to do things in a big way!

Before we left Germany, we had the opportunity to visit the Dachau concentration camp. I felt led to hand out tracts and waited for God to tell me when. I felt led to stand at the front gate. I had some bicycle tracts Betty had given me. As I stood at the Gate on this gravel road, I was down to the last three tracts when a young man came by walking his bicycle past me. My mouth hung open as I handed him one of the bicycle tracts. I couldn't believe it! What was he doing at Dachau with a bicycle? I watched him walk away and read the tract and put the tract in his pocket.

First Baptist Atlanta

After we returned from Germany, we gave a home concert at First Baptist Atlanta on a Sunday night. They had some of us share during the concert. I was given the privilege of sharing. I was wearing a tuxedo and was feeling rather overheated. When I walked up to the pulpit, I took a drink of water and everyone laughed because it was Dr. Stanley's water that I had taken. Someone told me Dr. Stanley said my testimony was one of the most powerful he had heard in a long time, and someone else told me there was a Jewish person at the concert who gave their life to the Lord!

The Coca-Cola Company

Two weeks before my temp job at Coke was supposed to end, the temp agency had an assignment in the staffing department. The people from the volunteer program released me from my obligations and took me out to lunch to thank me and say goodbye.

I worked at the new job in staffing for a couple of days and did not have peace. You are not supposed to leave one temp job for another, and here I was short-circuiting God again. I was so miserable, I knew it wasn't God's will for me to be there; so I quit, knowing that I would be burning my bridges at the Coke temp agency. Even though I no longer worked there, I went back many times, over the years, to have lunch with former co-workers.

DESIRES OF YOUR HEART

Atlanta, Georgia

It was time to start a new chapter in my life. I registered with a recruiter, who used to work at the Coke temp agency but was now working at another temp agency. I asked what companies she had accounts with, and it turned out they had an account with BellSouth which had taken over the phone company right across the street from my apartment.

I asked if they had any opportunities for placement at that location, but they didn't. I went home and checked my voice mail messages. In the 30 minutes or so it took to go from her office to my apartment, the recruiter called saying, "You're not going to believe this, but BellSouth just called with a one-day assignment!" Of course it was at the location on my street that I had asked the Lord for five years before! I literally **walked out of my building and crossed the street to go to work!**

BellSouth

I worked in a marketing department assisting the clerical help with photocopying, faxes, mail, and similar tasks. The one-day job was extended for a week and then indefinitely. I was assigned to assist one of the directors and his managers. The person who had the job before me would let the faxes fall on the floor and then step on them. I hand-delivered the faxes for the entire department, to each manager personally, and prayed for each manager as I delivered them.

They discovered I knew how to use a computer and started asking me to do presentations. First, I did presentations for my director and his managers. Soon word got out, and they had me doing presentations for our whole department. When managers from other departments started asking me to do presentations, I demanded a raise and got one.

The finance manager wanted me to help her with a special project to clean up the advertising financials in addition to all my other responsibilities in the department. I was planning to go on a two-week mission trip to Israel and told them I would be looking for a permanent job when I got back. I had come to work in jeans and a T-shirt because it was casual Friday. They didn't want to lose me so they created a contract position working with the finance manager and the advertising director. I interviewed for the job in jeans and a T-shirt and was hired. The position was from when I got back from Israel to the end of the year, and it paid $10,000 more a year then I made at Coke.

Israel Mission Trip

How exciting it was to be going on a mission trip to Israel in June of 1997! It was my first time in Israel, and I was somewhat apprehensive. I was going with a couple of other Jewish believers from my church and sixteen other believers from throughout the South.

While at the Atlanta airport, someone told me they heard on the news that a bomb had been found on the Tel Aviv beach where we would be ministering. You might think that would deter me from going; but in actuality, I felt safer. The Israelis brought security to the beach and made sure there were no other bombs.

People are always concerned about the constant wars in Israel. If the planes are not flying, don't go. If the planes are flying, go; unless you know for sure God is telling you not to go. Nevertheless, I know the safest place to be is in God's will.

On the way to Israel, we had a 12-hour layover in Amsterdam, Holland. We toured the Anne Frank Museum, which is the house she and her family hid in during the Holocaust. It brought the realities of the Holocaust and sinful humanity to the forefront of our minds, as we have the solution for sin and deathJesus, Yeshua the Messiah!

There were 19 of us on our team. We stayed at Yakov Damkami's house in Joppa near Tel Aviv and slept on mats in his backyard. Yakov Damkani is an extremely well-known Israeli believer who evangelizes all over Israel. Joppa is mostly Muslim, and we were constantly hearing calls to prayer blasted on loud speakers at various times throughout the day and night.

Between the jet lag, hot temperatures, getting bitten by bugs overnight and loud calls to prayer, it was hard to get rest. We had netting, but my arm fell out during the night, and I counted at least 30 bug bites. The food we ate was a shock, since there was no meat, only occasionally tuna fish. Most Israelis eat a lot of vegetables, hummus, falafel and the like.

We stayed there for two weeks and distributed Gospel books at the beach. No one is allowed to give out pamphlets on the beach, only books. We gave out pamphlets on street corners, army bases, near malls and wherever we could. We went out three or four times a day and gave out thousands of Gospel materials and received contact information from over one hundred people who wanted more information.

It was such a blessing to share in Israel. A printer who was a Jewish believer lived in Jerusalem. He supplied most everyone who evangelized in Israel with free materials. One time, his house had been blown up because of his evangelical work. Orthodox Jews are extremely hostile to the Gospel and will persecute believers.

I'll never forget the first time we went out on the streets in Israel. We had a Gospel tract asking, "Where do you store up your treasure?" The verse on the tract was from Matthew:

"Do not store up for yourselves treasures on earth, where moth and rust destroy and where thieves break in and steal. But store up for yourselves treasures in heaven, where neither moth nor rust destroys and where thieves do not break in or steal."

-Matthew 6:19-20

The first person we encountered had just dropped her change purse. Her coins rolled all around the ground. We helped pick them up and shared a tract with her.

We went to a protest rally. The secular Jews were protesting the Orthodox because they don't serve in the military and usually don't work, just study. Most of these protestors were atheists. My teammate called me over to share with a young man who wanted to talk to a Jewish believer from New York.

The man was from Brooklyn, New York. He had two brothers. One was a believer in Jesus and the other was an Orthodox Jew. They had sent him to Israel to figure it out, he met us, and we were happy to explain it to him! I

83

met an Austrian man who was working on his thesis, which raised the question: "How Was the Universe Started?" So I told him! Ironically, you go to witness to the Jews, and you end up witnessing to many Gentiles (non-Jewish people) along the way.

In the middle of our two weeks, we took two days to go sightseeing. We left early Sunday morning and came back late Monday night. We traveled all around Israel and saw many of the sights like Caesarea, Tiberias, the Sea of Galilee and En Getti. I put my arm in the Dead Sea and it practically cleared up all the bug bites! In Jerusalem, we were given a special tour underneath the Temple area.

We experienced opposition while we tried to distribute Gospel materials. Orthodox Jews do not want proselytizing to other Jews. They harassed us, and one man followed me into a mall and assaulted me. Security got him off of me, and we were able to escape out the back exit of the mall where lots of people were waiting on line for a movie. We gave them Gospel tracts, which they would not have received if I hadn't been attacked! I was so exhausted on the flight back from Amsterdam to Atlanta, I slept the entire time!

BellSouth

After Israel, I started my new job at BellSouth. They were reorganizing our department, and my manager promised to get me hired permanently as the Accounts Payable manager. At the same time, a friend from church was serving as a missionary in England. The Lord put it on my heart to financially support her on a monthly basis. I prayed about the amount and couldn't believe the Lord would have me give so much.

"Bring the whole tithe into the storehouse.
Then there will be food in My house.

Now test Me in this"says ADONAI-Tzva'vot
"if I will not open for you the windows of heaven,
and pour out blessing for you,
until no one is without enough."
-Malachi 3:10

I really struggled with sending in so much money, and at first I didn't. I was supposed to be hired at BellSouth, but for some reason it was being delayed. As soon as I started sending in the missionary financial support, I was hired by BellSouth. There were three levels of manager, and I was brought in at the lowest level at the lowest pay scale, which was still $10,000 more a year then I had been making as a contract employee. My manager said, "Don't expect any raises for a while."

BellSouth

Our church moved to the north side of Atlanta, and I would take a train and a bus to get up there. *Branches*, our drama ministry, would meet at the new location, and my friend Gina would drive me to the train afterwards. She was struggling at work because her boss was having issues and taking it out on her. We prayed many times for that boss. Eventually, the boss went away!

Gina got a new boss, Greg, and told me there was a new problem. She told me the new boss would stare at her all day. Eventually, he asked her out on a date and had me go too for safety. They eventually got married and have lots of kids! He has a telecommunications background, so I passed his resume around at BellSouth, but nothing happened. Ironically, he had some meetings with people from my department and ended up getting a job in my department anyway!

Even though my manager told me not to expect any raises for a while, shortly afterwards I got one. They raised all the company pay scales to incorporate cost of living and had to bring me up to the new minimum for my management level. Then I had my review and received a raise on top of that. This enabled me to pay off my college loans!

Greg had a position open under him at the next management level. We were not allowed to switch jobs unless we had been there for more than a year or it was at a higher management level. My boss didn't want to lose me, so she had me promoted to the next management level, as a Budget Planner, and the minimum pay scale was more then I was making. Then they raised all the minimums again for cost of living. Then I had another review and received another raise! Now I was making about $15,000 more a year then when I got hired on at BellSouth!

My sister had moved to Florida and was working about 80 hours a week for very little money. I helped her get into BellSouth as a contractor making twice what she did in Florida. She wanted me to share an apartment with her in Dunwoody near my church. So I finally bought a car and moved in with her. Even with a car, it made more sense to take the train to work every day. I noticed a large menorah on the side of the road and prayed every day that God would send someone to that synagogue to witness to the people there.

SEND ME

"Then I heard the voice of ADONAI saying: "Whom should I send, and who will go for Us?" So I said, "Hineni. Send me.""-Isaiah 6:8

The Call to Jewish Outreach

In 1998, God called me to Jewish Outreach. How did He call me? Circumstances, a sermon, a feeling, a Jewish Evangelism newsletter, all of the above. I just knew I was supposed to reach out to Jewish people more than I was doing at the time, and things started happening.

For I am not ashamed of the Good News, for it is the power of God for salvation to everyone who trusts—to the Jew first and also to the Greek.
-Romans 1:16

My friend Yolanda called and begged me to go with her to an audition at the 14 Street Playhouse in Atlanta for a Christian drama company called *ArtWithin*. I really didn't want to go, but Yolanda showed up at my door and practically dragged me to the audition. I went with her and thought it might be fun to audition, too. When the casting director heard I was a Jewish believer in Jesus, he and the rest of the staff were most excited.

I know it's special to be Jewish and believe in Jesus, but they were very excited for some other reason. Apparently a Jewish non-believer, had shown up for the audition after seeing an advertisement in the newspaper. Ironically, she was in the acting class that our director's wife attended. We realized that God had drawn this Jewish woman to the class. Needless to say, I was cast in the play, and Yolanda wasn't.

Who Knew?

The Christian drama company had strong ties to a local church. I went to a prayer meeting at the director's house. His wife suggested I join that local church because it was in a Jewish neighborhood. I told her I wasn't looking for a new church.

Six months later...I started volunteering with Jews for Jesus and went for training in Chicago. After I finished the training, I knew I was supposed to join the other local church, Mount Vernon Baptist, and did so on July 5, 1998.

A Russian Congregation met at my new church on Sunday afternoons. It turned out the Russian church had a big outreach to Russian Jews I only learned about after joining the church. They held various concerts at the church and bussed in hundreds of Russian Jews. Speakers would give testimonies, and we would distribute Gospel materials and share with people.

Years later I met Igor Ashkenazi, a world famous Russian gymnast who was on staff with Jews for Jesus at the time. I arranged for Igor to speak at my church. He gave a Russian *"Christ in the Passover"* presentation to over 500 Russian Jews and some 50 of them prayed to receive Jesus!

You Never Know?

I started doing various volunteer activities with Jews for Jesus while I worked full-time during the day. I distributed their Gospel tracts at various events and signed people up for their newsletter. I kept a poster of Jerusalem in my cubicle, and it gave me opportunity to share with just about every Jewish person on my floor.

I drove to Nashville and helped Moishe Rosen, the founder of Jews for Jesus, represent them at a National Religious Broadcasters convention. A woman saw my Atlanta name tag and started to ask if I knew someone but hesitated. Apparently a Jewish believer from Atlanta shared his testimony in her Sunday School class in Mississippi, but she didn't know how to get in touch with him as she wanted to have him on her radio program which was aired in 70 markets nationwide.

It turned out she just happened to be looking for my friend Josh! She gave me her number to give to Josh, and I called him. He had been praying about the promise she made to put him on the radio program right before I called! He later went on the radio show and shared his testimony with millions!

Anti-Missionaries

The volunteer coordinator at Jews for Jesus called me to follow up with a man from Atlanta who wanted to volunteer with them. The person claimed to be a believer in Jesus, but was an Orthodox Jew living in Atlanta. He was an anti-missionary (someone who dissuades Jewish people from believing in Jesus) who heads up an anti-missionary organization. Apparently, he wanted to see what would happen if he called Jews for Jesus.

I would meet Anti-Missionary #1 for lunch at various kosher restaurants. He would speak loudly so everyone in the restaurant knew what he was trying to do: talk me out of my belief in Jesus! I loved to meet with him and answer his questions because it gave me an opportunity to pray over the people in these places and share the Gospel in the context of answers to his questions! He would e-mail me questions and that forced me to buy books and look up the answers. E-mailing was a great way for me to learn and grow and have time to pray about and research answers. This went on for many months and ended when I asked him who Isaiah 9:7 was talking about?

"Of the increase of His government and shalom *there will be no end on the throne of David and over His kingdom to establish it and uphold it through justice and righteousness from now until forevermore. The zeal of the ADONAI-Tzva'ot will accomplish this."*
-Isaiah 9:6

He said the verse was talking about King Hezekiah. I said it couldn't be because the Kingdom was established from that time on and forever, but King Hezekiah died and his kingdom was not established forever. He never answered that e-mail, and that was the end of our question and answer Internet exchanges! I credit Anti-Missionary #1 for training me as a missionary!!! Although our Internet exchanges ended, he would continue to invite me to his synagogue and home for Shabbos meals (meals shared on Saturdays, which is the day Jews observe for worship and rest) and other events which I continually bathed in prayer.

Anti-Missionary #1 invited me to hear a world-renown Anti-Missionary from New York. The meeting just happened to be taking place at the synagogue I had seen from the train and had been praying for! I went to the meeting and was immediately befriended by Anti-Missionary #2. He decided he was going to make me his "project."

The world-renown Anti-Missionary boasted about his activities. He mocked the Christ in the Passover presentation that Jewish believers observe, but, in essence, shared the Gospel! If you put the blood of the Passover lamb on your door post, the angel of death passes over. If you put the blood of Messiah Jesus, the Passover Lamb, on the doorpost of your heart, death passes over you.

The local Anti-Missionaries bragged about a Jewish woman they were able to get to renounce faith in Jesus. They helped her become Balteshuvah, which means they turned her back to Rabbinic Judaism. Rabbinic Judaism refers to the current practice of Judaism that depends on the teachings of Rabbis, since the Temple was destroyed in 70 AD and the biblical way of obeying God no longer could be followed. Rabbis began to teach that the Jewish people could be made right with God by doing good deeds (charity), praying (devotion) and studying Torah (the first five books of the Bible) rather than through the Temple sacrifice system. They talked her into moving to New York and attending a woman's Orthodox Yeshiva (school). My heart went out to her, and I began to pray for her.

The world-renown Anti-Missionary could care less about meeting me, until Anti-Missionary #2, told him I was Jewish and believed in Yoska (derogatory slang for Jesus). He insisted I take his phone number and call him. I called him that week and spent over an hour sharing my testimony, and we exchanged many e-mails and instant messages for years.

Anti-Missionary #2 put me in touch with an Orthodox Rabbi who invited me over to his home to discuss anything I wanted to. I asked to discuss Messianic prophecy, and he said, "Anything but that!" As time went on, I soon discovered this Orthodox Rabbi to be Anti-Missionary #3! I also found out he worked with Anti-Missionary #1.

Anti-Missionary #2 invited me to his house for Shabbos dinners. (The term Shabbos is used by Ashkenazi Jews often with an Eastern European heritage, while Shabbat is the preferred term used by Sephardic Jews, typically Israelis and Spanish-speaking Jews. Both terms means the same thing.) We would discuss Scripture and go round and round and round. He tempted me with sweets, but no sweets can dissuade me from the sweetest Name I know! I loved going to his house for Shabbos meals because he would invite others and tell them about my belief. When he would walk out of the room, his guests would ask me why I believed in Jesus, giving me an opportunity to share! One time he gave me a book to read and the world-renown Anti-Missionary's tape collection concerning Isaiah 53. A great many Jewish people come to faith after reading Isaiah 53. I did.

The book Anti-Missionary #2 gave me was written by an elderly Orthodox Rabbi in Toronto, Canada. Some say there are two Messiahs. One is the suffering servant Messiah, called Moshiach ben Joseph so named because of Joseph's many hardships in Egypt. The other is the conquering hero Messiah, called Moshiach ben David, referring to David's reign as King of Israel. The Rabbi said Isaiah 53 was talking about Moshiach ben Joseph. The Anti-Missionary's tapes say Isaiah 53 is talking about Israel, a more common belief among Jewish people. I went back to Anti-Missionary #2 and told him about my findings. He immediately called the elderly Rabbi in Toronto and asked him why he wrote a book saying Jesus is the Messiah!

Many Rabbis do believe Jesus is the Messiah. There was a famous Rabbi in Israel named Yitzhak Kaduri. He claimed that he knew who the Messiah was. He wrote the name of the Messiah on a piece of paper and told them not to look at it until a year after his death. When they looked at the paper, it said that Jesus is the Messiah!

Anti-Missionary #2 spent the next seven years trying to talk me out of Jesus. He would call me and leave hostile messages. He would send me hostile e-mails. He would go on and on in endless instant messages over the Internet. He even invited me to his synagogue to meet his Rabbi who asked me why I believe in Jesus, in earshot range of several other congregants! That turns out to be an incidental way to share the Gospel with by-standers. Finally, Anti-Missionary #2 decided I was hopeless and gave up on trying to get me to renounce Jesus.

Meanwhile, Anti-Missionary #1, called me and wanted to meet for lunch again. At lunch he suggested I speak with a friend of his who used to believe in Jesus. He gave me the phone number and to my total joy and amazement, it was the young Jewish woman who renounced Jesus that he wanted me to speak with. What an answer to prayer. I called her and she asked me why I believed in Jesus. We exchanged e-mail addresses and debated many Scriptures concerning Messiah for many months until we lost touch.

Jesus Loves You

A friend and I represented our church at the Georgia Baptist convention in Savannah. My friend needed to go to Savannah to pick up a van from a church for the drug and alcohol rehabilitation ministry he was involved with. He had wanted me to drive him there so he could drive the van back to Atlanta. It gave us an opportunity to represent the church at the convention, get the van and do some Jewish ministry while I was there.

The three main branches of Judaism are Orthodox, Conservative and Reform, and Savannah offered all three in easy proximity. My friend and I went to the service at the Orthodox Synagogue, and they wanted to know why we were in Savannah, so we told them and shared about our belief! We went to the Conservative Synagogue and picked up a directory of all their members, and I prayed over them! We went to the Reform synagogue which is the third oldest Jewish congregation in the United States. It was closed so we couldn't go on a tour. We prayer-walked it seven times. On the seventh time around, the door opened and they let someone in, so I reached in and gave them a tract!

We went to the church to pick up the van on November 15. I mentioned to the pastor that this day was the anniversary of my baptism and also the anniversary of my Bar Mitzvah. The pastor said when he was located in Atlanta, a Jewish man attended their services. I just happened to know of him and told the pastor I had heard Steve had renounced his faith in Jesus. This miraculous meeting prompted me to start praying for him again.

After the trip to Savannah, I started immersing myself in Atlanta's Jewish life. I took various classes at synagogues and Jewish centers, and I joined the Jewish centers. I also began to visit Atlanta's synagogues, to eat at kosher restaurants and to go to various "lunch-and-learns" at different Jewish places, basically doing whatever I could do to be around Jewish people so I could pray for them, ask challenging questions and share with them.

At the Orthodox synagogue where I was taking a class, I usually sat in an empty area praying God would bring who he wanted me to share with. During one class, I sat down and was joined by an Orthodox man and another woman sitting down next to him. As the two of them began talking, I realized the Orthodox man sitting next to me was Steve, the one I had been praying for who renounced his belief in Jesus! It turned out the woman was a Jewish believer in Jesus!

"For God so loved the world that He gave His one and only Son,
that whoever believes in Him shall not perish
but have eternal life."
John 3:16

For God so loved Steve that he sent two Jewish believers in Jesus to wrap Messiah's love around him in the middle of an Orthodox Synagogue. I made sure to introduce myself, tell him about my belief in Jesus and tell him that I had been praying for him. I ran into him later at some Jewish Singles functions and reminded him that Jesus loves him and died for his sins.

Is Jesus the Messiah?

I made it a habit to work out at the gym at the Jewish Center. I was in the locker room and Anti-Missionary #3, the Orthodox Rabbi I had met earlier, came up to me and said he noticed I signed up for his class, "Is Jesus the Messiah?" Of course he already knew I was a believer in Jesus. Anti-Missionary #3 told me if I dared to open my mouth about Jesus, he would have me removed! I brought my friend Josh, another Jewish believer in Jesus, to the class, and he shared his testimony!

This was a three-week class, and the next guest speaker was Steve, the Jewish man who had renounced Jesus whom I had been praying for. The anti-missionaries had him speak at their men's meetings and different events around town. Someone asked him why they should believe what he was teaching. Couldn't he change his mind again and believe in Jesus? It turned out he eventually started dating a Gentile believer, and from what I heard she took him to church and he did give his life back to the Lord but continued to live in the Orthodox world. Unfortunately, the pressures of him living in two different worlds caused him to commit suicide?

"Finally, be strong in the Lord and in His mighty power. Put on the full armor of God, so that you are able to stand against the schemes of the devil. For our struggle is not against flesh and blood, but against the rulers, against the powers, against the worldly forces of this darkness, and against the spiritual forces of wickedness in the heavenly places." -Ephesians 6:10-12

Oy Vey!

I signed up for a five-week beginner's Hebrew course on Monday nights at a local traditional (somewhere between Orthodox and conservative) synagogue. The visiting teacher was Orthodox. There were about 25 people in the class and we started by introducing ourselves and saying what congregation we belonged to. I told them my congregation was my Mount Vernon Baptist Church! Needless to say there were gasps, horrified looks and questions as to why I was there. Whenever I made any reference whatsoever to Christianity, you could hear the murmuring begin.

After the five weeks were over, it was decided the teacher would continue for anyone who wanted to keep studying. The class dwindled down to about eight but went on for another three months until the teacher needed to step down for a maternity leave. There was an Orthodox Rabbi that would be willing to take over the class if he had at least a few students willing to commit to it. A woman who had been most antagonistic to me being there actually called me and was so very friendly because they needed me to stay in the class, and I did.

Available to Serve

About this time, I hit a glitch with my employment. I was let go from my job at BellSouth, but I was given two months' severance pay and six months of unemployment benefits. This enabled me to minister full-time while job searching and seeking the Lord for my next steps.

I had lost my job during the "Days of Awe." This is a 10-day Jewish observance between Rosh Hashanah (the Jewish New Year) and Yom Kippur (the Day of Atonement) that focuses on repentance. I visited Beth Hallel on Yom Kippur. At Messianic Congregations, Jewish and non-Jewish believers in Jesus worship together.

After the service I stood up to leave. The Lord sat me down and told me to pray for the parents of the man sitting in front of me whom I had met but barely knew.

Later, a friend called me and told me she met a Jewish believer in Jesus at her church. I took down her information, but didn't feel I should contact her then. A month later another friend called from the same church and told me about this same Jewish believer in Jesus so I called her. I met with this Jewish believer, and we prayer-walked synagogues around town together.

Not too long after that, the same Jewish believer called me and asked if I could pick her up (her car was broken) and take her to witness to an elderly Jewish woman dying of cancer. We went to visit the woman, shared our testimonies and the woman prayed to receive Jesus! She was the mother of the man sitting in front of me at Beth Hallel on Yom Kippur!

Temple Sinai

There was a Reform synagogue near my church, and they actually used our church parking lot during the High Holidays. I started going to that synagogue for services, classes and events. I told Rabbi Krantz about my belief in Jesus and asked if it was ok for me to be there. The Rabbi allowed me to be there, and I actually went there seven days a week for something or another. I would go to Sunday School at the Temple (Reform synagogues are often called Temple) and then to my church afterwards. I really fell in love with the people there, continually prayed for them and went every day for two months. Word got out about my belief. A visiting "New Age" Hebrew teacher would follow me around and got me to share Jesus with her just so she could run to the Rabbi and say I tried to convert her. Sadly, the Rabbi left me a voice mail telling me not to come back.

B'Nai Torah

I really felt burdened for Rabbi Radler at the Traditional synagogue where I was taking the Hebrew course. I called the Rabbi, I e-mailed the Rabbi and even sent him a letter, but there was no response.

Rabbi Radler was teaching a class at the Jewish Center called, "What Do Jews Believe?" Most Jews don't even know what they believe. They look to their Rabbis for all the answers. I once asked an Orthodox Jew, "What if your Rabbi is wrong?" His reply was, "Hashem will move heaven and earth to make what the Rabbi said come true." *Hashem* translates from Hebrew to English as "the name," meaning *God,* whose name is above all names. They don't use His name out of reverence. So this man was telling me that he believed God would intervene to make what his Rabbi said to be true. He put his faith in the Rabbi's words rather than God's Word.

I took that class, and there were all kinds of questions. Someone asked what Jews believe about heaven and hell. The old adage is you ask three Jews a question and you get five opinions. Someone else asked what Jews believe about Jesus!

After the class, I introduced myself to the Rabbi and told him I had been trying to meet with him. He gave me his card and told me to make an appointment with his secretary. I had to go to the bathroom really bad, but I was just dying to talk to someone about the Jesus question that was raised. I prayed the entire time I was in the bathroom to be able to witness to someone.

As I walked out of the bathroom, the woman who had asked the question about Jesus was walking by! I walked out to the parking lot with her and shared my faith. Her car was parked right next to mine.

I began praying for this inquiring woman after that class. I went to a dinner party at a friend's apartment, and she was also invited. I went into the store, and she was at the cash machine in front of the store. I went to a Jewish lecture, and she was there, too. I visited her synagogue, and when she sat down on the pew next to me and realized it was me, she freaked out. She had to be calmed down by her boyfriend. I think I counted a total of eight divine appointments.

I set up an appointment and met with Rabbi Radler who had taught the class at the Jewish Center on what Jews believe. We used his Tanakhs (Old Testaments) for our discussion. He had the *Stone Edition* (Orthodox) and gave me the Jewish Publication Society edition (Reform). Being new to this, I just threw everything I could at him, hoping something would take root. He asked how a man could be God, and I showed him the following Scripture:

*"For to us a child is born, a Son will be given to us,
and the government will be upon His shoulder.
His Name will be called Wonderful Counselor,
Mighty God My Father of Eternity, Everlasting Father,
Prince of Peace.*

*Of the increase of His government and shalom
there will be no end."*
-Isaiah 9:5-6a

He read it in his *Stone* edition and didn't think much of it, so I showed him the JPS edition. The Rabbi got very nervous, started sweating and began rubbing his finger between his neck and his shirt collar. He immediately did something very smart. He looked up the verse in the original Hebrew. He kind of looked at me and smiled as if to say, "You may have something here." This Rabbi was only in his forties, but died a few years later. Praise God for pushing me so hard to meet with him!

Funny You Should Mention That

I worked various temporary jobs while I waited on the Lord for my next steps. I took a one-day temporary job in my neighborhood. The job was right near an Orthodox café, so I went there for lunch. The café was crowded, and seating was limited. Since I was by myself, there was an extra seat at my table. An Orthodox woman asked if she could sit there since there was nowhere else to sit. She said she was married to a doctor who traveled to various medical offices all around the state.

She complained to me that her husband was constantly confronted by Christians. I said, "Funny you should mention that," and shared my belief with her. You should have seen her face! I began praying for her and her family, and after that we kept running into each other around town. I ran into her at the mall, at the Jewish Center, at the grocery store and at a Kosher Festival at an Orthodox Synagogue, at least seven divine appointments with her and her family all over Atlanta.

God Had Different Plans

I had been volunteering with a friend's Drug and Alcohol Rehabilitation program by participating in their weekly Bible study. I gave Jewish perspectives and encouraged the guys to witness to their Jewish acquaintances. We were in a Jewish area, so almost everyone had Jewish acquaintances.

My friend's director offered me a live-in job doing fundraising for the Drug and Alcohol Rehabilitation program. Since the program was housed in apartments located in a Jewish neighborhood, I thought this would allow me the opportunity to continue my Jewish Outreach because I would be living in the program apartments.

I gave up my apartment, gave away my extra clothes, and gave away all my furniture. I called my friend's director to make the final arrangements to move in. Apparently the money they had received to hire me was used for something else? I had no job, and I was now homeless?

DIRECTION

Destin, Florida

It was summer 2000. I packed all my earthly possessions into my car and headed south to our church Singles retreat in Destin, Florida, that I had already planned to attend. I had hoped the Lord would give me guidance and direction while I was there, and I believe He did.

I was supposed to eventually go back to my church in the middle of Jewish Atlanta, but first I was to go to Tampa to stay with my parents for a time. They had a T-shirt business and very much wanted me to live and work with them. I really didn't want to, but thought it was a viable option until the Lord showed me the next steps.

> *"Call upon Me in the day of trouble.*
> *When I rescue you, you will honor Me."*
> *-Psalm 50:15*

Tampa, Florida

My parents sold all kinds of touristy Florida T-shirts and arranged for me to have a flea market booth that could be rented on a monthly basis until I decided what I wanted to do.

They had gone to an auction and bid blindly on a box of T-shirt decals which turned out to have hundreds of Christian decals. I figured, if I'm breathing I should be witnessing. I took the Christian decals, put them on T-shirts and made a big display of Christian T-shirts at my booth. A busload of girl scouts from Alabama arrived at the flea market and started buying everything on my tables! My sales were almost twice that of my parents!

My parents couldn't believe how much money I made and asked how I did it. I told them it was the Christian T-shirts. They immediately made displays of Christian T-shirts at their flea market booths, which were by both main entrances to their flea markets. My father displayed a T-shirt with Jesus on the cross which said, "Thank You Jesus!" right over the doorway. My uncle once asked my mother how business was and she said, "Praise the Lord, Jesus saved us!"

For the next 10 years, Christian after Christian would witness to my parents and give them Gospel tracts. Thousands upon thousands of flea market customers were witnessed to by those T-shirts. Thousands of Christians purchased those T-shirts to use as a witness to others, sending the Gospel message literally all over the world! My homelessness became an incredible blessing I could never have thought of!

"But as it is written, "Things no eye has seen and no ear has heard,
that have not entered the heart of mankind
— these things God has prepared for those who love Him."
-1 Corinthians 2:9

My friend Mark Landrum, a Jews for Jesus missionary in London, England, at that time, asked if I wanted to volunteer for a two-week street evangelism campaign in London preceded by a week of training in Paris.

There was no doubt this was God's next step for me. I was so excited! I bought the cheapest plane ticket I could get from Tampa to London, but had to make stops in Miami and New York. I had never been to either London or Paris so this really was an adventure for me.

Paris, France

Both the London office of Jews for Jesus and their Paris office had two-week evangelistic outreaches in the summer. They combined the training for both outreaches in Paris because it was more economically feasible to have all the training staff in one place. We spent a week being trained day and night at an old Bible college. One morning at breakfast, one of the French volunteers said to me, "But you are an American. What can you do in Paris?" I just looked at her and said, "I can't do anything, but Jesus can!"

"'Not by might, nor by power, but by My Ruach (Spirit),
'says Adonai-Tzva'ot (the LORD Almighty)."
-Zechariah 4:6b

Later that afternoon, we finally got to go outside and do some evangelism. I had been assigned to hand out broadsides (Jews for Jesus term for

Gospel tracts) on the Champs Élysées and couldn't have been more excited.

Ironically, I had been paired up with that same French volunteer from breakfast. Five minutes into it, she came running over to me and said, "Steve, there are four Israelis and they don't speak French. Can you talk with them in English?" So I did.

Later on, two tourists, a husband and wife, walked over and asked if we were with *Jews for Jesus*. Our T-shirts said, "Juif pour Jesus." I told them we were. He said they were Christians and had supported *Jews for Jesus* for years! I asked him where he was from, and he said the United States of America. I asked where, and he said they were from Atlanta, Georgia. I said, "Me too!" They volunteered to pick up discarded broadsides for us as they walked up the street.

London, England

After the training in Paris, we went back to London. We went to Speaker's Corner in Hyde Park. It's a place where people stand on soap boxes and talk about whatever they want, kind of like Venice Beach in California.

Someone from Jews for Jesus was on a soap box proclaiming Jesus. The woman next to me asked, "How can you be Jewish and believe in Jesus?" I turned to her and said, "I'm Jewish, and I believe in Jesus!" Right as I turned, I noticed the couple from Atlanta whom I had met in Paris! The woman from Jews for Jesus on the soap box started talking with the Jewish woman next to me, and I spoke to the couple from Atlanta.

I asked the man what kind of job he had that he could fly around like this. It turned out he was a pilot for The Coca-Cola Company. A while back, some of my Christian friends at Coke had come to my apartment in Atlanta for a prayer meeting. We specifically prayed God would give a mutual co-worker a Christian pilot to witness to them, and this man, George, turned out to be that pilot, and God wanted to make sure I met him.

We spent two weeks distributing broadsides, showing off our evangelistic T-shirts, and sharing the Gospel with people all over London. We would get up early in the morning and minister until late at night six days a week. I went to the Orthodox neighborhood and shared the Gospel with a man who was a Gentile, and he prayed to receive the Lord.

After the campaign was over, the Jews for Jesus team asked me what I was doing next. I told them I was waiting on the Lord, and they suggested I volunteer on their New York City campaign which was still going on for another week. Since my plane ticket just happened to have a stop in New York, I got off the plane and volunteered for another week in New York City!

New York City, New York

The very first place they sent me to share the Gospel was the World Trade Center. I immediately prayed, "Lord don't let this be the day they blow it up again." Most people forget the World Trade Center had been previously bombed in 1993, and I had no doubt it could happen again.

Later that same day, I distributed broadsides in Greenwich Village. A Jewish man stopped to tell me he had seen me earlier before going to his job at the World Trade Center, and he thought it was amazing that he saw me again! I told him God was trying to get his attention, and he needed to get right with God.

Another time, I was being harassed by someone passing by in one of the New York City subways where I was distributing broadsides. The man kept harassing me and walked right into a pole!

"Do not touch My anointed ones,
and do My prophets no harm."
-Psalm 105:15

While I was volunteering on the New York City campaign, I was told there would be a two-week campaign in Toronto, Canada, right afterwards.

Toronto, Canada

So, I hopped on a bus, and up north I went! Almost every time we went out on the streets in Toronto, a group of anti-missionaries would follow us around and harass us. Apparently they had a network of people that would alert them to our presence whenever we would start distributing tracts.

Many Orthodox women would walk up to me and all of them would say the same thing, "You should be ashamed of yourself!" I replied with, "I am ashamed of my sins, but my sins are forgiven. How are your sins forgiven?" They would gasp and walk away.

"For the life of the creature is in the blood, and I have given it to you on the altar to make atonement for your lives—for it is the blood that makes atonement because of the life."
-Leviticus 17:11

The Toronto anti-missionaries took my picture and put it in their magazine. I received an e-mail from Anti-Missionary #1, asking me if I had been in Canada that summer. You sneeze in New York, and they say *gesundheit* (God bless you) in Miami!

Marietta, Georgia

After Toronto, I flew back to Florida. Although my parents were disappointed I would be leaving, I knew it was time to go back to Atlanta. My pastor's secretary told me one of the seniors at the church had a furnished basement in Marietta to rent out for only $300 per month. She kept the price cheap because she liked to rent it out to men from the church, so I moved in.

A few years later Jews for Jesus had a campaign in Los Angeles. That same picture of me was on the cover of the Jewish Journal of Greater Los Angeles with a readership estimated at 160,000. There was a caption next to my picture saying, "Guess who's coming to town?" and they made the shadow of my body into the shape of a cross.

THE JEWISH JOURNAL
OF GREATER LOS ANGELES

Guess Who's Coming to Town

As Jews for Jesus mounts its largest-ever Southern California campaign, local leaders prepare to fight back.

ENDS OF THE EARTH

Marietta, Georgia

My summer boot camp adventure hadn't quite ended. My friend Mark who had invited me to London also invited me to the Jews for Jesus campaign in Sydney, Australia, taking place during the 2000 Summer Olympics. When I found out it was a 19-hour plane flight to Australia, I was awed by how far away it was. I had never been that far away from home.

I knew I was going to the ends of the earth! Friends gave me a buddy pass to fly to Australia, and it only cost $500 roundtrip to fly from Atlanta to Sydney with stops in California each way. The only catch was, I had to arrive two weeks early in order to be able to get a seat, since so many travelers were going to the Olympics.

San Francisco, California

Apprehension, anxiety and nervousness about flying so far from home kept me up the entire night before I was to leave. I had an early morning flight to San Francisco with a 14-hour layover before flying to Sydney.

I was absolutely exhausted. I had been up all night, barely slept on the plane and was jet-lagged from the cross-country flight.

As I walked off the plane, a woman stopped in front of our gate to fix her shoe. I recognized her, it was my friend Saheen, whom I knew from First Baptist Atlanta. She had just broken up with her Jewish boyfriend because he wasn't a Christian and gave me his contact information so I could send him Gospel materials. She just happened to be flying in from Los Angeles and God made sure her shoe broke in front of my gate.

That day churches from all over the Bay Area just happened to be having a citywide day of prayer. A friend picked me up at the airport, and I went with her to a church to be assigned a street to prayer walk.

I was standing on the street we were assigned when God literally forced my head to turn to the high-rise at the end of the street. "Pray for your cousin." I shook it off and went back to what I was doing. I'd been told, my cousin had moved to Northern California, but I had no idea where.

My head is once again, forced to turn to the high rise, "Pray for your cousin." *I must be imagining this.*

A third time, God forced my head to turn toward that high-rise and again told me to pray for my cousin! I did, even though I had no clue why. (I later learned that very building is where my cousin lived at the time.)

Sydney, Australia

I arrived two weeks early for the Olympic Outreach. A local family didn't want to be in Sydney during the Olympics and gave us their house to use while they went on vacation. Before our outreach started, I distributed Gospel tracts and helped the printer who was behind in printing the thousands of tracts we planned to use.

I would eat lunch at an Armenian luncheonette near the printer. I became friendly with my waiter and started witnessing to him. The owner came out, and it turned out to be the waiter's father. The waiter left, but the father sat down with me and wanted to hear what I had to say.

Apparently, he had just received a letter from his mother-in-law in Armenia telling him that she had become a Christian and that he needed to become one, too! I shared the Gospel with him, and he prayed to receive Jesus! A few days later I ran into the waiter on the street, shared the Gospel, and he too prayed to receive Jesus!

It was so exciting to be able to stand in one place and distribute Gospel tracts to people from literally all over the world who had come to see the Olympic Games. My favorite place to distribute tracts was at the train station. Thousands upon thousands of people would walk by and be challenged by our evangelistic T-shirts, and we could distribute as many as 1,800 tracts in one two-hour period!

One day I was distributing tracts at the train station and noticed a former co-worker from Coke who once expressed a desire to ask God if He was real. I made sure to give my former co-worker a broadside!

Los Angeles, California

I flew back from Sydney with a stop in Los Angeles. My plane was filled with Olympic medal winners. When we arrived in Los Angeles, crowds awaited our plane at the airport to greet the medal winners. The crowds cheered, applauded and mobbed the medal winners.

Marietta, Georgia

I had just completed 10 weeks of grueling street evangelism and training. I had been to five cities in five different countries on three different continents. I was physically and emotionally drained. I had been physically assaulted, spit at, cursed at, had rocks and bottles thrown at me, had people yell at me, had my tracts ripped up and thrown at me, was stalked by anti-missionaries and questioned by police almost everywhere I went.

I couldn't help but feel somewhat discouraged because there was no one to meet me at the airport and no one there to cheer me on. But I knew I had done what God had called me to do, and I must find my significance in serving Him, not from others. I had also learned that you cannot take the spiritual and physical abuse personally. It is Jesus they have a problem with, not me or you.

> *"Happy is the one who endures testing,*
> *because when he has stood the test,*
> *he will receive the crown of life,*
> *which the LORD promised to those who love Him."*
> *-James 1:12*

In all, I spent a week in Paris, two weeks in London, a week in New York, two weeks in Toronto and four weeks in Sydney. During these weeks, hundreds of thousands were challenged by my evangelistic clothing, tens of thousands were given tracts, I verbally shared with many and several prayed to receive Jesus. Friendships were made that will last a lifetime. My experiences had shaped me, preparing me for future ministry and I will cherish all these experiences and relationships for eternity. It is so exciting to serve the Lord!

MY JERUSALEM

Lucent

My summer adventure 2000 was over. I came back to my apartment in Marietta, Georgia, and began looking for work and found a temp-to-perm job at Lucent Technologies in Norcross. The office manager called me into the conference room to orient me to the group. She began to tell me about Jesus, and I told her I was Jewish and believed in him, too. She was so excited she started screaming and telling everyone!

The two of us made up gift cups with a cross and candy inside each one. We got to work really early and put one on each person's desk for Christmas. I asked her if anyone was Jewish, and she didn't think so. Later that day a new employee from Chicago slammed the gift on her desk and said he was Jewish! I tried to give him a Hanukkah gift, but he refused it.

Marietta, Georgia

I worked during the day and evangelized at night and on weekends. One Friday night, during Sukkot (the biblical Festival of Tabernacles), I got into my car and prayed about what I was going to do. I decided right then and there I would give Friday nights to the Lord by going to different synagogues and allowing God to use me. I thought about going to the main synagogue in the Orthodox neighborhood, but the Lord reminded me about going to my Jerusalem, my own neighborhood, first. I knew that meant going to the Orthodox synagogue in my town.

> *"But you will receive power when the Ruach ha-Kodesh has come upon you; and you will be My witnesses in Jerusalem, and through all Judah, and Samaria, and to the end of the earth."*
> *-Acts 1:8*

As divine providence would have it, there was a group of Jewish singles visiting this same synagogue that first Friday night. The leader of this group had an e-mail list of about 1,000 Jewish singles.

Every Friday night they would meet at a different synagogue and either have dinner before or after the service as well as other functions within the Jewish community. I was invited to be part of this group. After the service, we'd go to someone's apartment for an Oneg (means "delight," usually refreshments).

When we went to the apartment the first time, there were some singles there I had witnessed to before, and they immediately told the leader of the group about my belief. I wasn't trying to hide my belief, but I didn't feel I needed to hit them over the head with it at the time.

The leader allowed me to be a part of the group because I was Jewish, and he wanted to try to win me back to Rabbinic Judaism. Over the years, many Rabbis and singles complained about me being there, but he defended his decision and allowed me to continue going around with them on and off for years.

Jewish Singles Group

Our Jewish Singles' group went to various synagogues all over Atlanta. I prayed for the people there and would share with them as the Lord enabled. One night after a service, we all went with the youth director to his parsonage house behind the synagogue, and he asked me why I believed in Jesus and allowed me to share in front of the entire group.

Another time we all went to a synagogue for a Passover meal. In religious circles, Jewish people pray before and after the meal (called "benching"). They usually have a Kohen (someone from the Levitical priestly line) do the closing prayer. Usually people with names starting with "K" like Kaplan, Katz, Kahn or Cohen are Kohens.

My grandmother and father told me I was a Kohen. The only way they could have known that is because it had been passed down from previous generations. Rabbis have also told me I am a Kohen because of the name Kaplan. The Rabbi asked for a Kohen to volunteer to do the closing prayers. I was the only one who raised his hand. The Rabbi looked around the room, ignored me, and said he would do it. Everyone who knew me laughed!

One night we met at a restaurant for dinner. One of the singles was sitting at a table by himself, and I felt led to join him. We started talking and he invited me to a class he was taking. It just happened to be the Monday night Hebrew course I used to be in! Apparently he joined it after I left for my summer adventure.

The New Apartment

About this time, I moved to a new living situation. Marietta is on the northwest side of Atlanta and my job was on the northeast side. The commute was horrendous during rush hour. I decided to move in with twin brothers Josh & Graham, both Jewish believers in Jesus, as they were more centrally located in Buckhead. I had a bed and bathroom in the living room and used their shower upstairs. It helped them to have another person sharing the rent.

Monday Night Hebrew Class

I started going back to the Monday night Hebrew course. The class had dwindled down to the Orthodox Rabbi, the Jewish single, the antagonistic Jewish woman, a hostile Jewish woman from South Africa and me.

I left the class early one night and made sure to tell them all why! David Brickner, the Executive Director of Jews for Jesus, was on *Larry King Live* debating Rabbi Shmuley Boteach. David did an awesome job, and I made sure to pray for both Larry King and Shmuley Boteach.

The Orthodox Rabbi teaching the Hebrew course wanted us to experience "Shabbat" so he invited us to his synagogue and to his home for Shabbat lunch afterwards. It was an act of God to coordinate all of us and the two women's spouses to meet on the same Saturday, but we finally did.

Shabbat Lunch

At the synagogue, they had a class for beginners taught by a popular local Rabbi. I attended the class. Afterwards, a young woman came running into the class. She had wanted to meet the Rabbi. As they began talking, to my total amazement, I realized this young Jewish woman was, the one the anti-missionaries got to renounce Jesus! Oh how I prayed for her!

> *"I called upon You, O God, for You will answer me.*
> *Incline Your ear to me, hear my speech."*
> *-Psalm 17:6*

111

This woman was absolutely shocked to meet me there. We exchanged email addresses and stayed in touch. She had moved to Jerusalem but happened to be visiting Atlanta that weekend. She was trying her best to be an anti-missionary.

You Believe What?

She wanted to meet me for breakfast and brought her sister. She wanted to show her sister how to "deprogram" a missionary. The sister wanted to know why I believed in Jesus and had me share my testimony. You should have seen her squirm as I shared the Gospel of Jesus Christ with her sister in the middle of a Kosher restaurant!

Full-Time Ministry

David Brickner, the Executive Director of Jews for Jesus, called me personally and offered me an eight-month ministry position as a "Tiger Team" missionary. I thought to myself, *Wow, I never met anyone who had been on Larry King, let alone have them offer me a job!* Jews for Jesus was organizing worldwide *"Behold Your God!"* campaigns in any cities with 25,000 Jewish people or more. We would be doing street evangelism in cities all over the United States for five months and then in South Africa for the last three months.

Lucent

My temp-to-perm job never did go perm, but they allowed me to stay on until I took the ministry position if I would be willing to work at their other location.

The other location just happened to be in Sandy Springs at what used to be the AT&T building and where I had worked before. My department was in the same place as that job I had quit after one day. At the time, I had asked God to put me back there if He wanted me to be there; and eight years later, there I was again!

I asked my boss for a half day off to go to a friend's funeral, and she asked me, "Who died?"

I thought, *Doesn't she believe me, why would she be asking who died? It' not like she would know my friend.*

"I told her who died."

She said, "Your friend was my next door neighbor. I know he died and that today is his funeral. I wanted to go too, but I'm too upset to go."

Of course she let me go to the funeral. And obviously, God sent me to this job to minister to my boss.

Since the company wasn't hiring me, they gave me a menial job to do, and I was so bored! I prayed the Lord would do something.

A friend called to tell me her friend was supposed to go on a mission trip to Portugal but got sick. The trip was already paid for. They wanted me to take his place, and my boss let me have two weeks off even though I was only coming back for one week before leaving for the ministry position with Jews for Jesus.

Newark, New Jersey

I had to fly to Newark, New Jersey, to catch the flight to Lisbon, Portugal. It was Passover time, and I had distributed Passover Gospel tracts at the airport in Newark. I just happened to give them out to passengers going to Ft. Lauderdale and primarily of the Jewish persuasion.

Porto, Portugal

After arriving in Portugal, our group of about 80 or so spent a couple of days in Lisbon for orientation. They sent us out in groups of two or four all over Portugal. I was assigned to a pastor in Porto, Portugal. It just so happened this particular pastor was from Brazil, used to run a camp there and had a great love for the Orthodox Jewish children who would come to his camp every year.

We met with different believers in their homes usually for dinner first. I have to admit it was somewhat of a cultural shock to see a carved up pig on almost every dinner table. They invited whoever they could, and we shared our testimonies with them. We also had our testimonies translated into Portuguese. This was very fruitful and several prayed to receive Jesus.

The pastor's daughter had wanted to visit the small synagogue of about 30 members, but never had. My being in Porto gave her a reason, and we went. Since this synagogue was small, there was no regular Rabbi, but a visiting one from Israel had come for their Passover season. They were so excited I was there!

An Orthodox Jewish man showed us around. After the service, I told the man about my belief and gave him a copy of my translated testimony. He began to read it, put his hand on his forehead and said, "Baptista, Baptista! Look what he gave me!" He ran around the synagogue and told everyone about my belief! Good news travels fast! I asked the Rabbi who he thought Jesus was, but he just smiled at me.

Monday Night Hebrew Class

After I returned from Portugal, I said goodbye to the people at my Hebrew course. They asked where I was going, and I told them California. Then they asked why, and I told them I got a job out there. Then they asked what kind of job, and I told them I would be working for Jews for Jesus! They were so mad. They said they thought I had come back to the fold and wanted to know why I came to the class for so long? I told them it was because God told me to, that I loved them and that I was there to pray they would meet their Jewish Messiah. The Rabbi mocked me for saying that God spoke to me.

California Here I Come

I finished my week at Lucent, moved all my stuff out except my bed (Josh asked if they could keep it for guests), sold my car and flew to San Francisco to start working with Jews for Jesus in April 2001.

TIGER TEAM USA

San Francisco, California

What an honor and privilege it was to be serving on the first United States Jews for Jesus "Behold Your God!" campaign in 2001. There were four of us on the first "Tiger Team," which may have been inspired by my outreach from the summer before. We started in San Francisco and went from city to city ending up in South Africa primarily doing street evangelism for eight months.

> "So go into the highways and byways,
> and invite everyone you find to the banquet feast."
> -Matthew 22:9

During the Jews for Jesus San Francisco "Behold Your God!" campaign, a homeless woman thanked me for giving her a Gospel broadside. She was living in a shelter with her four-year-old son. She said others would keep stealing her Bible and the broadside was the only Scripture she had to read to her son!

My team leader was a Jews for Jesus missionary in Maryland. I asked him if he happened to know one of my Jewish friends from Maryland, but he didn't know her. Later that night he handed me a stack of contact cards so I could call people, and I went through them. Miraculously, the woman I had just asked him about had moved to the Bay Area and I was able to reconnect with her!

On the National Day of Prayer, Jews for Jesus headquarters staff partnered with us in prayer while we shared with people. I distributed Gospel tracts on the campus of San Francisco State University while a staff member prayed. A student from Singapore walked past, and I asked him who he thought Jesus was. He shrugged his shoulders and apathetically guessed, "Savior?" I shared the Gospel with him and asked him if he wanted to pray to receive Jesus to which he replied, "I guess so." As we finished praying, he grabbed my hand, started shaking it vigorously and kept thanking me over and over!

On the last day of the campaign, we ministered at the "Bay to Breakers Race." Some 28,000 people participated in this event. There are a lot of people who wear costumes or nothing at all as well as some serious runners. We had a team behind the finish line handing out broadsides or giving foot massages and sharing the Gospel to a captive audience.

My cousin, whom God told me to pray for the year before, was a serious runner. I did a Google search and found his name in several races. I had hoped he would be in this race and prayed I would run into him. The people who were supposed to pick us up to take us to the race were 90 minutes late because of all the traffic from the race. I was rather upset because I didn't want to miss a chance to see my cousin.

We had to park several blocks from the finish line and zigzag through several side streets to get to the race. By the time we actually made it, the serious runners were already finishing the race and were leaving the area. As we walked up one side street, I noticed one of the runners walking toward us. To my absolute joy and amazement, it was my cousin. He was just as excited to see me as I was to see him. He gave me his phone numbers and told me to make sure I contacted him!

After the campaign ended, we were given choices of where we could work for a month until the next campaign. I stayed and worked out of the San Francisco branch of Jews for Jesus. There was a game at Giants Stadium on Father's Day. It was sold out to capacity, and I brought about 4,200 broadsides with me, the most ever! I stood on a narrow walkway by a bridge from the parking lot to the stadium. Streams of people kept coming by and taking broadsides. I stayed there almost three hours until I gave away every broadside I had with me.

I spent a lot of time at the trolley turnaround and witnessed to people from literally all over the world, praying with many people to receive Jesus. One guy was on his cell phone and ended his conversation so he could talk with me. He told me his sister had been taking him to church, and he knew by seeing me it was time for him to pray to receive Jesus.

I met my cousin for dinner, but the name of Jesus didn't come up. I met him again later, with his girlfriend, who was also Jewish. She had a good friend who was Jewish and believed in Jesus and wanted to know why I believed in Jesus. After dinner I went with my cousin to his apartment. It was in that building God turned my head towards when He told me to pray for my cousin the year before on my way to Australia when I flew through San Francisco.

Milwaukee, Wisconsin

My team drove across the country to the next outreach in Milwaukee, Wisconsin. Mark Landrum led the two-week campaign, which was centered around Summerfest, which is billed as the world's largest music festival complete with baseball games, crowded shopping malls and busy street corners all over the city.

While distributing broadsides on a street corner, I noticed a woman nearby watching me. I walked over to her, and it turned out she was Jewish. She told me she had been visiting a Messianic Congregation, but she didn't understand about them. I explained the Gospel. I shared how God is Holy, man is sinful and we are separated from God by our sin. I told her how God came to earth in the body of Messiah, died for our sin and rose from the dead. She prayed to receive Jesus!

On the way back from distributing broadsides at Summerfest, my teammates stopped at the drugstore. I didn't need anything, but the Lord told me to go in and buy a postcard to send to my pastor. The young woman at the cash register was a Russian Jew. She attended church but didn't claim to have a personal relationship with Jesus. Later that night, my team went to buy custard and happened to run into her again. I explained the Gospel to her, but she didn't want to pray to receive Jesus in public. I told her Jesus said:

"Therefore whoever acknowledges Me before men, I will also acknowledge him before My Father who is in heaven.

But whoever denies Me before men, I will also deny him before My Father who is in heaven."
-Matthew 10:33

The cashier from the drugstore prayed with me to receive Jesus right there in the custard place.

I was distributing broadsides, and a Jewish man approached me. He inquired about Ceil Rosen, who was married to the founder of Jews for Jesus. The man told me Ceil Rosen was his aunt and that Ceil had asked his mother to secretly buy her a Bible, which led to her salvation even before her husband, Moishe Rosen, became a believer in Jesus. Next, he asked me if I knew his cousin Lynn, and I grabbed his arm and took him right over to her as she just happened to be my partner on the outreach that day.

The Baha'i faith was having an international convention while we were in town. I was assigned to a street corner in front of their convention center. There were several Jewish people of the Baha'i persuasion that we shared with. I shared with a Black Hebrew Israelite, explained the Gospel and prayed with him to receive Jesus as hundreds of Baha'i walked by in amazement!

New York City, New York

After Milwaukee, we had a few weeks before the next "Behold Your God!" campaign, and I chose to minister in New York. The regular Jews for Jesus New York Summer Witnessing event was still going on. They sent me to hand out broadsides in the subway underneath the World Trade Center. People down there seemed hard-hearted and took less broadsides than in most places around New York. On the other hand, several sweet-spirited Black women walked right up to me and whispered, "God bless you!" as they passed by. We were there just weeks before 911, and I prayed for all those we tried to reach. After the campaign ended, I got to serve as a camp counselor in the Jews for Jesus camp in upstate New York.

Minneapolis, Minnesota

After New York, we went to Minneapolis for a two-week campaign. We did a lot of ministry in the Mall of America and around the city. While I was distributing broadsides, I saw a temp I worked with at The Coca-Cola Company in Atlanta. She didn't remember me or claim to know Jesus.

Thank God for a local church that allowed us to use their church as a base camp. They were a tremendous blessing to the campaign. The Minneapolis/St. Paul Ecumenical Council had issued a statement saying they didn't want our campaign in their city.

Chicago, Illinois

Next, we drove to Chicago for a four-week campaign. My team leader was a Palestinian believer married to a Jewish believer. We were distributing broadsides in Daley plaza the morning 9/11 happened. There was pandemonium all over, and we didn't know what was going on. A woman tried to grab my broadsides and then dug her fingernails into my arm so hard my arm bled. They were evacuating Chicago because at the time, they mistakenly thought the plane that went down in Pennsylvania was headed for the Sears Tower.

Atlanta, Georgia

After Chicago, I had two weeks before the next outreach with Jews for Jesus. I decided to go to Atlanta and use those two weeks as a vacation. I took a bus and stayed with my old roommates. I went to visit friends at The Coca-Cola Company. While I waited for them in the lobby, the one I ran into in Sydney, Australia, and had been praying for, just happened to walk by during the five minutes I was in the lobby. I asked if they were ready to receive Jesus? My former co-worker said, "Here in the lobby? Come to my office when you're done with lunch." I did, explained the Gospel and my former co-worker prayed to receive Jesus!

TIGER TEAM SOUTH AFRICA

Johannesburg, South Africa BYG

After Atlanta, I traveled to South Africa with Jews for Jesus to minister for three months, from the beginning of October to the end of December, 2001. We spent two weeks in Johannesburg as part of a focused evangelism campaign followed by eight weeks more of ministry before going to Cape Town for the last two weeks for another evangelism campaign. We stayed in a hotel for the first two weeks, and then in a church missionary house for the next eight weeks.

Anti-missionaries harassed us at the malls and on the college campus we visited. Even though the college was public, they got the college to forbid us to be on campus but gave us one day of grace to be out there. We took a team of 14 people and blanketed the entire campus.

They placed me at the main gate, and I ministered with a boldness like there was no tomorrow! I gave out hundreds of broadsides and stopped almost every person who walked by me. I prayed with nine people to receive Jesus and obtained contact information from almost 200. I actually did meet one Jewish young man named Daniel. He gave me his e-mail and we stayed in touch for several years until his e-mail no longer worked?

I was talking with a Gentile man, and the leader of Jews for Judaism came over. Jews for Judaism is an anti-missionary organization that refutes Jews for Jesus and other Messianic Jewish organizations who point to Jesus as the Jewish Messiah. The leader interrupted our conversation and offered the man I was speaking with an anti-missionary pamphlet. I slapped the pamphlet and it fell to the ground. Let's just call it "righteous indignation." Even though they continued to harass my teammates in Johannesburg and Cape Town, no one bothered me for the rest of the campaign.

Johannesburg, South Africa

Ministering in Johannesburg was somewhat different. Most people spend their time at the malls because their businesses and entertainment are there as well. A lot of our ministry consisted of wearing evangelistic T-shirts, walking around malls and sharing with people. I'll never forget going into a store, having the two clerks comment on my T-shirt, sharing the Gospel with them and then squeezing into a changing booth with the two of them and praying with them to receive Jesus.

One time I met a devout atheist at the mall. He asked me to meet with him and his friend. They were part of a group list on the Internet and would debate religious topics with others including a Christian and an Orthodox Jew with whom one of them worked. As a result of meeting them, I got on their group list and debated with them and prayed for the Orthodox Jew.

One night I wore my evangelistic T-shirt to the movies. I noticed two Orthodox couples going into the movie. I made sure to go over to them and show off my T-shirt. I got to share with them. One of the Orthodox men just happened to be that Orthodox Jew from the group list.

One of the local anti-missionaries wanted to meet with one of our female missionaries, but we didn't think it would be wise for her to meet him. They let me meet him at the mall in the Orthodox neighborhood. He asked if he could bring a friend (an anti-missionary-in-training), and I said yes, of course (two for one, such a deal). Well, the friend turned out to be that Orthodox Jew from the group list.

The anti-missionary started by telling me all his reasons that Jesus wasn't the Messiah. After about 90 minutes, they asked me why I believed in Jesus. Of course they just dismissed my experiences as delusional and refuted my interpretation of the Scriptures as incorrect. As we sat there, I prayed that God would give me a question to ask him that would touch his soul. God told me to ask him, "If Orthodox Judaism is the only way to God, how do Gentiles go to heaven?" When I asked him, he just looked at me and said, "You know, I really struggle with that question."

I purchased a two-month membership to the gym which allowed me to work out at any location. I wore my favorite "Jews for Jesus" evangelistic T-shirt to the gyms where there were many Jewish people. It was red with big letters saying, "Jews for Jesus." One day a woman said to me, "I can't believe you are wearing that shirt!" It turned out she was a believer and had a Jewish plumber working at her house. She invited me over to share with him, and I remained friends with him long after.

At the gym location near the financial area, a Jewish man cursed me out in the locker room because of the T-shirt, and he got several of his friends to complain about me. The manager of the gym came over to me with his staff and offered me another T-shirt to wear, but I refused to switch. A few weeks later the manager of the gym asked me if I would be willing to file a complaint about the hostile Jewish man because he had been causing others trouble at the gym and they wanted to get rid of him.

The director of the Jews for Jesus branch was also leading a Messianic Congregation in Johannesburg. We would attend services on Friday nights. I met a Jewish believer named Leona, and she asked us to pray for her non-believing daughter as well as minister to her. We went over to their apartment and shared with the daughter and also prayed for Leona's grandson Stephen who wasn't there.

Mary, an American missionary invited us over to her apartment for Thanksgiving. She invited some of the other American missionaries working in Johannesburg. One of the other missionaries had just received a care package from a church group of "Mission Friends" in Atlanta who just happened to be former students from a class of 12 kids I helped with on Wednesday nights at my church!

Cape Town, South Africa BYG

We spent the last two weeks of our three months in South Africa in Cape Town. Cape Town is at the southern tip of the African continent (the end of the earth) where the Atlantic and Indian Oceans meet. It is one of the most beautiful places I have ever visited. On our day off we went to the Cape of Good Hope, which overlooks the meeting of the two oceans. We stopped to take a picture, and a Jewish woman saw my evangelistic T-shirt. I was the only one wearing one that day, and she wanted to talk to me because of it.

> *"Get yourself up on a high mountain,*
> *you who bring good news to Zion!*
> *Lift up your voice with strength,*
> *you who bring good news to Jerusalem!*
> *Lift it up! Do not fear!*
> *Say to the cities of Judah:*
> *'Behold your God!'"*
> *-Isaiah 40:9*

When we got to the top of the overlook, the Jewish woman asked me about my belief. I shared the Gospel with her, and she asked how it worked. As she prayed with me to receive her Jewish Messiah, she cried. It was glorious!

During the outreach, several of us attended a lecture at an Orthodox Synagogue entitled: *"Jews for Jesus: The Ultimate Contradiction."* The Rabbi said, "I would love to meet a Jew for Jesus who can tell me why he believes in Jesus." Afterwards, I walked up to the Rabbi and told him why I believe in Jesus. This ignited a discussion with some 50 on-lookers. After he finished with me he went to the next person in the crowd who just happened to be Devorah an Israeli Jewish believer with our group. She's a lawyer and defended Jesus. The discussion went on for over an hour. Many people were open.

We did an outreach on New Year's Eve; and as we were going back to the student hostel where we were staying, we decided to stop and do some more outreach. A drunk, glassy-eyed man came over to me. I shared the Gospel with him, and he bowed his head and prayed with me to receive Jesus. When he lifted his head, his eyes weren't glassy anymore. As I explained the responsibilities of being a Christian, his friends called for him. He told his friends to wait because he needed to hear what I was sharing!

We visited a local Messianic Congregation, and I was asked to share my testimony about our outreach. Afterwards, a woman came up to me and asked if I could minister to her stepson. She was a Gentile, but was married to a Jewish man who had a son. The son was in jail in Peru, where he met Jesus! As soon as she told me about him being in Peru, I had absolutely no doubt I would be going there one day. The stepson didn't have e-mail or a phone. All she could give me was the e-mail of someone who was trying to minister to him.

Right after visiting the Messianic Congregation, I went back to the streets to distribute Gospel tracts. I met a young Jewish man who introduced me to a hostile Jewish man. I did not know it at the time, but this friend of his had just tried to crash his car into the Jews for Jesus van. I shared with the young Jewish man and his friend (who was holding a beer in one hand and a cigarette in the other), and both prayed with me to receive Jesus. The young Jewish man suggested I talk with the Jewish waitress working in the café across the street. The waitress sat me down, asked me to share my testimony and told me her daughter was a believer. Then she told me about her son who was in jail in Peru (for drug smuggling) and it turned out to be the stepson of the woman I had just met. I couldn't believe it!

A group of us went to the mall to show off our evangelistic T-shirts, and I met a Jewish non-believer named Richard. I shared with him, and he gave me his email address to keep in touch, and we did keep in touch.

The plane ride home was the longest I had ever been on: 25 hours! We flew from Cape Town to Johannesburg without getting off the plane and stopped to fuel up off the west coast of Africa. You really need to walk around and drink a lot of water on those flights to prevent blood clots, but I didn't know? Many have died going back and forth to South Africa. My leg hurt so much, I went into the bathroom and cried. When we got to Atlanta, it was snowing and the plane had to circle for 30 minutes. I was finally back home once again. I moved back in with my friends, and it took about a month to recover from the eight months of ministry.

HOME SWEET HOME

MVBC Jewish Outreach

In April 2002, my church appointed me as a faith-supported missionary to the Jewish people. This enabled me to be in full-time ministry as well as still volunteer with Jews for Jesus, Rock of Israel and other organizations. I sent out support letters, and people sent in donations to enable me to minister full-time. My friends gave me their 1986 Cadillac to use.

Jesus Loves You T-Shirts

I prayed about an evangelistic T-shirt I could wear to minister in. I believe the Lord had me to use a Jewish Star, which would draw the attention of a Jewish person. The Jewish Star is the six-pointed shape on King David's shield when he went into battle. I view the Jewish Star as God (Father, Son and Holy Spirit) reaching down to man while man (body, soul and spirit) is reaching up to God. The combination of this is Jesus, and His message is *"Jesus Loves You!"*

> **"For God so loved the world that He gave His one and only Son,**
> **that whoever believes in Him shall not perish**
> **but have eternal life.**
> **God did not send his Son into the world to condemn the world,**
> **but in order that the world might be saved through Him."**
> **-John 3:16-17**

Because of my experience working in my parents' T-shirt business, I knew how to print T-shirts relatively inexpensively. My father ordered decals, and my mother ordered T-shirts for me. After an outreach in South Florida, I went to their house and made our first *"Jesus Loves You"* Jewish Star T-shirts. I try to wear one of these T-shirts and hand out Gospel tracts everywhere I go. At first I put some of my testimonies into a Gospel tract and printed them on our church risograph machine (a high-speed digital printing system). Later, I ordered "Do You Know the Messiah?" tracts from www.gtpress.org. I started going to street corners, malls, sporting events, movies, plays, trade shows, college campuses, bus and train stations, etc.

Jewish Doctors

The first time I went out to share in Atlanta, in a *"Jesus Loves You"* Jewish Star T-shirt, I prayed about where to go. The Lord led me to the street corner in front of the Hard Rock Café in Atlanta. There just happened to be an International Convention of Cardiologists having a private party at Hard Rock Café. There were so many Jewish doctors, I stayed an extra hour and handed out over 1,000 Gospel tracts. I couldn't have planned it better if I tried.

The Nanny

Fran "The Nanny" Drescher was in Atlanta for a book signing. I went and wore my *"Jesus Loves You"* Jewish Star T-shirt. She's Jewish, and most in her entourage were Jewish as well. I waited on line to have my book signed, and when I walked up to Ms. Drescher, there was dead silence. She couldn't look me in the eye; but she grabbed my hand, thanked me for coming, and I said, "GOD BLESS YOU."

As I walked away, I heard people whisper about me being a Jewish Christian, giving me an opportunity to share with a Jewish woman and her daughter.

I had no idea my fraternity brother Reid Drescher is actually Fran's first cousin. Reid is married to Aviva Drescher and they both appear on that show *The Real Housewives of New York City*.

Marlene

I went to the bank inside the Kroger. There was an older woman, Marlene, working at Kroger, and she was wearing a Jewish Star and had a New York accent. She noticed my *"Jesus Loves You"* Jewish Star T-shirt and told me she liked it! I asked if she liked what it said inside as she seemed to be squinting and probably only saw the Jewish Star. She asked what it said inside, and I told her. She said, "Oh!" She never learned how to drive and had just lost her husband the month before. She was happy to give me her phone number so I could drive her places.

Although Marlene was not yet a believer in Jesus, she had been to church many times with her daughter who was a believer! I would take Marlene to the doctor, to the store, to church, to restaurants and to our weekly home fellowship.

Birthday Party Outreach

I threw myself a 40th birthday party, which was really an outreach to my Jewish friends and acquaintances. Several Jewish people came, including our neighbor Doug who was also from New York. I had never met Doug, but my roommates knew him and invited him to the party. Doug had a brain tumor removed when he was a child, and this caused him to lose his peripheral vision. He wasn't able to drive, so he had moved to Atlanta where he could depend on public transportation. We stayed up until 3 AM talking with Jewish unbelievers and had a great time.

Kosher Day Outreach

The Atlanta Orthodox Jewish community organized "Kosher Day," a fundraiser benefiting Jewish charities, by selling tickets to a Sunday baseball game at Turner Field. Before my friends and I started distributing Gospel materials at the event, a man saw my *"Jesus Loves You"* T-shirt, approached me, allowed me to share and prayed to receive Jesus!

Many Jewish people walked past us and some took the tracts. When they didn't, I proclaimed, "JESUS IS MESSIAH! SHALOM ALECHEM! (Peace to you!) JESUS IS MESSIAH!!!" Some would stop and talk, either to argue or discuss. One of the Chabad Rabbis I knew and his group walked by and asked if I was working overtime.   I told him, "JESUS IS MESSIAH!" I asked if he wanted a tract, and he said "No" but then turned around and took one, saying it was one less that I would have to give out. I thought he would rip it up, but he folded it and put it in his pocket.

Another Orthodox Rabbi I knew walked by with his group. I told them, "JESUS IS MESSIAH!" and the Rabbi said, "He wasn't." I asked the Rabbi who he thought Jesus was, and he said, "Jesus never existed." I turned as the Rabbi walked down the street, and said, "I LOVE YOU, Rabbi!" It was as if the Lord Himself just spoke through me directly to the Rabbi's heart because the Rabbi turned around and smiled at me.

I saw Anti-Missionary #2 with his wife and their two boys. I offered him a tract, but he just slapped it and kept on walking. I proclaimed, "JESUS IS

MESSIAH!" The wife smiled and graciously said to call her about coming over for Shabbos lunch as we had previously discussed.

Another man prayed with me to receive the Lord on Kosher Day. My friends and I took him to lunch, gave him a Bible and encouraged him in his walk with the Lord.

Mike

After the event, as I walked through the cobblestone streets of the tourist area of Underground Atlanta to catch a train, I passed by several kiosks. I couldn't help but notice the kiosk with a man dressed as a clown painting faces, because he was wearing a huge Star of David. As I waited for him to finish with one of his customers, I noticed he had a rainbow sticker on the side of his kiosk. I prayed God would save him and use him to minister right where he was already working! Mike was very friendly, let me share, accepted a Gospel tract and gave me his contact information for follow-up. It turned out even though Mike was nine years older than me, we had both graduated from Jericho High School in New York!

Home Fellowships

Marlene, Doug, I and others who stopped by, started having weekly gatherings at our apartment. One night we would have dinner and a Bible study, and on another night we would have dinner and game night. I would pick people up, make the food, teach the lesson, clean up and then drive people home. Eventually, others came alongside and started helping. At first there were only a few of us. Sometimes it would only be Marlene and me at the Bible study. I would constantly invite people, and, eventually, six months later Mike, the Jewish man at the kiosk who painted faces, started coming to game night.

Morris and Sarah

While distributing Gospel tracts at the Lindbergh Marta Station near Toco Hills, which is the Orthodox Jewish community in Atlanta, an autistic Jewish man, Morris, walked by and commented on my Jewish Star *"Jesus Loves You"* Tshirt and took a Gospel tract. Later that night he left me a voice mail saying he wanted God in his life.

When I called him back, I explained the Gospel to him, and he prayed to receive the Lord. His father was deceased and he lived with his mother, Sarah. He had a fight with his mother and moved into a halfway house. When I met Morris at the halfway house, he was despondent and really didn't understand what I was saying to him. I asked the Lord if ministering to him was a waste of my time. The Lord gave me the following verse:

"And answering, the King will say to them, 'Amen, I tell you, whatever you did to one of the least of these My brethren, you did it to Me.'"
-Matthew 25:40

Although Morris and his mother were not Orthodox, they were very much a part of the Orthodox community. Morris would often wear our T-shirts in the Orthodox neighborhood. I eventually met his mother and shared with her as well, and she prayed to receive her Messiah. They went on to introduce me to people they knew in the community.

One day Morris and I went to the mall together. I was disappointed not to be able to witness to any Jewish people during our visit. As we were pulling out of our parking space to leave, Morris started yelling, "Stop the car! That's my uncle's wife's brother and his family!"

Ironically, they were having a Bar Mitzvah at the Reform synagogue I had been asked to leave some years back. Nevertheless, I attended the service (which is open to the public) and the Rabbi didn't remember me, and I was able to share my faith with Morris' family and some extended family. He was so happy for them to hear the Good News message.

Car Trouble

Returning home after one of my trips, I discovered my car was nowhere to be found. Apparently it had been stolen, and the police were able to catch the man in the act. Unfortunately, when I retrieved it, I found the window was broken and the starter was as well. You could actually start the car by turning the starter without a key.

I told my Missions pastor I needed a new car. It just so happened that my senior pastor was leaving to take a bigger church in another state, and the church needed someone to assume the payments on my pastor's car. Praise the Lord for His provision and my new car!

Sandy Springs Apartment

We called the courtesy officer for our apartment complex to complain about a late-night noisy party in the day care center next door. We were surprised to find out he organized it. We seemed to have constant noise behind our apartment and decided to pray about moving. One of my roommates went out to confront a person blasting their car radio, and he was punched in the face. It was time to move.

My roommates and I wanted a three-bedroom apartment for less than $1,200 per month within walking distance of a train station. I went to an apartment-finder store, and they found us a beautiful apartment in Sandy Springs, a Jewish neighborhood just north of Atlanta, that met all these requirements and just happened to be where my church was located. A few months later Doug, my former neighbor, moved into our new apartment complex as well.

I advertised our Bible Study Home Fellowship and our other outreach parties on the apartment complex bulletin board near the mailboxes. Almost every day the advertisements were ripped down. I kept a stack of photocopied advertisements and a stapler in the car and put them back.

Todd

An autistic Jewish man named Todd worked near our new apartment. I tried reaching out to him, but he was somewhat apprehensive about meeting with me. My friend Scott lived nearby and befriended Todd. Scott brought Todd over to one of our game nights. When Todd walked in and saw Marlene, he was most excited because they used to work together and shared lunches. After this meeting, Todd became my friend and eventually prayed to receive his Messiah!

Mike's Salvation

Our little home fellowship group in Sandy Springs started to grow. People would bring their friends and relatives, and we would have as many as twenty people or so. One night, two missionary friends of mine from Hope of Israel came to visit our Bible study. Their organization gives away free Bibles to Jewish people. They didn't say a word the whole time, but I know they were praying because that was the night Mike asked, "Ok, so how does it work? What do I need to do to be saved?"

I began meeting with Mike one on one. I gave him various books to read, and we studied the Bible. He wore a *"Jesus Loves You"* Jewish Star T-shirt and took Gospel tracts to give out at Underground Atlanta, just as I had prayed. I prayed for his needs. He had lost touch with his stepfather after his mother died. Mike knew his stepfather lived in Sandy Springs but hadn't spoken to him in years and didn't know how to get in touch with him.

I hosted a 50th birthday party for Mike and invited his family over. Mike's brother had told the family not to attend in fear that I would try to convert them; but the family came, and it was a really special time. Not only are Mike and I from the same hometown and high school, but we actually went to the same elementary school. My sister and Mike's sister really hit it off. It turned out Mike's sister was already a believer! Mike's stepmother pulled me aside and asked what I did to Mike? She said, "Mike was full of anger. Now he is full of peace. He's not the same person!" I told her she should thank God as He is the one who transformed Mike's life.

Lunch With Lee

I went to the mall on the other side of Atlanta to meet with one of my Jewish contacts. While I was at the mall, I ran into my friend Lee's wife. She suggested I have lunch with Lee since he was working in the Orthodox neighborhood.

Lee and I started meeting for lunch at the Kroger in the Orthodox neighborhood so I could show off my *"Jesus Loves You"* Jewish Star T-shirt while we ate. We would sometimes meet with Morris who moved back home and lived near there. Whenever I was out of town on mission trips, Lee would disciple Morris.

Lee is a gifted teacher and has a real handle on the Jewish customs of the Old Testament. Eventually, Lee taught our weekly Bible study, and people would often bring food. Lee would start with prayer requests and pretty much everything we prayed for was answered!

New Year's Eve

Marlene invited me to a local Senior Center for a New Year's Eve celebration. We sat at a table with another couple, a Jewish woman Gloria and a Gentile man Hank. The Jewish woman attended a Conservative synagogue which is one of the largest in North America. Later, she told me she asked her Rabbi if she should come to our group, and he said no. She came anyway! I was kvelling! (So proud of her!) Would you believe Hank turned out to be Mike's stepfather whom Mike was trying to find?

Hank started coming to our weekly home fellowship. You should have seen Mike's face the first time Hank showed up! The second time he came, he began asking Lee some real questions after the study finished. Lee was able to share with him, and a teary-eyed 89-year-old man prayed to receive Jesus.

Ministry House

When Josh, one of my two twin roommates got engaged, I believe God led me to look for a house, but mainly because our ministry was growing. We were having as many as 25 at our Bible Study Fellowship, and we had little space to make "Jesus Loves You" T-shirts.

I looked at many houses before going on a mission trip to Israel in February 2007 but couldn't find the right one and was frustrated because our lease was ending at the end of March. When I returned from Israel at the end of February, I had a feeling God would bless me with the right house because of all the persecution I had endured while ministering in Israel.

I went back over the listings of houses I had discarded and cried out to God. I found a house I had looked at from the outside but not the inside. As I took a closer look, I realized this house had everything I prayed for. As soon as my realtor took me inside, I knew it was the house God wanted me to buy!

It had a big, open living room next to the kitchen with lots of seating space and lots of bedrooms to rent out to help me afford it. Graham, the unmarried twin brother decided to move in, too. The next door neighbor looked at my "Jesus Loves You" Jewish Star T-shirt, told me he was Jewish and didn't believe in Jesus and said, "I hope you buy the house so we can talk about your shirt."

I took Todd to look at the house, and he was most excited because his cousin lived on my street. It turned out that the woman that oversaw classes at the Jewish Center and didn't like all the questions I would ask, lived on this street with her family! I ran into a Jewish non-believer friend we'd been reaching out to for years, and discovered he lived on the next block from my house.

"From one He made every nation of men to live on the face of the earth, having set appointed times and the boundaries of their territory. They were to search for Him, and perhaps grope around for Him and find Him. Yet He is not far from each one of us,"
-Acts 17:26-27

You Be Quiet

Several years ago, my friend David who used to drive me to that Navigators Bible study we were in, picked me up one afternoon. On the way to the study, he stopped at a client's house, Mrs. Adler, to do some work while I waited in the car. He told me he thought Mrs. Adler was Jewish, so while I waited for David, I prayed for Mrs. Adler and her family.

My friend, who is a Gentile Christian woman married to a Jewish believer in Jesus, requested prayer for a meeting she was having with her Jewish sister-in-law and Anti-Missionary #1. Since I happened to know Anti-Missionary #1, my friend took me to their meeting.

My friend and Anti-Missionary #1 began their discussion, and when I tried to interject, he told me and the sister-in-law we were simply there to observe? The sister-in-law and I looked at each other, started laughing and just had a great conversation. The sister-in-law asked why I believed in Jesus, which gave me an opportunity to share with her.

After we met, the sister-in-law suggested that my friend and I visit her father, who was also my friend's father-in-law, who lived nearby. When we pulled up to the house I was shocked because it was Mrs. Adler's house! It was eight years later and it turned out Mr. Adler passed away and my friend's father-in-law had married Mrs. Adler. She wasn't home, but we did get to share with the father-in-law!

Double The Fun

While buying flowers for Todd's grandmother, a Jewish non-believer who was in the hospital, I ran into another Jewish non-believer from a Jewish Center class. She said, "I'm glad to see you're not wearing that "#X%X" shirt! I tell everybody about you!" I almost always wear an evangelistic t-shirt of some kind unless I am meeting with a non-believer because I don't want them to feel trapped.

Todd's mother (Jewish non-believer) was at the hospital and overwhelmed that I had come to visit her mother. She introduced me as Todd's Jewish friend. They asked if I had someone else in the hospital. Coincidently, my pastor's wife was there. The grandmother was shocked when I said "pastor." When she asked me to share my belief, Todd's mother told her, "You don't want to hear that," but the grandmother told her to shut up and let me speak.

My friend Shelley, a Jewish believer in town ministering with me, and I met Todd and his mother, brother and sister-in-law at a restaurant for Todd's birthday. Todd's brother wanted to know why I believed in Jesus, and Todd's mother had to hear my testimony again!

Did You Hear?

One of my friends who used to live in Atlanta, asked me to try to witness to his former neighbors in Atlanta who are Jewish. I contacted them and tried to reach out in different ways. They owned a music store, so I purchased a trumpet from them that our ministry donated to a congregation in Arad, Israel. I visited them a couple of times, and they invited me to the father's 80th birthday party.

I prayed to God to have opportunity to share with an entire house filled with 80-year-old Jewish people and others. I met this one woman, and she asked what I did for a living, so I told her. She yelled across the room, "Hey, Irving! Come and meet Steven. He's a Jew for Jesus just like my niece!"

You could have knocked me over with a feather! We are sinful vessels made righteous by Messiah's atoning death on the tree (cross). We only have to be available to be used by God. Trust Him and He will amaze you!

"Fear not, for I am with you;
Be not dismayed, for I am your God.
I will strengthen you.
Surely I will help you.
I will uphold you with My righteous right hand."
-Isaiah 41:10

JEWISH VISITS

Anti Missionary In Training

The Lord led me into the beginners class at a large Orthodox synagogue in Atlanta one Shabbat morning. As I walked by the man at the door, I realized I had met and witnessed to him at Anti-Missionary #1's house. He recognized me, too, and asked where I was working, and I told him I was a missionary to the Jews. He shrugged and asked if I would like to have lunch at someone's house after Shul.

After the class, Anti-Missionary #3, came up to me and asked why I was there. I told him it was because I loved him! Then he asked why I was specifically at his Orthodox synagogue, and I told him because I loved the people there. He said I could stay as long as I behaved. My former Hebrew teacher came by to say "Hello," as I am sure the others told him I was there.

Afterward, an anti-missionary-in-training took me to his house for lunch. As we were leaving the synagogue, Anti-Missionary #1, saw me and almost had a stroke. As he questioned me, he stopped in the middle of his interrogation to thank me for the post card I had sent from Florida, and then started in asking me questions again.

The anti-missionary-in-training spent lunch asking me questions about my belief in Jesus in front of his wife and their guests. He told me he wanted to be an anti-missionary with Anti-Missionary #1 and Anti-Missionary #3, but he was told that there wasn't enough work in Atlanta for three people.

His wife went into the kitchen and yelled at the anti-missionary-in-training for bringing me over and then walked back out smiling like nothing happened even though we could hear everything she said. It was like a scene right out of a movie. As we were talking together, they mentioned at least five Jewish people; and boy were they surprised that I knew all of them.

Shabbaton

One Friday night, I went back to the same Orthodox congregation. I sat behind some guys I knew and said "Hello." The service began, and the liturgy was being recited in Hebrew. The people were speaking so quickly that it was hard to keep up with what was going on, even though the young boys put up page numbers at the Bema or pulpit, so I used the time to pray for people, especially all the ones I knew.

I asked the Lord if He wanted me to be at this synagogue, because it was hard for me to be there and not be allowed to openly witness. Within 30 seconds I had my answer. Anti-Missionary #1 came running over to sit next to me. He looked like he was ready to attack me verbally. I stuck out my hand and said, "Good Shabbos!" He was taken aback, and his whole demeanor changed. After the service, he became my own personal escort. I felt so special.

As I walked out, we met various people, and he introduced me to each one as a Jew for Jesus (PRAISE THE LORD). I ran into another Rabbi who taught a class that my roommate and I had attended at the Jewish Center. He is such a nice man and was so excited to see me. He kept shaking my hand. I hadn't seen him since the day I wore my *"Jesus Loves You"* T-shirt to the Pizza Palace when he was there with 50 of his students.

He asked me what kind of work I was doing. When I told him I was a Christian missionary to the Jewish People, he stopped shaking my hand (but was still holding it); go figure. Anti-Missionary #1 was standing there and told me he was having a Shabbaton, a weekend of learning, at his house. He had invited Gentiles who had been members of a now-defunct Knoxville Messianic Congregation who wanted to convert to Judaism. He told me if I was to behave and act as an Invited Observer, I would be allowed to join them. I promised to be good.

As I walked into Anti-Missionary #1's house, I saw the young woman he had talked out of believing in Jesus. I had been praying for her as well as Anti-Missionary #1's wife and family. Anti-Missionary #1 and his wife were also there as well as another dozen or so guests. I made sure to sit with the woman from Israel I had been praying for, and we chatted the whole evening. She mentioned in the general conversation going on that she had been offered a job as an assistant to a world-famous anti-missionary. She didn't know if she should stay in Israel, where she currently lived, or move to the USA to work for him. I told her to ask Hashem, and everyone looked at me as if I were crazy.

During dinner we went around the room and introduced ourselves and told about our work. Since I promised Anti-Missionary #1 I would behave, I told everyone I was an Invited Observer; and they all laughed. Later on, several people wanted to know what I was doing there, so I told them I was there as an Invited Observer and was praying they would all know Jesus.

One woman at the event had a Jewish biological father and had been adopted at two days old by a Jewish family. According to Rabbinic Jewish law, since her biological mother wasn't Jewish, she wasn't Jewish either. She said she received a revelation about becoming a Christian and then received another revelation about becoming an Orthodox Jew. She said she just hopes she doesn't receive anymore revelations!

As we began the closing prayers for the meal, Anti-Missionary #1 asked if there were any Kohens present; and, as usual, I was the only one who raised my hand. Anti-Missionary #1 came over, put his hands on my shoulders and said, "I'm sorry, but you disqualified yourself...unless of course you want to...," and I said, "NO!" After dinner Anti-Missionary #1 taught on the Ten Commandments and used that time to criticize the Christian interpretation of them.

The next morning I went back to the same Orthodox synagogue. The Rabbi's sermon was about Ilan Ramon, the Israeli astronaut who died on the Space Shuttle. Apparently, although Ramon had not been a particularly observant Jew, he had ordered kosher meals for the flight. While flying over Israel, he had recited the Shema, a central teaching from the Torah:

"Hear O Israel: The LORD our God, the LORD is one. Love ADONAI your God with all your heart and with all your soul and with all your strength."
-Deuteronomy 6:4-5

The Rabbi praised Ramon for using his influence to be a light to millions of Israelis who had probably never heard the Shema before.

After the service, Anti-Missionary #1 invited me back to his home for the continuation of the Shabbaton. A young woman joined us, and as far as I could determine, she was a Jewish college student who believes in Jesus but was encouraged by her parents to meet with Anti-Missionary #1 to return her to the fold of Orthodox Judaism. I asked the couple sitting next to me why they were there, and they said they wanted to find the Truth. (Let's pray that they do.)

After lunch, the people went around the room and shared why they didn't believe in Jesus. My job was to intercede in prayer for the college student, and I know that is why I was there. I kept smiling at her and watching her as they made light of Jesus with their attitudes and words. The college student had absolutely no reaction. She didn't react to my smiles, and she didn't react to their disrespect.

There was a break between the afternoon session and the evening one. Both the college student and I decided to leave at that time. She told us her friend had been killed in a car accident the day before, and that explained her countenance. It is sad she lost a friend, but praise God He used it to protect her from their evil.

As the college student and I walked out, Anti-Missionary #3 and his wife followed. He told me I had a very unique opportunity by being there and wanted to know what I thought. I told him I wanted to cry because of the way they spoke of Jesus, and I wanted to leave but didn't. I asked him if criticizing others is what Orthodox Judaism is all about. He admitted he would have preferred it not to be like that. I told him my job as a missionary to the Jewish People is to point people to Hashem, and encourage them to read the Tenach (Old Testament). He seemed surprised by what I said and wanted to meet to discuss it further.

The Most Infamous Christian Missionary

One Sunday night, after I returned to town, I felt led to do something in the Jewish community and noticed that the Rabbi I had met at the Jewish festival was teaching classes at a local Orthodox congregation. When I met the Rabbi in the Shul lobby before the class, he asked why I was there. I said to better understand why he rejects our Jewish Messiah. At first he was going to let me stay but then was afraid I'd befriend people. He told me to leave. As I left, he asked, "Where does the Bible say Messiah must die for our sins, rise from the dead and we must ask him into our heart for atonement?" I said, all over the Old Testament! He said that's the answer he always gets, and then incredibly he invited me to his class for a debate!

The Rabbi introduced me as the most infamous Christian missionary in all of Atlanta, clearly stated the Gospel and asked if it's what I believed. Everyone laughed. Deuteronomy 30 was the weekly Torah portion teaching. It says one must keep the Law. I asked why he has no High Priest, and he said because there was no Temple. I had him read Jeremiah 33:15-18, which says there will always be a High Priest, but he said that was talking about the future. I challenged him with Isaiah 53, and he read it saying it was about Israel in the future. I asked three times how Gentiles could go to heaven, since he was saying that Isaiah 53 wasn't talking about atonement through Jesus, but he wouldn't address my question.

The Rabbi asked his question again about why I believed in Jesus, and I said Deuteronomy 18 says God will send a prophet like Moses to whom the people must listen. I said Jesus is the Prophet in Deuteronomy 18 and quoted to his class of 15 what Jesus said in John 14:6: "I am the way, the truth, and the life! No one comes to the Father except through Me." Some laughed; some were shocked. The Rabbi wanted me to come back when there were more people, but he would have to get permission from his boss.

It was now time for their prayer service, and for a few minutes I was the tenth man needed to make up a minion (Jewish Prayer Group). A debate erupted as to whether or not I was Jewish. The teaching Rabbi said according to the Law, I was Jewish! The head Rabbi (the one who had previously thanked me for my postcards) came in and smiled at me as the Rabbi told him what had happened. A man blasted me as we went to pray! He said I must really hate the world renown anti-missionary, and I said I send him postcards all the time and love him and pray he meets his Messiah. This man couldn't accept that I believed in Jesus and kept trying to debate me with Rabbinic interpretations, but we had to leave for the prayer service.

As I sat in the back of the room and they all prayed, I prayed for them! Amazingly, their prayers do not contradict the New Testament for the most part. After the service, the man who blasted me apologized and gave me his card. When I looked at his face I realized I had witnessed to him last summer at Stone Mountain and had been praying for him. He continued to debate Scriptures with me, but it was time for the Over 35-Year-Old Singles' class with the Rabbi.

As I walked into the Singles' class, there was the usual gasp of recognition from people I have witnessed to. I began talking with a woman there whom I had met before, and the Rabbi told me this is why I had to leave. He didn't want me getting friendly with people, but I told him it was too late as I already knew half the people in the room.

You Go To Church?

At the request of my friend, I visited a nearby Chabad House, which is a Jewish Center focusing on family-oriented educational activities. Chabads come from the Chasidic Orthodox persuasion, which is the only evangelistic branch of Judaism. They believe in a Messiah, but do not embrace Jesus.

As I walked in, I sat on the end of the third row from the back, but the Holy Spirit prompted me to sit on the end of the fourth row from the back. At first, there were few people for the 7 to 8 PM service I was attending, but as it got closer to 8 PM, the sanctuary filled up. Many people pointed at and commented about me. When I didn't see my friend, I felt I was alone in the lion's den; but I knew God was with me.

As I looked around the sanctuary, I thanked God for all my supporters. They had made it possible for me to witness to so many people in that room over time. I have witnessed in various places around Atlanta to groups of Americans, Australians, South Africans and Israelis. My friend finally showed up and sat next to me across the aisle in his assigned seat. (In synagogues, worshippers pay for their seats in a similar way to a season ticket-holder.) He didn't realize I was already there.

Once the sanctuary was almost filled, I became physically ill from the demonic forces in the room. After the service, I said "Hello" to the Rabbi. He was Orthodox and was the Rabbi who had asked me to leave another Sandy Springs synagogue when it changed from reform (more liberal concerning how to interpret Torah adherence) to conservative (somewhere between the stricter Orthodox and more liberal Reform factions). I had been burdened for him and had sent him my testimony letter recently. He didn't recognize me at first, but later asked if I had sent him a letter.

After leaving the sanctuary, my illness went away. Two other men and I walked with my friend to his house for dinner. On the way, my friend told me even though he was Jewish, he was raised in a Christian home. His father, although Jewish by identity, was a Charismatic pastor. Once we arrived at the house, we had a discussion about belief, and I found out why one of the Israeli men with us was acting cold towards me. Apparently I had witnessed to him at the Pita Palace.

By the time dinner started, a total of nine Israelis had arrived. One of the Israeli women wanted to know what I did for a living and gave me an opportunity to share in front of the whole group. Every time our host and his wife left us to walk their guests to the door, the Israeli woman would ask me questions. She couldn't believe I went to church on Sundays.

Are You A Kohen?

The following Monday morning, I attended the 6:30 AM prayer service at the Chabad House. People were surprised to see me there, but were most welcoming. The Rabbi made sure I put on a tallis (prayer shawl with fringed corners) and tefillin (strapped-on prayer gear), which made me look like one of them. A Rabbi who didn't know me asked if I was a Kohen (from the priestly line, and I am), so I said, "yes." He asked me if I would read from the Torah; but another Rabbi spoke to him, and I didn't get to read from the Torah. Afterwards, I spoke to my friend, and he asked if I would be interested in studying Torah with him.

Rumor Has It

There were four synagogues in the main Orthodox neighborhood. I had been to three of them and prayed for an opportunity to go to the fourth. I was ministering to a Jewish man one night, and we stopped for pizza in the Orthodox neighborhood. While there, we met a Rabbi, and he invited me to his synagogue, which just happened to be the one I had been praying about going to. My belief didn't come up in our initial meeting, so I just showed up at their service one night.

It turned out that the Rabbi's Orthodox Congregation was made up of people mostly from Iran, and they met in a house across the street from a synagogue I attended frequently. When I walked in, I noticed an Orthodox Jewish man I know who is very hostile to the Gospel; and of course he noticed me. He very much dislikes my belief. He lived near Anti-Missionary #1, one of the anti-missionaries who was always concerned to win me back to Judaism.

After the service, the Rabbi and I were the only ones left in the building, so we chatted. He said that people had told him I have a tendency towards Jews for Jesus, and I said, "I am a Jew for Jesus!" We had a really good conversation and talked for some 20 minutes. His biggest objection was: How can a man be God? I told him a man can't be God, but God can come to earth and dwell in the body of a man.

In turn, I asked him why he followed Rabbinic Judaism, and he told me because his father did and his father's father did and his father's father's father did! I challenged the validity of Rabbinic Judaism and told him how one Orthodox Jew lied about me and the *Atlanta Jewish Times* published a false and inaccurate article relating to that. He asked to see the article, and I later mailed him that one and several others as well as some items from the Internet. He told me he could possibly meet with me one on one, but he couldn't allow me to come back to his synagogue. I told him I'd been thrown out of much better places than his synagogue, and we both had a big laugh.

For Such A Time As This

My Jewish Singles' group invited me to a Purim Party at a local banquet hall. Purim is a Jewish celebration of the book of Esther. My goal in going to these events was to pray for my Jewish people and be available to God. After arriving a few minutes early, I was approached by the drummer of the band, an Israeli now based in San Francisco. Somehow the conversation got around to the Gospel being shared as well as his e-mail address.

The leader of the Singles' group arrived slightly intoxicated. We said our hello's and then he stood next to me and began introducing me as a Christian missionary to whoever walked by and then asked people if they wanted to convert. I had the opportunity to share with dozens of Jewish people and stood there praising God from my heart the entire time. Later on that night, the Orthodox Rabbi overseeing the party confronted me with my beliefs in front of a crowd, giving me an additional opportunity to stand up for Jesus. I took care to give one-word answers and smiled so I wouldn't get thrown out.

After the Purim party, I waited at the bus stop, and one of the Jewish singles I had witnessed to before gave me a ride home. We spoke about God on the way and spent several minutes talking in front of my apartment. He said he would consider studying Scriptures with me, but never did?

No Missionaries Allowed

My Jewish Singles' group invited me to an all-night Shavuot study session at a Reform synagogue. Shavuot is the Jewish celebration of the giving of the Law on Mount Sinai. The event was advertised as a joint effort between several synagogues. I knew the Rabbi who had asked me not to come back to his synagogue would be there, so I really didn't want to go. However, I learned that the chairperson for the event was a former co-worker from The Coca-Cola Company. I had never witnessed to her, and I knew I had to go.

Sure enough, when I walked in, the Rabbi who told me not to come to his synagogue anymore saw me and ran right over to the Rabbi hosting the event, but nothing happened. We had choices for the classes we could attend, so I picked a certain Rabbi's class entitled *Peace Vigil*. The Rabbi looked at me and did a double-take as I had once witnessed to him at a train station, and he remembered me. He asked if I was there to cause trouble, and I told him I was there to pray for peace! He ran over to consult with my former co-worker, but nothing happened. Again, I was allowed to stay.

After the Peace Vigil, I ran into the leader of the Singles' group. He told me, right in front of some of the other singles, that a man from B'Nai Torah had sent him an e-mail wanting to know about me being a missionary.

Next I went to my former co-worker's challah-making class, and it was just the two of us, giving plenty of room for conversation. She said she had converted to Judaism and then married a Jewish man. She asked why I believed in Jesus, so I told her. Then she asked if I was on a mission, and I told her I was there to tell her what I had just shared with her. She was very nice and told me to go downstairs for the next class after we finished up.

The assistant Rabbi from the synagogue I was banned from taught a class on Reform Judaism: How Reform Should We Be? Because our Singles' group was there as well, we had a mix of backgrounds, some Orthodox, some Conservative and some Reform. Each person asked the same question, "How can we know how observant we should be?" Someone even asked about Temple sacrifices.

After 45 minutes of this same question coming up, I identified myself, answered their questions in the context of the class, shared the Gospel and told them God gives the Holy Spirit to guide us. The host Rabbi told me someone in the class said that it was as if I had spiritually raped her, and it was time for me to go. The Rabbi walked me to the door and thanked me for going peacefully. I quoted the following verse, to him, and he said he was familiar with that verse:

"We all like sheep have gone astray.
Each of us turned to his own way.
So ADONAI has laid on Him
the iniquity of us all."
- Isaiah 53:6

What A Nice Man

A Jewish day school held a fundraiser to honor Anti-Missionary #1 and his wife for 18 years of service. Somehow I was invited, and even though the tickets were $90, I paid it and attended.

An elderly woman was looking for a place to sit and asked me where she might be able to find a seat, so I pointed her to a chair. Anti-Missionary #1, brimming with anti-missionary zeal, came running over to us demanding to know what was going on! I had no idea the elderly woman was his mother. She told Anti-Missionary #1 that this nice gentleman (meaning me) was helping her to find a seat.

Many people were challenged by my presence, including the ones at my table who wanted to know what I did for a living. The couple sitting next to me told me their daughter used to be a Christian, and I almost fell out of my chair when I realized their daughter was The young Jewish woman who renounced Jesus, whom I had been witnessing to and praying for, for several years.

Kosher Festival

What a blessing it was to attend the annual Southeastern Kosher Festival again. Various organizations were giving away food samples, selling Judaica or promoting their organizations. It reminded me of an ingathering of the Jewish people to the land of Israel.

One of the Rabbis I was taking a class with had sent out a group e-mail inviting everyone to the festival, and this was the first time I'd attended one of these events with a complete sense of peace. I could never be sure how I'd be received. Praise God, I had the opportunity to interact with many Jewish people. In addition to the tables in the main hall, they had an outside tent area for Israelis and South Africans.

A former co-worker was doing security and was friendly. Another man was happy to see me. He had expressed interest in my belief previously and talked with me for a while. The woman who once sat next to me at a Kosher Café and complained about all the Christians who try to convert her husband the doctor, was there and somewhat polite. I've run into her so many times I've lost count.

A man thanked me for the postcards and was somewhat friendly until I ran into him later and he tried to talk me out of my belief. Another man used to be somewhat friendly towards me but did his best to ignore me. The anti-missionary-in-training from the congregation was very friendly but said he preferred the postcard from Rio de Janeiro I sent him better than the one I sent from Miami. Several others I knew were also friendly.

While walking around I ran into Anti-Missionary #1. He wanted to know what I thought of his class and gave me an opportunity to share my belief in front of his son. (I've lost count of how many of his friends and relatives the Lord has given me opportunity to witness to.)

I noticed a man wearing a University of Miami hat, so I told him I went there and started a conversation. He wasn't a religious Jew but came to the festival because his friend invited him. He asked what I did for a living;

149

and as I began to tell him, the Rabbi who had debated me in front of his class came running up to us and asked if I had told the man about my belief? I said yes, and the Rabbi said "Ok," and went back to minding his table. My fellow alumnus from the University of Miami said he wanted to hear more about my belief, so I gave him my contact information.

The Rabbi who debated me in front of his class was at a table with my friend's sister promoting his organization. I visited with them for a while. As people walked by, the Rabbi would introduce me as a believer in Jesus. My friend's sister gave me information for taking Hebrew classes, as they keep telling me if I read the Bible in the original Hebrew, I wouldn't believe the way I do.

I walked around the festival several times praying (and ok, eating the free samples) and talking with different people. I met a man who was stationed by the entrance and was able to share with him a little. I kept stopping by the Rabbi and eating a mint each time from his table. On the third time around, he told me not to eat anymore of his mints. I thought my sampling too many mints may have hurt my witness, so I went over to the Krogers to buy more mints.

While at Krogers, I ran into the doctor's wife, again! This time she just laughed when we bumped into each other. On the way back from Krogers, I ran into the man who went to my college, whom I had just witnessed to, and his wife. Since we were outside, I was able to open up more about my belief with them.

As I went back into the festival, I ran into the wife of Anti-Missionary #2, who had had me over for Shabbos dinner many times and went to law school with my cousins in New York. He had given up on winning me back to Judaism and asked me not to contact him anymore. His wife was happy to see me, spent a lot of time talking and told me she saw my letter to the editor in the *Atlanta Jewish Times* defending myself against their accusatory article that falsely said I was trying to convert minors from Judaism to Christianity. It was good to know that someone had read my rebuttal.

I gave the Rabbi with the mints the bag of chocolates I had bought at Krogers. It was the only kosher candy I could find, and he was most appreciative. Just then, I noticed Anti-Missionary #2's wife talking to security people and pointing to me, but nothing happened.

I saw the woman from my lunch-n-learn who always drove a green Volkswagen. I pray for her every time I see a green Volkswagen. She was happy to see me and asked me if I wanted to buy a cooking demonstration ticket. I had the opportunity to interact with other Rabbis I knew as well as other Jewish acquaintances. Praise God for this awesome opportunity! I pray each one of those I met will be filled with the joy, love and peace they can only receive through knowing Jesus personally.

What Are You Doing Here?

Another evening, I arrived at the 8 PM anti-missionary lecture at a nearby Chabad at 7:45 PM. I was surprised to see Marlene there. She was with her Jewish, former co-worker who had a negative attitude towards me. Marlene asked what I was doing there, and I told her I assumed God sent me to take care of her. I asked what she was doing there, and she said her friend invited her.

A hostile Jewish man I witnessed to before demanded I pay the $10 (suggested) donation, so I did and then ate some of the refreshments they had. After he took my money, he ran and told all the organizers I was there. Marlene asked me to get her some fruit, and when I came back to my seat, her co-worker actually stuck his foot out to trip me! It was that kind of night.

The speaker was a Gentile who served as a missionary in Israel and other places and then converted to Orthodox Judaism. There were about 100 people in attendance. The speaker clearly shared the Gospel from 8:15 to 9:30 PM and then trashed Christianity until 10 PM. His justification for missionaries was that they sincerely believed what they were sharing. He asked for questions to be written down and then read. I knew this would be my opportunity to at least share with whoever read the questions. I felt led to ask, "Did you know Jesus loves you and is waiting for you to come to Him with His arms outstretched?" The speaker read my question aloud, and many people gasped. He said he wanted to talk to whoever wrote this afterwards, and several people turned and looked at me; but I did not feel led to reveal myself at that time.

Afterwards, the hostile Jewish man verbally attacked me. This upset Marlene, and she left. Several of the group stayed and chatted until 11 PM. I got home by 11:30 PM and called Marlene to make sure she was ok, and we spoke until 12 AM.

Because It's True

The world renowned Anti-Missionary was speaking at the Chabad closest to my home. I decided to go and sat in the back. The hostile Jewish man was there and asked me to sit in the front with him, and he was actually very friendly. I noticed several Jewish people I knew. The men in front of me were talking about the previous anti-missionary lecture, and remarked that someone had sent in a note that said, "Jesus Loves You." I leaned forward and told them it was me. They asked me why I said that, and I told them, "Because it's true."

I noticed people standing at the door and pointing at me. The world renowned Anti-Missionary was supposed to speak at 7:15 PM but hadn't, and at 7:45 PM I was approached by several people and asked to step outside where there were police. They told me this was a private event and I needed to leave. We had a short conversation, I said, "God bless you!" and left.

Towards Tradition

Ironically, the very next week, the same Chabad held another event by a group called "Towards Tradition." This group is made up of Orthodox Jews who partner with Christians to fight for our same religious freedoms. One of my prayer and monthly financial supporters was at this event. She had happened to be sitting next to their vice president on a plane to New York, and he had invited her.

They started the meeting by asking who had seen The Passion of the Christ, and many hands went up. Then they asked who had seen it twice, and I was the only raised hand. They mentioned how supportive Evangelical Christians are, and the need to partner together to accomplish our goals.

As we were walking out, I got into a discussion with the presenter about Jesus being the Messiah. We got into a somewhat heated debate, and many people stopped to listen. My friend and I started tag-team witnessing, and it seemed to be very fruitful. As my friend was leaving, she had the opportunity to share with a Jewish man who wanted to know about her beliefs. After this event, my friend began doubling her donations to me.

Jewish Festival

In honor of Israel's 60th Birthday, the Atlanta Jewish Center had their annual Jewish Festival in May instead of August. Thousands of Jewish people attend this event. A volunteer and I went to distribute Gospel tracts. Several Jewish people walked by. Some took Gospel tracts, and some even talked to us. After 20 minutes, an irate Orthodox man ripped up a tract, and then security came with police.

We were clearly on public property, but the police said we were not allowed to distribute Gospel tracts anywhere in the county and needed to leave, so we left. We came back later, and the same volunteer as before dropped me off down the street.

I held up a banner I brought with me proclaiming Jesus as the Jewish Messiah. After two hours of holding the banner across from the college parking lot where most people parked, a van drove by, and Anti Missionary #2, stuck his head out and called me a loser.

Shortly after that, the police showed up again. The officer was extremely aggressive and cited me for soliciting without a permit. The ordinance for soliciting in that county talks about not going door-to-door selling things, and I clearly didn't break the law. The officer told me if I didn't leave right then, he would arrest me, so I left.

On the way to my car, a Jewish man lowered his car window and said, "I don't agree with your beliefs, but you have the right to be there." I said, "God bless you!" and he said, "God bless you!" too!

I e-mailed Jay Sekulow's office of the American Center for Law and Justice (ACLJ), and he referred me to local attorneys with the Alliance Defense Fund who took my case. The attorneys went to the Jewish Center and showed security that I had every right to distribute Gospel materials on the public sidewalk in front of the Jewish Center. When my case came before the judge, it was thrown out because the police officer who cited me was no longer on the force!

JEWISH CLASSES

Lunch-N-Learns

I attended various lunch-n-learns at different synagogues and other locations around Atlanta. We would usually meet at noon and bring our lunches for an hour of teaching from various Rabbis. I attended the Thursday lunch-n-learns at the Chabad nearest my home for some five years. I would pray over the synagogue and for the people in the class.

At one lunch-n-learn, the Rabbi once asked everyone to sum up Judaism in three points and write it on a piece of paper. I wrote, "Love God and love your neighbor as yourself." The Rabbi said I was wrong but read my answer to the class. They sum it up with Torah Study, Prayer and Acts of Kindness, which is the Rabbinical Interpretation that was formulated to replace the sacrifice system after the Temple was destroyed.

My friend and I were out witnessing one Saturday and went to services at a Traditional synagogue, which is midway between Orthodox and Conservative. A young man was having his Bar Mitzvah, and they had an Oneg (refreshment time) that was open to the entire congregation in the fellowship hall afterwards. One Orthodox young man at the Oneg was dressed like a Chabadnick (an endearing term for a young religious man wearing a black hat and suit, flowing hair and sideburns) and stood out like a sore thumb among the others. He was actually the brother of the Bar Mitzvah boy, and I felt burdened to pray for him. Let's call him, "The Chabadnick"!

One Thursday, I was greeted at the door by a young man who informed me the Rabbi was out of town and the lunch-n-learn was cancelled. He and another young man asked if I would like to join them for study. After several minutes of studying, they wanted to know what I did for a living, so I told them. It actually took several minutes to convince them I was truly a missionary wanting to share the love of Jesus with them; and to demonstrate that I was, I shared the Gospel with them. They asked why I went to the lunch-n-learns, and I told them, "To better understand why they reject their Jewish Messiah and to pray that they would meet Him."

One young man asked for my e-mail address and told me he wanted to meet with me again to hear why I accepted Jesus. The other young man was moving to New York City, and he, too, gave me his e-mail address. Because he was dressed more normally, it wasn't until later that I realized he was, "The Chabadnick" I had been praying for!

Judaism And The Messiah

I learned that the Rabbi at the large Orthodox synagogue was going to teach a three-week class called *"Judaism and the Messiah."* Reservations could be made with his program director (one of my former Hebrew teachers). Here is the e-mail she sent after I e-mailed her to register for the class:

"Great! See you there! I really appreciate the note you sent me. It was completely unexpected and unnecessary, therefore, much more wonderful." She was referring to a thank you note I sent her after her Hebrew class concluded, thanking her for teaching it. Postcards, holiday cards and notes are great ways to reach people. She once said to me, *"We could be such good friends if it weren't for...."*

Although I usually learned something at all these classes, my main reason for attending was for intercession and evangelism. I usually tuned out the speaker when they blasphemed against Messiah, but looked for ways to share and discrepancies in what they said while I prayed for the people in the class. For anyone interested, I recommend Rachmiel Frydland's book *What the Rabbis Know About Messiah: A Study of Genealogy and Prophecy* (Clarksville, MD: Messianic Jewish Resources, International, 2002) as it covers a lot of the material this class did.

When I arrived at the shul, the doors were locked. Several other Christians I know happened to be at this class as well and arrived when I did. They were concerned about being able to get in, and I said, "Don't worry about it," punched in the security code and let us all in. They were astonished and asked how I could possibly know the code. I asked, "Don't all missionaries to Jewish people have the code to the main Orthodox Synagogue in their city?" In all seriousness, I was given the code to attend a class I used to take there.

The following is a summary of the three-week class:

WEEK 1 – There were approximately 100 seats set up; and by the time it started, there was standing room only. As is my custom, I sat in an empty area and waited for God to send the ones He wanted me to minister to. As I looked around the room, I saw many familiar faces of people I had previously shared or interacted with or for whom I had prayed. Right before it started, the anti-missionary-in-training sat next to me. The Rabbi started by asking what questions we would like to have answered through this class, and he wrote them all down on the white board in the front.

- What is a Messiah?
- Why do we need one?
- Is the Messiah an era or a person?
- What will the Messiah accomplish?
- What does Scripture say about the Messiah?
- What does the Talmud say about Messiah?
- How will we recognize Messiah when he comes?
- When will Messiah come?

A man sitting one seat away from me asked about all the Jews for Jesus, and how they were supposed to answer them. The anti-missionary-in-training told him about my belief, and I knew the main reason for my attendance at this meeting was for this man. The Rabbi smiled when the man asked about Jesus and drew a big "J" on the whiteboard under topics for the third week.

We spent most of the first class with the Rabbi writing down questions. He talked about Rambam's view of Jesus. Rambam is one of the most famous Jewish Sages (philosophers) of the twelfth century who wrote a lot of the Talmud, a commentary on the Torah. The Rabbi said that Rambam had thirteen principles of faith and taught that Jesus was not the Messiah. He also went on to say that some of the other Sages don't agree with the Rambam. Most Orthodox Jews give more credibility to the Talmud, which is a commentary on the Jewish Scriptures, than to the Scriptures themselves. The Rabbi also said that the Anointed One in Scripture refers to the Messiah. The answers to the first class could be summed up by saying that Jewish people are waiting for a king-like person who will lead the world into a Messianic era of peace after a great war. That belief is most closely associated with Orthodox Judaism.

Afterwards, I drove over to the Kroger and walked around wearing a *"Jesus Loves You"* T-shirt. There were many people from the class shopping there who were challenged by the T-shirt.

WEEK 2 – There weren't as many people the second week, but it was still fairly full. Although the Rabbi said that the Talmud teaches that if you calculate the coming of the Messiah, your soul should rot, he said that the earth is 5764 (Jewish Calendar) years old, and Messiah will come in about 240 years (around the year 6000). The Rabbi said that Adam was supposed to have lived for 1000 years, but since he sinned, he only lived for 930 years and the Messiah will get the remaining 70 years. Lord only knows where they get this stuff.

After the class, I asked the Rabbi why the Talmud would say not to calculate the coming of the Messiah. I reminded him that we are commanded to read the Tenach (Old Testament), and the Tenach includes Daniel chapter 9 which calculates the coming of the Messiah. He said that was an excellent question and he would get the answer.

WEEK 3 – The Rabbi discredited Jesus being the Messiah by saying that a trinity didn't make any sense. A man couldn't be God, and there is no world peace. He stopped for questions, and I asked, "Isn't it possible for the God of the Universe to indwell the body of a man? He's God, so can't He do anything he wants?" The Rabbi replied, "If you want my opinion, I can give it to you some other time." The Rabbi made mention of Rabbi Svie, who in 1200 AD was thought to be the Messiah but converted to Islam upon threat of death. The Rabbi also made mention of the Rebbe Schneerson, who many Orthodox (Chabad or Lubavitcher) followers worship as Messiah. The Rabbi said he never publicly denounced those who follow Schneerson until now! A Chabad Rabbi and some of his people were at this class. The Orthodox Rabbi gave the Chabad Rabbi a chance to give his point of view, which was that not all Chabadnicks view Schneerson as Messiah. The Chabad Rabbi claimed that even though Schneerson died some 10 years ago, couples that are married today receive personal letters from him blessing their marriages.

During the class, I felt burdened to pray for the man who had inquired about Jesus. When the class ended, he immediately turned around to me and started asking me questions. Praise God, I was able to share with him and answer questions while the anti-missionary-in-training listened in and then joined in, questioning me about the vision I had seen which led to my salvation. I told him the Book of Joel says young men will see visions.

Anti-Missionary #1, came up to me and also started asking questions. He hurled the apparent discrepancy in Matthew 2:23 at me: "and He went and lived in a town called Nazareth. So was fulfilled what was said through the prophets: He will be called a Nazarene." God had told me to brush up on that one a couple of days before. The operative word is *prophets*, because Nazareth is not mentioned in the Old Testament. I told him over and over it wasn't one prophet who said it, but an accumulation of several prophets determining He would be from Nazareth. Some other explanations are that people from Nazareth are despised, and Jesus was despised, and the Hebrew root *Neser* is the same root for *branch* as found in Isaiah 11:1:

"Then a shoot will come forth
out of the stem of Jesse,
and a branch will bear fruit
out of His roots."
-Isaiah 11:1

After 10 minutes of heated discussion (in front of others), I told Anti-Missionary #1 I loved him and to have a good evening. Afterwards, I asked the Rabbi if he had an answer to my question from the week before, and he said, "Although Daniel 9 calculates the coming of Messiah, you aren't calculating it, you're just reading about it." I prayed the Rabbi would read about the Messiah coming before the destruction of the Second Temple in 70 AD!

Jewish Center Class

Sometime later, I took a Hebrew class at the Jewish Center. Our assignment was to write down 10 sentences in Hebrew. Our Israeli teacher asked me to read a sentence, so I read, "Yeshua hu Hamasheach!" He asked if I was trying to say, "Joshua is the Supervisor"? I said, "No. I said, 'Jesus, He is the Messiah!'" The class was stunned!

MEDIA OUTREACH

Atlanta Jewish Times

There was a time when my name was getting into the *Atlanta Jewish Times (AJT)* almost every week. Sometimes it was good, but sometimes it wasn't so good.

The *AJT* did a story on Beth Hallel, a local Messianic Congregation, accusing them of purposely and deceptively naming their MJCC (Messianic Jewish Community Center) after Atlanta's Marcus Jewish Community Center (MJCC). I called the Marcus Jewish Community Center and learned they named their center years after the Messianic Jewish Community Center was named. I wrote a letter to the editor, and they published it.

Another time the *AJT* requested jokes. I sent this one in, and they published it:

> A man goes to see Mel Gibson's new movie, *The Passion*, and is inspired to take his family to Israel to see the places where Jesus lived and died. While on vacation, his mother-in-law dies. An undertaker in Tel Aviv explains that they can ship the body home to Wisconsin at a cost of US$10,000, or the mother-in-law could be buried in Israel for US$500.
>
> The man says, "We'll ship her home."
>
> The undertaker asks, "Are you sure? That's an awfully big expense, and we can do a very nice burial here."
>
> The man says, "Look, 2000 years ago they buried a guy here and three days later he rose from the dead. I just can't take that chance."

Once, as I attended the Jewish Festival at the Jewish Center by myself, dressed in plain clothes. I walked around and looked at all the exhibits and prayed for people as I walked through. There were people who knew me and were a little agitated that I was there. Anti-Missionaries #1 and #3 had their anti-missionary table up and running. Just as I was leaving, I saw AntiMissionary #2 talking to security and pointing at me. I actually went back into the festival and asked the security guard he was talking to if there was a problem. She said there wasn't.

I had gone on a mission trip and was out of town when the *Atlanta Jewish Times* called my church looking for me. Unfortunately, they had published a false article about me and my conduct at the Jewish Festival without actually verifying if it was true. They had an article entitled: "JCC (Jewish Community Center): No One Will Scare Children on Our Property." They accused me and another woman of going around the festival and telling little children that their parents lied to them about Jesus. They had people in the article saying, "Yes, I saw him going around."

I was at the festival by myself and never spoke to any children. This was the most ridiculous thing and was used to highlight the anti-missionaries. It is so sad that they have to make up lies to promote their ungodly agenda.

When I returned from my trip, I spoke to the *Times* editor who wrote the story and assured her it wasn't true. They allowed me to write a letter to the editor saying I did not do those things, and that I had forgiven the people who falsely accused me. I shared the Gospel in the letter; but, of course, they edited it out.

It really hurt me that I was subjected to such lies and innuendoes. I really love the Atlanta Jewish community and pray for them constantly. The following Sunday I was invited out West to one of my supporting churches. They had me speak and blessed me with a $12,000 offering. The one who wrote the misleading article no longer works for the *Atlanta Jewish Times*.

"... and he said: 'Listen all Judah and inhabitants of Jerusalem and King Jehoshaphat. Thus ADONAI says to you: Do not be afraid or dismayed because of this great multitude, for the battle is not yours, but God's.'"
-2 Chronicles 20:15

Messianic Jewish Times

A Gentile believer who attended our weekly Bible study at my home said she didn't know any Jewish people she could invite to the study, so we prayed she would meet some. Lo and behold, an Israeli Jew started attending her church with his girlfriend. I called the Israeli and sent him e-mails, but he wouldn't respond to me. I sent him yet another e-mail, and he finally responded because his sister, a believer living in Tel Aviv, sent him a copy of the *Messianic Jewish Times* that had me quoted on the front page. He was so excited he knew my name that he e-mailed me to say he wanted to meet me.

Internet Jewish Outreach

The Internet is a great way to reach out to people. Thanks to Facebook and other social media, I'm back in touch with hundreds of friends and family members with whom I can share. Our website, www.savethejews.org, has generated many contacts with people seeking the Lord, and we have been able to share with them. There was a Jewish woman from Canada that called and allowed me to share with her for over an hour! There was a family in New York whom we now supply with evangelistic T-shirts and Gospel materials. We have no idea how many people have read the testimonies from our Internet presence.

I used to go into chat rooms and witness to people. There was one woman who would identify me as a missionary every time I came in and would be very hostile. One night she was saying how she used to live in Maryland. One thing led to another, and we discovered that her doctor was my cousin! For two days she was very friendly and allowed me to share my testimony!

Another time, I was reaching out to people using instant messaging and got into a conversation with a gay Jewish man from San Francisco. He asked me what we could possibly have in common. I prayed! I asked where he was from originally, and he turned out to be best friends with my sister-in-law in high school in Queens, New York. He couldn't ask me questions fast enough, he was so excited.

I had various other conversations with Jewish people on Instant Message. Sometimes I would be able to meet with local people I met this way, and some of them would actually come to our Bible studies! Here's part of a conversation I had with an Israeli:

Me: Who do you think Jesus is?

Israeli: During this season he is a baby in the boxes on church lawns.

Israeli: I don't see how he could be messiah though. No king would have been born in a barn.

Me: That is the beauty of Hashem. He humbled Himself by taking on humanity.

Israeli: Do not speak blasphemy to me. Hashem is not a man.

Me: Sorry you feel that way. I didn't mean to offend you. How do you explain Isaiah 9:6?

Israeli: I don't know what it says.

Me: It talks about the son being called God!

Israeli: Type it out for me.

Me: For to us a child is born, to us a son is given, and the government will be on His shoulders. And He will be called Wonderful Counselor, Mighty God, Everlasting Father, Prince of Peace."-Isaiah 9:6

Israeli: Is that in the Bible?

Me: Tanach

Israeli: This verse?

Me: Yes in the Tanach.

Israeli: I thought it was only part of Handel's Messiah. Music.

Me: Where do you think Handel got it from?

Israeli: I assumed he made up the lyrics.

Me: I believe the whole Handel's Messiah is from the Tanach!

Israeli: You are sure of this?

Me: Yes, have you ever read Isaiah 53?

Israeli: I do not think so.

Me: That is the verse which really made me consider Jesus!

Israeli: Type it out please.

Me: I just emailed it!

Israeli: Todah. How can Hashem be a baby? Who ran the world while he was on earth?

Me: He did! Have you read the first chapter of Genesis: God created the heavens..., the Spirit of God hovered over the waters...Genesis 3:8 the voice of God was heard walking in the Garden.

Israeli: Yes. Steven, I am interested in what you have to say, but it is late and I need to go to work tomorrow. Can we finish this some other time?

Me: Sure, Baruch Hashem!

Israeli: Thank you

Me: Shabbat Shalom!

Israeli: I do want to ask one last question. Does Jesus help people to deal with anger?

Me: Yes, once you believe in Him, you receive the Holy Spirit to live through you. That is what is meant by Born Again. You die to your sinful nature and allow Hashem to live through you.

Israeli: I have a lot of anger and hatred inside me against the dogs known as Palestinians.

Me: Pray for your enemies! Many Palestinians love the Jewish people and Hashem!

Israeli: I cannot believe that. They only want to blow us up.

Me: Not all! Many love us!

Israeli: It would be worth it to me to get rid of the hatred I have inside. It is eating me up.

Me: Jesus can take away that hatred! He took away my desire for alcohol.

Israeli: When you stopped drinking, was it all at once or gradual?

Me: It was gradual for three months, then I just stopped, had no desire. I had hatred towards someone in my life, but because of the Holy Spirit, I could forgive and love him!

Israeli: Steven, thank you for talking to me.

Me: Any time, [xxx-xxx-xxxx my phone number], if you want.

Israeli: I need to sleep and think about this.

Israeli: You are sure Jesus is our Messiah? How can he be? Where is the peace?

Me: I have peace in my heart!

Israeli: But isn't he to bring peace to the world??

Me: He did give individual peace, and when He comes back, the entire world will have peace!

Israeli: When is he to come back?

Me: No one knows. But there are signs it will be fairly soon.

Israeli: What signs?

Me: Earthquakes, famines, floods, plagues, Israel becoming a nation as well as many Jews becoming believers in Jesus.

Israeli: It says these things in the scriptures?

Me: The New Testament. Did you read Isaiah 53?

Israeli: I haven't read it.

Me: It is important!

Israeli: Alright, alright already. I will go read it. I need to find my book.

Israeli: Please excuse me. I must go. What I just read is too much for me.

...A few days later...

Israeli: I've spent the last few days thinking about things. I think Jesus was probably the Messiah.

> Me: Do you believe Hashem came to earth in the body of Jesus and died for our sins?

Israeli: I think so.

> Me: Would you like to ask Him into your heart right now to forgive you?

Israeli: Yes, but I don't know how.

> Me: I can type a prayer, and you can repeat it to Him!

Israeli: Alright.

> Me: God, I know I have sinned against You and I want to turn from my sin. I believe You provided Jesus as payment for my sin. With this prayer, I receive Jesus as my Savior and Lord. Thank You God for forgiving me of sin and for sealing my name in your book of life forever. Amen.

Israeli: Omein.

> Me: Did you pray that prayer?

Israeli: Yes.

> Me: If you really meant it, God will give you His Holy Spirit to guide you in all truth!

Israeli: Is there anything I need to do besides that?

Me: There are four things in following Yeshua, like the four legs that hold up a chair: Praying, reading your Bible, fellowshipping with other believers and telling people how Jesus changed your life.

Israeli: The Gentile Bible?

Me: The Jewish Bible, both Testaments. I will help you if you want!

Israeli: Only Gentiles read the second part, don't they?

Me: All read it! It is the fulfillment of the Scriptures.

Israeli: I will have to go look for one of those soon then.

Me: Please call me with questions [xxx-xxx-xxxx] or I will be glad to call you or write you.

Israeli: I do not want my wife to know. I would rather you didn't call.

Me: You can call me.

Israeli: Alright, but not right away.

Me: Ok, I have friends in NY who can help you as well if you want.

Israeli: Alright.

Me: Please feel free to email or IM me with questions.

Israeli: Yes.

Me: Hashem wants the best for your life!

Israeli: I need to sign off if you don't mind. My wife is in the room

Me: God bless you!

Postcards

While on mission trips, I would maintain a list of about 200 Jewish people/ families to whom I would send postcards. This turned out to be a great relationship builder. Someone sent me a syndicated column about Israel written by a Jewish woman who lived in California and was originally from Atlanta. It also mentioned this woman was related to Anti-Missionary #1.

I started sending her postcards and signed them, "Love, your adoring fan, Steve." It was three years before we actually met while she was visiting in Atlanta. Although it started out as a joke, we remained friends for many years, and I often visit with her when I'm in Los Angeles or she is in Atlanta. She has made it very clear she is Jewish and does not believe in Jesus. Whenever someone calls and I am with her, she tells them she is with her "Jews for Jesus" friend.

My journalist friend is somewhat famous and was asked to be on a Messianic television program in Birmingham, Alabama, and asked me to drive her there. While we were there, the host of the show invited me to come back to share my testimony. Over the years I've been blessed to share my testimony on various television and radio programs throughout the United States.

Evangelistic Mailings

I wrote a letter to the Jewish community and included my testimony. Each month we would mail copies of the letter to people with Jewish names in each of the zip codes around Atlanta. In 18 months, we mailed out a total of 5,000 letters. We received numerous phone calls, letters and e-mails. Most were hostile, but some were positive.

An Orthodox Jewish doctor called with some questions. I showed up at his house, but he really didn't want to talk. I mailed him a copy of: *Jewish*

Doctors Meet The Great Physician. I visited another Jewish man I met from the mailing, and we have remained friends.

Fox News

We supply a Messianic Congregation in Washington, DC with evangelistic t-shirts. They are specially made with "*Yeshua Loves You*" inside a star of David on the front and "*Jesus Loves You*" inside a star of David on the back.

Apparently, someone from the congregation was wearing one of these t-shirts while distributing Gospel tracts at the Capitol building because they were in the background of a Fox News telecast. I actually saw this myself and received numerous e-mails from friends all over the country. While speaking at a Messianic Congregation in Tucson, Arizona, Rabbi Michael said he had seen this man on tv as well

A NEEDLE IN A HAYSTACK

While visiting Aron HaKodesh, a Messianic Congregation in South Florida, I told my friend Jamie Lash (Jewish Jewels Television Host) I was planning to do an outreach at the University of Florida. She told me I should visit a Jewish missionary friend of hers, so I did. He told me about his daughter. She was dating an Israeli non-believer named Tom who lived in Ohio. I immediately started praying for Tom.

I began preparing for a five-week evangelistic outreach in Israel. I returned home from a whirlwind weekend in California that I had squeezed into my schedule when a friend and her pastor invited me to their church in Cape Girardeau, Missouri, and a pastor friend invited me to minister at his storefront church in Warren, Ohio. The last thing I wanted to do was embark upon a 2,000-mile road trip right before the five-week evangelistic outreach in Israel. Yet when God calls, I must answer because His Word says:

> *"I have been crucified with Messiah; and it is no longer I who live,*
> *but Messiah lives in me. And the life I now live in the body,*
> *I live by trusting in Ben-Elohim* [the Son of God]*who loved me*
> *and gave Himself up for me."*
> *-Galatians 2:19b-20.*

As I drove to Missouri, I visited friends at a Messianic Congregation in Cartersville, Georgia, just in time for Shabbat prayers and Oneg. They prayed over me and blessed me immensely!

The invitation to the church in Cape Girardeau, Missouri, came from Betty. She had been on 30+ trips to Israel and on one trip saw an 85-year-old mutual friend wearing a *"Jesus Loves You"* T-shirt and wanted one. She wore it to her Missions meeting, and they wanted T-shirts too. Then other people in her church wanted them. When people in other towns asked for T-shirts, she invited me. After I spoke, Betty cried because I was the first Jewish person to ever walk into her church!

On route to Ohio, I drove to St. Louis and stayed with my friend Shelley's Jewish non-believing father who claimed to be agnostic. I've stayed with him many times before. Shelley is a Jewish believer, and I made arrangements to meet Micah, another Jewish believer and his family who happened to be in town, at the only kosher deli in St. Louis. When we arrived there happened to be another Jewish believer at the restaurant. Micah showed up with his family, and now there were seven Jewish believers sitting in the middle of a kosher restaurant wearing evangelistic T-shirts! Dozens of Jewish people were challenged and some let us share.

My next stop along the way was to visit with a friend in Bloomington, Indiana, who had invited me to his house. As we prepared to reach out to the many Jewish and other people at Indiana University, my cell phone rang. My friend in Indiana (near Bloomington) called me to ask when my Israeli friends, the Beckfords, were going to be in Bloomington. She had no idea I was in Bloomington at the moment. When she learned of our impromptu outreach to the university, she asked to join us and brought along a Jewish believer who brought a dog and a guitar (great for bringing people over). Many were challenged by our T-shirts, hundreds of tracts were given out and many conversations took place.

After our outreach, we went to lunch, and Jewish people were challenged by our T-shirts. I was dying to share with the three Jewish students next to us and prayed for an opportunity. When their food came, I asked what they ordered and where they were from. They were from Chicago, Los Angeles and Miami. I told them I was just in Palm Springs, and it turned out they were too. They saw my friend's evangelistic booth at the street fair in Palm Springs and said they had asked about it giving me an opportunity to share!

My last stop was Warren, Ohio. My friend, Pastor Scott, wanted to bless Israel and had invited me to share testimony at his storefront church and do outreach. He had me set up sales tables on the sidewalk in front of his church and hang Israeli flags on the front of them. It was promoted all over town, and we were photographed by the local newspaper reporter for the "Faith and Values" section.

I didn't understand why a missionary to the Jewish people was doing an outreach in front of a black church in a black neighborhood, but trusted God for the results! While I was selling our merchandise, many people came by and we shared with them. One man allowed me to share the Gospel with him and prayed to receive Jesus.

Two women stopped their car and started laughing. I walked over and asked what was so funny? They said they were from Israel, were looking for challah bread and got lost then noticed our Israeli flags! Praise God!

Pastor Scott kept calling people in his congregation and told them to come by and buy something from me. He wanted to make sure I would go home with at least $1,000!

On the way back home, I called my friend Robert Specter, who heads up Rock of Israel Ministries near Cincinnati and asked if he wanted to meet for dinner. Robert told me he was on the road and asked where I was? It turned out he was about an hour behind me on the same highway. Robert told me to get off at a certain exit and meet him for lunch.

When I got off at the exit, I noticed a mall and immediately thought about witnessing to Israelis while waiting for Robert to arrive. Israelis often sell Dead Sea products, hair curlers, massage gadgets, toy helicopters and other items at kiosks in malls.

I walked up to one Israeli and said, "Yeshua HaMashiach!"

He said, "I know."

I said, "What do you mean you know?"

He told me he had a Messianic girlfriend and she told him all about Yeshua!

I asked what his girlfriend's name was, and he told me I couldn't possibly know her.

I said, "Why not?"

He said, "Because she lives in Florida. But maybe you know her father who is a minister?"

I asked his name, and it turned out to be the man I met with at the University of Florida, and this was Tom, whom I had been praying for! (The missionary never told me what city Tom was in, he had just told me Tom lived in Ohio)

I told Tom I had been praying for him and asked why he didn't believe in Jesus. He said he needed a sign. I asked, "Don't you think a 400 pound man wearing a *"Jesus Loves You"* Jewish star T-shirt that had been praying for you is a sign?" He said, "No, I need a real sign."

"Furthermore Adonai spoke to me saying, 'I have seen this people, and it is indeed a stiff-necked people.'"-Deuteronomy 9:13

FAMILY REUNIONS

A cousin organized a family reunion for anyone related to my great-great-grandparents who came from Borisov, Belarus, just outside of Minsk. (This was my mother's mother's family. Ironically, my father's father's family was also from Belarus, a city called Pinsk.)

I had never met this distant cousin. We spoke on the phone and each shared our family "secrets," that she was a Lesbian and that I was a born-again Christian. She and her friends were hosting the reunion at her home in Connecticut, and I think she wanted to make sure I wouldn't cause any trouble. God calls us to love everyone. He is the judge, not us!

In the process of preparing for the family reunion, I found out I had cousins living in Atlanta. To my surprise, not only did we sometimes shop in the same Kroger, but my cousin's wife did contract work for my old department at The Coca-Cola Company. It was so nice to actually have family living in Atlanta!

The family reunion was awesome! I got to see relatives I hadn't seen in a long time and got to meet many relatives for the first time as well. It turned out one of our cousins, Stephen Weiss, had been married to Donna Karan, the founder of DKNY, the famous New York fashion house. Barbra Streisand apparently knew him, and had dedicated a song to him on one of her albums after he passed away. I got a little closer to my relatives and had a chance to share with one about my belief in Jesus.

While distributing Gospel tracts with my friend Dennis in Provincetown, Massachusetts, on Cape Cod, a woman walked up to me, poked me in the chest and demanded to know my name. I told her it was Steven, and she said, "It's me, don't you recognize your cousin?" She had lost 75 pounds, and I had only met her once at the Family Reunion in Connecticut, so I didn't recognize her! She invited us to her summer house, which was on the Cape, for a party but told me I couldn't proselytize. She also said there would be 10 women there, but none of them would be interested in me.

When we arrived at the party, my cousin's partner of 16 years gave me a big hug, as I knew her from the reunion. They loved Dennis because he is a handyman, and they needed work done on their homes. They asked what we were doing in Provincetown. I told them we were handing out Gospel tracts. They asked what Gospel tracts were, so I gave them some!

WHAT GOES AROUND COMES AROUND

PHOENIX, ARIZONA

In March 2009, I attended the 26th Annual Lausanne Consultation on Jewish Evangelism (LCJE). This annual event gathers together ministers doing Jewish evangelism for networking and presenting educational papers on Jewish Evangelism. We equipped many with *"Jesus Loves You"* T-shirts and Gospel tracts.

Six of us from all over the USA, including Moishe Rosen, the founder of Jews for Jesus, knew each other from the same Internet chat room and had dinner. Moishe asked me if he could be on my ministry's Board of Directors and wrote a beautiful letter of recommendation for me and my ministry!

Phoenix was thought to have one of the fastest growing Jewish populations in the United States, so I arrived early and stayed after the LCJE meeting to show off my T-shirt and distribute Gospel tracts at college campuses, malls and street corners. At one shopping mall, a Russian, Jewish non-believer saw my *"Jesus Loves You"* Jewish Star T-shirt from upstairs, ran down and told me she had never met a Jewish believer in Jesus.

We gave out shirts and tracts at a skateboard park. I offered one of the skateboarders a shirt, but he threw it back at me and said he didn't want it because he was Jewish! This enabled me to witness to him and his mother, who was in a parked car nearby. I also got to visit a family of Jewish believers and ministered at a church.

I spent some eight hours distributing thousands of Gospel tracts at Arizona State University. I witnessed to many Jewish and other students, faculty and campus workers from all over the world. There were three Jewish students who were hostile towards me, but when I ran into them a second and third time while walking around campus, they were more open; and two actually took Gospel tracts.

My friend (a Jewish believer) asked me to reach out to her non-believing family while I was in Phoenix. I had lunch with her family (father, mother and sister) and was able to share some. My friend's father went to medical school in Munich, Germany, after World War II and had a friend from that school who lived in Atlanta. They were surprised I knew of him. It turned out his wife was the mayor of my town, and I actually met him later at a political Hanukkah party!

While we were at the LCJE meetings, our group went over to Jewish Voice Broadcasting for a tour by Jonathan Bernis, the president. My father had prayed with me to receive Jesus and constantly told me he watched Jonathan on tv.

ASTORIA, OREGON

Soon afterwards, a Christian women's group was having a retreat in Astoria, Oregon. They had decided they would take up an offering for Jewish Voice Ministries. When the guest speaker was told the offering was for another ministry and not theirs, she decided not to attend. I was asked to take her place and share my testimony. Since I was familiar with Jewish Voice Ministries and the wonderful work they do, I was more than happy to step in and take up the offering for JVM.

There were two other Jewish believers taking part in the retreat. It turned out Lyn was actually from my neighborhood in Atlanta, and she lived on the other side of the main road by my house! Heidi was from Harrisburg, Pennsylvania and used to attend the Bible study fellowship Lura Beckford used to host. Not only that, Heidi told me she had been downtown one day and met some Orthodox Jewish men from Atlanta and let them stay at her house. Turns out one of them was "The Chabadnick" I have been praying for!

TUCSON, ARIZONA

A year later, Jews for Jesus had an outreach in Phoenix. While we were there, they asked me to lead a team to do some outreach in Tucson. We went to the college campus, and I stationed people at various locations. I passed a group of about 20 cyclists having drinks outside of a café. They all looked at my T-shirt as I walked by, so I stopped to talk. They were visiting from Canada and allowed me to share about my T-shirt.

Afterwards, I took a Gospel broadside and handed it to one of the men in the group. The entire group burst out laughing. I asked what was so funny. Someone said I had handed the broadside to the one Jewish person in the group.

Next, I felt led to distribute broadsides in front of the student union. When I arrived, there was a Hillel group (Jewish educational and welcoming outpost for college students) set up and promoting a Purim Party right in front of my spot, and there were some 30 Jewish students standing there. Many asked me questions and took broadsides. Later, a Rabbi came by, and we had a nice interchange. There were Hare Krishnas set up across the way from the Hillel group. When they saw how many broadsides were being taken, they moved right near me to try to take advantage of the flow of interested passers-by.

Just as I was about to leave, a young man with a skateboard walked up to me. He told me he had the same shirt? I asked him where he got the shirt from? He said that I had given it to him in a skateboard park in Phoenix last year! You could have knocked me over with a feather! I asked if he knew Jesus personally, and he said no. I shared the Gospel with him, and he prayed to receive Jesus!

IRVINE, CALIFORNIA

Years later I began driving out west every February. There is a trade show in Las Vegas, Nevada, a Messianic Conference in Irvine, California and Ambassador Month for a supporting congregation in Tucson, Arizona as well as a Gem Show that usually takes place around the same time. Depending on the exact dates of these events, I will go to each city accordingly.

One year I went to the Messianic Conference in Irvine before going to Tucson. I usually sell evangelistic t-shirts at this conference. We usually set up the marketplace near the hotel lobby. There are always non-believing Jewish people staying at this hotel, and they often come into the marketplace.

A man, not wearing a conference badge, purchased one of my t-shirts? I didn't recognize him from the conference, and we didn't really say anything to each other. The next morning, I happened to run into this man in the hotel lobby during one of my breaks.

The man told me he was from Tucson, Arizona and was in Irvine visiting his daughter at college. He told me he was Jewish, and even though he was not a believer in Jesus, he was curious about the Saturday morning Shabbat Services we were having. He also told me he purchased the t-shirt for a Christian friend of his.

The next day, while on another break, I ran into this same man and his non-believing Jewish wife in the hotel lobby again. It turns out his wife lived in the same neighborhood on Long Island in New York that my parents had lived in for a year after they sold their house and before they moved to Florida.

I asked the man why he didn't believe in Jesus, and he told me he wasn't ready. I told the man that I was planning to be in Tucson in two weeks, and we exchanged numbers so we could meet for lunch.

When I got to Tuscon, I invited the man to my supporting congregation Sar Shalom, and he came. It turned out one of the people from the chat room I knew and was at the LCJE meeting in Phoenix, was part of this congregation and was actually good friends with the man that bought the t-shirt! The leadership invited me to lunch as always, and we invited this man as well.

I kept in touch with this man, and he continued to visit the congregation. Even though he made a profession of faith, he took me to lunch a year later with the man he bought the t-shirt for, and insisted I pray with him to receive Jesus! The rabbi from the congregation started discipling him!

ODESSA, UKRAINE

Several years later, it was a blessing to join Jonathan Bernis' Team (Jewish Voice Ministries) for Jewish festivals in Odessa, Ukraine. Our team of seventy-three joined over 200 local volunteers and distributed over 250,000 festival invitations. We had many interactions on the streets leading up to the festivals and gave away some 15,000 Gospel books to people who came. Many Jews and Gentiles prayed to receive their Messiah.

A Gentile believer had seen festival advertisements and wanted to go because her daughter married a Jewish man and she wanted to learn more about the Jewish roots of our faith. She literally cried when I gave her a festival invite! I was able to share with and get contact information from an Israeli Arab man who was studying medicine in Odessa. As we were leaving the congregation for outreach, an American Jewish man was parking his car. He was most interested in our festival T-shirts and gave us his contact information for followup. When he happened to pass by where I was distributing invitations later on, he told me he wanted to come to Atlanta.

The festivals, which included wonderful concerts, music and dance, were held at an ornate Opera House most would not be able to afford themselves; but the festivals were provided for free. It is our understanding this was the first time the Opera House ever had evangelical music. Over 2,000 Jewish people gave contact information for the local Messianic congregations to follow up with.

While waiting on the ticket line at the airport to come home, one of my team members told me the couple next to her saw my *"Jesus Loves You"* Jewish Star T-shirt and said, "Maybe he knows something we don't know." Another team mate struck up a conversation with this couple. The woman was Jewish and originally from Odessa, and the man was a Catholic Australian.

Afterwards, my team mate told me about the interaction and said she wished she had a tract to give the couple. I gave her one I had, and she gave it to the couple. Then the couple wanted to meet me! It turned out the couple lived across the street from friends of mine in Sydney, Australia! We spent some 30 minutes sharing the Gospel with them, and the man prayed to receive Jesus.

VACATIONS

PALM SPRINGS, CALIFORNIA

My sister asked me to join her on vacation in Palm Springs, California. When I realized it was the week before I was flying to the West Coast for an outreach in Portland, Oregon, I decided to extend my mission trip to go with her as I had never been to Palm Springs.

I asked the Lord how He would have me serve Him in California, and He told me to do everything my sister did! She's Jewish, and she will do things on her vacation that other Jewish people do!

On the way to the hotel from the Palm Springs Airport, we stopped off for something to eat at one of the only places that were open at that late night hour. I wore my *"Jesus Loves You"* Jewish star T-shirt to the buffet inside the Agua Caliente Indian Casino, and people just burst out laughing at it (that was a first).

Our cousins came from San Diego to visit us at the pool of our hotel in Palm Desert. My cousin's wife was intrigued by my T-shirt, allowed me to share in front of everyone and later told me several of her relatives were believers.

I noticed women in the hot tub whom I suspected were Jewish, and my cousins, who are Jewish, let me share with them! I distributed Gospel tracts at a flea market and shared with Jewish people, including a vendor at the flea market who used to live next door to my mother's old boyfriend in Brooklyn, New York!

My sister and I drove to Los Angeles, and I distributed Gospel tracts on Hollywood Boulevard and shared with Jewish people. We spent the afternoon with my friends Cyril and Rhonda Gordon who were Jews for Jesus missionaries at the time. Later that night, while my sister went shopping, I distributed Gospel tracts on the Santa Monica Pier and 3rd Street Promenade and shared with Jewish people and prayed with a man to receive the Lord!

I shared with a Jewish man in our hotel pool and followed him into the hot tub, where he spent 20 minutes asking me questions about Jesus. Later, I wore my *"Jesus Loves You"* T-shirt to the mall and wrote postcards to over one hundred Jewish people I know. We went to the Palm Desert Visitors Center, and I shared with a Jewish man from Long Island, who asked me to mail him my testimony.

My sister and I went to a Thomas Kincaide Gallery, and the saleswoman said she liked my T-shirt and told me her husband is Jewish, but not a believer. Just as we discovered we had both been in Israel for a mission trip in June of 1997, the phone rang! The saleswoman answered the phone, looked at me and said, "I think this is for you," and handed me the phone!

The woman on the phone was calling to speak with the Jews for Jesus volunteer who used to work at that store. The employee no longer worked there. The woman on the other end had just moved to Orange County, California, and wanted help witnessing to her Jewish neighbors (on both sides). I gave her Jews for Jesus contacts and later sent her some materials.

While in Palm Springs, I visited a Messianic Congregation nearby. The leader was very friendly, and the whole congregation was a blessing. They appreciated my Jewishness and made me feel welcome.

On Thursdays they close off five blocks of the main road in Palm Springs for a street fair. Fairs are great because you can stand in one place and almost everyone will walk by at some point. The Lord led me to stand on the corner in front of the Starbucks. Later on I had to move because I was in a reserved place (who knew?) where an Orthodox Rabbi sets up a table called, "Ask the Rabbi!" Standing near his table was great because it showed me who was probably Jewish and gave me many opportunities to witness to Jewish people, including the Rabbi!

I distributed 1,000 Gospel tracts, shared with many Jewish people and prayed with one man to receive Jesus! The Libraries in Cathedral City and La Quinta let me display Gospel tracts!

The last night, I shared with a Jewish waiter and a Jewish woman my sister had met. I spent several hours distributing Gospel tracts at the LA Airport and was challenged by 11 different people. If you have a valid plane ticket, you can distribute literature in the public areas. I shared with some Jewish people. A Catholic man from Mexico City with a Jewish Grandmother prayed to receive Jesus.

On the way to a plane connection in Utah, I was able to share with some Mormons. Mormons do not accept that Jesus is God, so I distributed Gospel tracts at Salt Lake City Airport for 10 minutes until the police said to stop.

I remained friendly with the leader of the Messianic Leader in Palm Springs. For 10 years afterwards, he would invite me out to Palm Springs the first weekend in December for the Festival of Lights Parade. His Congregation had a float in the parade and everyone would wear our *"Jesus Loves You"* Jewish Star T-shirts, which were seen by hundreds of thousands along the parade route.   We would sing Gospel songs and distribute Gospel tracts.

This same Messianic leader also organized an annual prophecy conference which met at a church using the backroom of a synagogue at the Jewish Center. He invited me to sell, *"Jesus Loves You"* Jewish Star T-shirts and other Judaica at the conference, which in essence was at the Jewish Center! Members of the Jewish Center were absolutely dumbfounded I was there. One Jewish man bought a Shema ring from me just so he could show other people what I was selling!

ATHENS, GREECE

My sister invited me to go with her on vacation to Greece. I used frequent flyer miles but had to fly from Atlanta to Toronto to London to Frankfurt before going to Athens. I couldn't resist wearing a *"Jesus Loves You"* Tshirt and distributing Gospel tracts as I went.

In Toronto, I ate dinner at an Airport restaurant and was disappointed the hostess put me in the back where the passers-by couldn't see my T-shirt, until I realized God might have a different plan. As I sat down, I noticed the woman across the way staring at my T-shirt. She looked just like my cousin's wife and was wearing a Chai (Jewish letters symbolizing *life*). My waiter turned out to be Jewish, let me share with him and took a Gospel tract! At the airline lounge, I noticed an Orthodox Jewish man using one of the computers; and I gave him a Gospel tract. I walked past three Jewish people who commented on my T-shirt, let me share and accepted Gospel tracts.

I arrived in London early in the morning with a 12-hour layover and took a train to Golders Green, the main Orthodox Jewish neighborhood. I arrived at 8:15 AM, in time for the morning rush, and began distributing Gospel tracts at the train station until the security woman moved me outside of the station area. I was glad to be moved because it was as if the Hand of God swooped down and put me exactly where I needed to be, across from the bus stop where hundreds of young Jewish men were going to Yeshiva (Jewish school). Many people took Gospel tracts and hundreds of Jewish people were challenged by my presence there as they walked or drove by. A Jewish man walked by and reminded me of our meeting in Melbourne, Australia, during the Jews for Jesus "Behold Your God!" campaign where I actually sat and shared with him at a restaurant. Daniel (United Kingdom Director for Chosen People Ministries) walked by and invited me to his home where I met his family.

I arrived in Athens two days before my sister did. I had planned to visit the Athens Synagogue, but my luggage hadn't arrived. I asked God why my luggage wasn't there, and He told me to wear my T-shirt to the Synagogue. There are 5,000 Jews living in Greece, and 3,000 of them live in Athens. The only two synagogues (both Orthodox) in Athens are right across from each other, with services taking place at only one of them.

When I arrived at the active synagogue, a non-English-speaking Israeli greeted me and took me into the sanctuary. I met another man, and he told me he was a "Christian" converting to Judaism, and I made sure to explain to him he is not a Christian, but a Gentile. (Jews usually consider anyone who is not a Jew to be a Christian, but not all Gentiles are Christians.) The leader came in and did a double-take of my T-shirt. A few minutes later he left and then came back with the non-English-speaking Israeli and the security guard. They wanted to know if I was Jewish, so I pulled out my passport and pointed to Kaplan, and they let me stay. It turned out they needed me for the Minion. (They need 10 Jewish men over age 13 in order to have certain prayers.)

188

A man walked over to me and wanted to know about my belief, so I shared with him. No one invited me to Shabbat dinner after the service, but as I walked from the synagogue I was behind three men: the leader, an Ultra Orthodox man who heads up the Athens Chabad and a man from LA who was studying at the local university. They walked down a different street but I ran into them again a few minutes later. The leader left them, and I was able to share with the other two!

I mailed out 200 postcards to Jewish people and families we minister to and spent over an hour putting stamps on the cards at the post office. A Greek Jew asked about my T-shirt, took a tract and asked if he could have a Hebrew one for his boyfriend in Israel.

My sister's flight was delayed 11 hours, so I hung out at the airport. I showed off my T-shirt to literally thousands of people from all over the world, shared and gave tracts to an Israeli and a Canadian Jew. I prayed with a British Gentile with Jewish roots who had seen me at the post office, to receive Jesus.

While standing in our hotel lobby, I heard people speaking in Hebrew. A tour group of thirty Israelis was staying at our hotel. I immediately ran up to my room and got my Hebrew Gospel tracts. When I came back down, most were out by the pool and more than half took tracts!

I had a great holiday with my sister, ministering whenever I could while doing the things tourists do. The vacation went by quickly, and it was time to return to Atlanta.

On the way home, I practiced airport outreach. I shared with and gave tracts to people in Athens who were waiting for a flight to Israel. At my stop in Frankfurt, I gave tracts to two French couples and an American Orthodox Jewish couple. I showed off my T-shirt in London and offered tracts to passers-by, and I gave out tracts to some Orthodox Jews in Toronto.

I noticed a Jewish looking couple and made sure to show off my t-shirt. The man said, "I like your t-shirt, I have the same one!" I asked where he got if from. He told me Carol (a friend of mine) in Alabama gave it to him. It turned out this couple was David and Joan Abramsky and they worked for JFJ in San Francisco.

VIVA LAS VEGAS

DID YOU GET HER PHONE NUMBER?

In 1993, while I was at First Baptist Atlanta, one of my friends from church told me he met Rhonda, a Jewish believer from California who was visiting the church. I asked if he had gotten her phone number, but he had not. At that time, I thought there were only a few of us Jewish believers in the world, and very much wanted to meet other Jewish believers. I figured if God wanted me to meet Rhonda, I would.

Some twelve or so years later, my friend Brooke suggested I start ministering in Las Vegas as there is no shortage of lost sinners there. At the time, Las Vegas was considered to be the fastest-growing Jewish population in the United States.

My sister just happened to be taking my mother to Las Vegas for Mother's Day for a concert by Johnny Mathis, my mother's all-time favorite singer. I decided to go minister in Las Vegas while my family was visiting there. Brooke put me in touch with her friend Rhonda who invites visiting missionaries to her house on Saturday evenings for a dessert social. She also invites area pastors and has the missionaries share about their ministry, hoping the pastors will invite them to speak at their respective churches.

Rhonda and her family invited me to speak while I was there, and a pastor invited me to speak at his church the next morning. Rhonda helped me get to speak at other congregations, and I have been going back to these congregations for years. Of course, Rhonda turned out to be the Rhonda from California who visited First Baptist Atlanta in 1993. Not only that, but she had graduated high school in Skokie, Illinois, at the same time as my ex-girlfriend and actually knew her!

WHO'S YOUR COUSIN?

It turned out my father's cousin, Joseph Barnard, was also living in Las Vegas, but I didn't know it at the time. Cousin Joey went to acting school with Marlon Brando and was the Executive Director and a teacher at the Lee Strasberg Theatre Institute in Hollywood. He appeared in the movie

Judgment at Nuremberg and had roles in *Star Trek, The Twilight Zone* and *Mission Impossible.* Unfortunately, Joey died, right when I started going to Las Vegas, while helping Jerry Lewis get ready for a television role in New York City.

Joey's parents (Beryl and Lena) were my godparents. Aunt Lena was my grandfather's sister. They lived a few blocks from my grandparents in Brighton Beach, Brooklyn, and they would often take me to their apartment. Aunt Lena always made me latkes even if it wasn't Hanukkah! Joey's granddaughter, Molly Kate Bernard, is a rising star and is currently in a television program *Younger.* Aunt Lena and Uncle Beryl would be kvelling!

YOU NEVER KNOW

My friend Shari also moved to Las Vegas. Shari was the administrative assistant for the San Francisco branch of Jews for Jesus, and we worked together back in 2001. We often prayed for Shari's mother, and what a blessing it was to be able to actually minister to Shari's mother in Las Vegas before she passed away as well as several other mother's of Jewish believers in Las Vegas.

Brooke, Rhonda and Shari and I met up at a mall food court to do some outreach. More Israelis work at malls in Las Vegas than almost anywhere else I had been outside of Israel. While we were at the food court, a young man noticed our Jewish evangelistic T-shirts and came over to talk to us. He was an Israeli who had just been released from jail for working in the United States without a proper work visa. After the outreach, we brought him over to Rhonda's house, shared with him and he prayed to receive his Messiah!

Another time, Shari and I ministered in Las Vegas during a Chabad Hanukkah outreach on the Fremont Street Promenade. (Hanukkah is a Jewish holiday that commemorates the rededication of the Second Temple in the second century BC.) I handed a Gospel tract to a man, and Shari told me I had just given a tract to Oscar Goodman (Jewish), the Mayor of Las Vegas.

I had lunch at Shari's diner (where she sold our t-shirts) and then we went out evangelizing and ran into the parents of Rich, a Jews for Jesus missionary. Rich had come to Atlanta in 1998. He grew up in Brooklyn, New York, and lived between Avenues J and K as had I. I had been praying for his parents since then, and this was the third time I had run into them in Las Vegas. We were actually at a casino looking for my friend's father, as he usually hangs out there, but didn't find him. When we went out to the car, Rich's parents came by and were parked right across from us; and we all knew it was a divine appointment.

Rhonda, Shari, Shari's grandson and I went to a Bagel Café one Saturday morning. Almost everyone was Jewish and stared at our t-shirts. We were seated in the back room. Old time Jewish comedian Marty Allen was in the room with his entourage. We went over and had our pictures taken with him and made sure to share Messiah. (Marty died within a year) Then we noticed billionaire Jewish casino owner Sheldon Adelson was also in the room with his entourage. We made sure to share with them as well!

MY FRATERNITY BROTHERS

After an outreach in Atlanta, I jumped on the train and ran into my fraternity brother Bobby! I didn't even know he was Jewish. It turned out he was in Atlanta for the Gift Show and had moved to Las Vegas. I always visited him at the art gallery he worked at and shared Jesus.

On one visit to Las Vegas, I visited Bobby and he told me, Todd, one of our other fraternity brothers who had actually been my roommate, happened to be in town. I met Todd at a bar. He's also Jewish and was amazed that I believed in Jesus. He went up to the woman next to him at the bar and told her about my faith. He asked her what she thought about it, and she said she thought it was great, as she was a Sunday school teacher!

On another trip, I called Bobby to tell him I was in town. Bobby told me, Mark,   another fraternity brother was also in town (and also Jewish). I called this other brother and to my total joy and amazement, he had already become a believer in Jesus! Apparently his Gentile wife had taken him to church and led him to the Lord! He wasn't able to meet with me, but when I went to a mall to witness to Israelis, I heard my name being called, and it was Mark both my fraternity brother and brother in Messiah!

HAVE YOU SEEN MY NEPHEW?

Lura Beckford told me she had a Jewish nephew she lost touch with, but she thought he was living in Las Vegas. She wanted me to share Messiah with him. I called this man and left a message. He called me back while I was sitting at a table at Shari's diner.

I asked about his faith in Messiah, and again to my total joy and amazement, he too had already become a believer in Jesus. I asked how he came to faith. He told me he was driving around Las Vegas and got lost. He just happened to come across Shari's diner and went in for directions. Shari sat him down, at the very booth I was sitting at when he returned my call, and led him to his Messiah!

PERSIAN PROSELYTIZING

When Jews for Jesus announced their "Behold Your God" outreach to any city worldwide with 25,000 or more Jewish people, Tehran, Iran didn't make the list. Their Jewish community had shrunk to about 20,000. I couldn't help but wonder how you would go about reaching these precious people? I know when I went on my first mission trip to Germany, I had thought I would rather go to Iran. In retrospect, Germany wasn't so bad. Iran seems like it would have been more of a challenge.

How do you reach Iranian Jews? Pray, pray and pray some more! Several years ago we had an outreach booth at the Sandy Springs Festival. An Iranian Jewish man came by and told me his family owned a local sports bar. I eat there all the time and have made friends with the Iranian Jewish owners. Even though I was wearing my "*Jesus Loves You*" Jewish star t-shirt, one of the owners complained to me his waitress was trying to proselytize him! Just by ministering around Atlanta, I have often run into and shared with several Iranian Jews as well as visit and pray over their two synagogues in the Orthodox neighborhood.

There is a trade show I go to in Las Vegas every year. The large majority of vendors and buyers are Jewish, and many of them are from the Los Angeles garment center, and are Iranian Jews. (The majority of American-Iranian Jewish people live in Los Angeles, California and Great Neck, New

York)   There are so many Jewish people at this show, they set up a kosher eatery.   My friends and I walk around with our evangelistic t-shirts and share with many of them.

WHERE IN THE WORLD IS GEORGE

MARSEILLES, FRANCE

This two-week Jews for Jesus "Behold Your God!" campaign had over 70 full- and part-time team members from several different countries displaying evangelistic T-shirts and sharing the Gospel with people all over Marseilles and other places in France. Over 300,000 Gospel materials were distributed, an airplane flew a "Juifs pour Jesus" banner over the city and many people were contacted by telephone. The Jews for Jesus Video, *Forbidden Peace* (testimonies of Jews and Arabs who have peace and reconciliation through Jesus) was shown at various locations, and teams went door to door inviting people to the screenings.

We made over 800 contacts (including information from over 300 Jewish seekers plus many Muslims) and prayed with 13 people (one Jewish person) to receive the Lord. Our church base was in an Orthodox Jewish neighborhood, which gave us additional opportunities to share!

Where in the world is George? I received an e-mail from my friend George telling me he would be in Marseilles the same time as me. George is The Coca-Cola Company pilot I met in Paris and then ran into again in London. We met at his hotel, and he treated me to a filet mignon lunch and Coca Colas. Yummy, yummy! George told me he was hanging out by the pool and saw a plane fly across the sky with a "Juifs pour Jesus" banner.

At one point during the outreach, I stationed my teammates at the entrance to a subway stop while I ventured out into the surrounding area. As I walked down the street, the doors of a building opened up and hundreds of men flooded out. I distributed over 200 Gospel broadsides within 10 minutes! After the crowd subsided, I looked up to see what kind of building I was in front of, and it turned out to be a Mosque! I had absolutely no idea I had just given the Gospel to over 200 Muslims. As Steve Urkel, from the *Family Matters* television program would say, "Did I do that?"

Jews for Jesus leadership told us there was a Jewish radio program interviewing people about our campaign. They questioned one Jewish woman, and she said, "I was walking down the street, and I was confronted by an American Colossus! I had no choice but to take what he was handing out!" My friends at Jews for Jesus said she was talking about me. Je suis colossus!

They asked for volunteers to minister in St. Tropez for one day. I don't know why, but I immediately said that I wanted to! St. Tropez is a beautiful tourist destination on the French Riviera. People from all over the world come to vacation there. I absolutely love locations like that because you see people from all over the world who are on vacation and more relaxed and more open. While distributing Gospel broadsides, I reached people from fourteen different countries within a short period of time.

While distributing Gospel broadsides in St. Tropez, a couple of young men walked by, and I offered them a Gospel broadside. They looked at it and said they didn't speak French. I said, "Neither do I." We all laughed. They asked what it was about, and I said, "It's about Jesus, the Jewish Messiah!" They asked if I was with Jews for Jesus and told me they were Jewish too. I shared with them. They said they were from New York and familiar with Jews for Jesus. They told me they were part of a tour group of about forty Jewish friends and family members. They were the ones who had organized the tour. The two guys started telling other people in their group about me, and I was able to share with several of them.

A woman from this group came by, and I asked where she was from. She said, "New York!"

I said, "Where?"

She said, "Great Neck."

I said, "Oh, my cousins live in Great Neck. Well, actually they live in Kings Point."

She said, "Actually, I live in Kings Point! Who are your cousins?"

I told her who my cousins are, and

she said, "Your cousin just married my cousin!"

The woman yelled out to the rest of the group, "Not only is this guy a Jew for Jesus, but he's related to us!"

This made people even more curious about my beliefs, and they started asking even more questions about Jesus.

When I got home from France, I called my mother. I asked her why she didn't tell me my cousin's wife had their baby. My mother said, "You were in France. How was I supposed to tell you?"

I said, "That's ok. I ran into her cousin, and she told me.

BUENOS AIRES, ARGENTINA

This Jews for Jesus "Behold Your God!" campaign was so much fun! We wore bright blue or deep red long-sleeve shirts that said, "Judios para Jesus" that could be seen from quite a distance!

One day, our team of twenty or so marched through the streets of the Jewish neighborhood. We had banners proclaiming Jesus the Messiah. We had banners challenging people to read Isaiah 53. We distributed hundreds of Gospel tracts to the many people who came to their doors or windows to hear our singing and to see what was going on.

One night, the Jewish community was showing a film at the mall where they had a kosher McDonalds. We arrived late, and the film had already started. After the film was shown we went into the lobby and hundreds of Jewish people were most surprised to see our team with our bright "*Judios para Jesus*" shirts. We shared with many of them and answered their questions.

On our day off, my friend and I traveled to a Jewish elderly care facility she used to send money to as a little girl. The Orthodox Rabbi working there was extremely nice, and he gave us a tour of the facility. My friend translated as I challenged the Rabbi about Jesus. Amazingly, this Rabbi had spent a lot of time volunteering with a Christian pastor who had witnessed to him for many years. We shared the Gospel with this Rabbi, and he prayed to receive his Messiah! Some plant seeds, others water them and God brings the harvest.

On the last day of the Campaign, a Gentile believer came up to us all excited! Her Jewish friend had received one of our Gospel broadsides and brought it to her. She told us she explained the Messianic prophecies in the broadside, and her Jewish friend prayed to receive Jesus.

Where in the world is George? I received an e-mail from my friend George telling me he would be in Buenos Aires the same time as me. George is The Coca-Cola Company pilot I met in Paris, ran into in London and then had lunch with in Marseilles. He told me to invite a couple of our evangelism team members to dinner with him and his crew, which included a Jewish co-pilot.

After dinner, George said, "You all have stories. Why don't you share them?" So we all gave our testimonies to the Jewish co-pilot, who seemed to appreciate it.

On the way to the airport for the return trip to Atlanta, we got into a conversation with our cab driver. He wanted to know what we were doing in Buenos Aires. We told him and shared the Gospel with him, and he prayed to receive Jesus! Then he said, "Did you know I am Jewish?"

We said, "What do you mean?"

He said, "I came from my mother's womb, and she came from her mother's womb who was Jewish!"

While going through the security line to my flight home, I met a man from Atlanta. We got into a conversation, and I introduced myself. He said, "I know who you are!" I asked how, and he said I had sent him one of my green testimony letters. A few months later, I was at the mall meeting with a new missionary to Jewish outreach who actually worked with this man's wife.

HOW DO YOU WITNESS TO JEWISH PEOPLE?

I decided to go to New York City and do an outreach. Although it was 10 years later, I wanted to tell everyone about my can opener and what God did. I printed 10,000 Can Opener Testimony tracts to bring with me!

Right before my trip to New York City, one of the post cards I sent to Joey, a gay Jewish man in South Florida, was returned? I called Joey to find out what happened. He told me he had moved to Rochester, New York. I asked him if I could have his new address so I could continue sending him postcards. He became somewhat agitated and asked why I was contacting him? I told him I was sharing the love of Messiah with him, and Christians might not be what he thought we were.

He wanted to know if his brother put me up to it? I asked who his brother is? It turns out his brother is Mark Greenberg, who's family was instrumental in putting together the Tree of Life Bible (which we used throughout this book). I didn't know his brother at the time. It turned out his brother was a Messianic Rabbi in Syracuse, New York back then and was actually led to the Lord by Jonathan Bernis! His brother and his congregation were praying, and God used me to reach out to Joey. Who knew?

The day before I drove up to New York, I went to check my mail at the church office. There was a letter from a 14-year-old Russian boy, Max, in Virginia. Somehow he got one of my Gospel tracts and wrote me. He wanted my advice on reaching Jewish people for Jesus. I took out the map and realized I could just stop at his house on the way up to New York, and I did!

Boy, was he surprised when I just showed up at their house! They invited me in and showed me a video of a Messianic Rabbi whom God had called to Belarus. My mother's mother and my father's father were both from Belarus, and I had wanted to go on a mission trip there. The Rabbi was shown preaching at a Russian Messianic Congregation in New York. He mentioned that he used to lead a Messianic Congregation in Syracuse, New York!

While in New York City, I took the Can Opener Gospel tracts to Times Square right before the Saturday matinees started. I knew I would be reaching many tourists besides the people of New York. As I distributed Gospel tracts, a woman walked up to me and tapped me on the shoulder. She said, "Thank you for being here. I so believe the same way you do!" I turned around and couldn't believe it. It was Mrs. Clamon, my Sunday School class teacher's wife, in town from Atlanta. She and her husband were the ones who had opened up their home for the singles fellowship 10 years earlier when I needed the can opener to make the broccoli casserole that caused the whole testimony to happen. Of all the people God would have me run into, it was the woman responsible for the testimony. You never know how your little acts of service will be used in God's kingdom!

When I returned home from the New York outreach, the Messianic Rabbi from Belarus just happened to be speaking at Beth Adonai, a Messianic Congregation led by Scott Sekulow, the only Friday night I was in town all summer. I found out when he went to Belarus, Joey's brother Mark took over the Rabbi's congregation. I put my name on their mailing list, and the following summer they had a mission trip to Belarus.

While in Belarus, the Messianic Rabbi took us to a weekly service in another town where a team from his congregation provided worship for a large group of Jewish people. At the service, the Rabbi had me share the Gospel in a Jewish way, through a translator, and then gave a salvation invitation. Forty Jews stood up and accepted their Messiah. What an incredible blessing we got to participate in because a 14-year-old boy was praying to reach Jewish people! What are you praying for?

YOU NEED TO GO TO IRELAND

Several years ago, God burdened me for Cork, Ireland, even though I had never been to Ireland. I had looked at Europe on a map, and my eyes were drawn to Cork, Ireland—not even Dublin—but Cork, the second largest city. Every time I flew over Ireland, I prayed.

I researched Cork on the Internet. There used to be a sizable Jewish community in Cork, and they even established a synagogue in 1886, the Cork Hebrew Congregation, which is still in existence today. A Jewish man had been the mayor of Cork. Now there were only seven people from two families that were members of the Cork Hebrew Congregation. I tried e-mailing Jewish people as well as churches in Cork, but no one responded.

It was five years before I actually flew to Ireland. I felt led to go to Cork for two weeks during the Jewish High Holy Days. I tried to reserve a Bed and Breakfast, but was unable to do so. It seemed God was sending me to a place I had never been before with only seven Jewish people at the synagogue and no hotel reservation. I told God, I'm buying the plane ticket, if this is all my imagination and you don't want me to do this, please stop me? Nothing happened so I decided to continue to trust God.

I flew into Shannon and then took a bus to Cork. I was up all night and completely exhausted. I had no idea where I was staying or why I was there? As I walked from the main bus station to the center of town wearing my *"Jesus Loves You"* Jewish Star T-shirt, I was stopped by a young women standing outside a building smoking a cigarette. She was an Israeli selling Dead Sea products, and the building had an indoor mall. She was so excited to meet another Jewish person! She took me inside to meet her three Israeli co-workers who all wanted to know why I was in Cork, allowed me to share with them and took Gospel tracts. I hadn't been in Cork for more than 10 minutes, and God had me meet and share with four Israelis.

The Israelis told me there was going to be a Rosh Hashanah luncheon, and they gave me the phone number of the woman organizing the luncheon. It was back-to-school week at the university, and most of the Bed and Breakfasts were full. I literally knocked on eleven Bed and Breakfast doors before I could find one with a room for rent. It cost 70 Euros per night (about $110). This was the most money I had ever spent for housing on a mission trip, making it the most expensive mission trip I had ever been on. I went up to my room and immediately called the woman organizing the luncheon. She said it was the very last day I could sign up for the luncheon.

As I ventured out onto the streets of Cork, I was somewhat clueless as to what the Lord would have me do. I went to look for postcards, but the Lord put it on my heart to distribute Gospel tracts in front of the post office. It was such a heavy feeling that I couldn't do anything else but go to the post office immediately. It was one of those times in my life I knew that I knew that I knew the Lord was telling me to do something!

As I began distributing Gospel tracts in front of the post office, a woman walked up to me and stopped. She looked at me and asked, "Are you Jewish?" I said, "Yes." She asked, "And you're telling people about Jesus?" She told me to wait right where I was and that she would be right back. She ran home and came back with the name and phone number of Esther, a Jewish believer living in Cork, and we met.

Esther was an elderly woman. She insisted we go to a store to visit an Israeli non-believer. When the Israeli saw my T-shirt, he jumped back and laughed. Esther took me to a prayer meeting for Israel where I met Ann, who asked me to record my testimony for a Christian radio program. Ann took me to Western Ireland to minister. She introduced me to her Ethiopian Jewish friend. We had lunch with him, but he wasn't very friendly. He attended church, but didn't seem to have a personal relationship with Jesus. We walked around with him, and the conversation got around to him praying to receive Jesus. He lit up like a fourth of July firecracker and couldn't stop smiling.

Ann took me to an Immigration house, where people from all over the world were living while trying to immigrate to Ireland. Six Russian Jews lived there, and we left tracts for all of them and shared with the ones who were home. We fellowshipped with believers from all over Africa; and when I returned home, I sent them Bibles and T-shirts.

There were about 100 people at the Rosh Hashanah luncheon. They had come from all over western Ireland. I couldn't have planned it better if I had tried. People asked me why I was in Cork, and I told them, "God told me to come to Cork to tell Jewish people about Jesus." They thought that was funny since there are few Jews in Cork. I thought it was insane!

There was an American Jewish man there. He actually lived in Dublin, but his wife was from Cork. She was about to give birth, so they had come to Cork so she could be with her family. I tried to share with him, but he wasn't interested, so I started praying.

I asked the father-to-be where he was from, and he said, "New York." I asked, "Where?" and he said, "Long Island." Again, I asked him, "Where?" He named the same town where one of my brothers lived. I told him my brother lived there, and he asked, "Where?" and it turned out they lived across the street from each other! Then he told me he had moved to Atlanta and gone to Georgia Tech. I asked what street he lived on in Atlanta, and it turned out we had lived on the same street. I offered him a Gospel tract. He said, "Ordinarily, I wouldn't take this, but this is just too weird!" and he took it.

The Cork Hebrew Congregation, the only active synagogue in Cork, was usually only open once a month for a Friday night service and on major holidays, but it was open six times while I was there. I went to synagogue every time it was open. The leader of the synagogue said I was welcome as long as I didn't preach. A Reform Rabbi flew in from England to conduct the Rosh Hashanah service. She wanted to know why I believed in Jesus, so I told her as well as the others who overheard our conversation.

In between synagogue visits, I distributed Gospel tracts in front of the university and on the streets of the Cork City Center. In all, I gave away about 2,000 Gospel tracts and got to speak with a variety of people. Surprisingly, I was able to share with many Jewish people (at least one Jewish grandparent) among them.

Ireland had an economic boom, and many Europeans moved there, some with some Jewish roots. Here is an e-mail I received from one of them:

"Hi Steven. I am the little, crazy Polish man. We met in Cork City on the street. I saw in your face and heart that you illimitably believe in Jesus. World needs people like you. I need, if it is possible, that you teach me to believe in Jesus. You are a very good man. Shalom Israel. I hope that you will write something to me. See you next time, please, Jesus."

A Jewish man who attends services at the synagogue gave me a tour of Cork and the surrounding areas. I met an Israeli musician who performed at a wine bar a couple of nights a week, and I went to support him from the audience.

I got bored one day and decided to mail 100 Gospel tracts to people throughout Ireland with Jewish surnames.

Five Ultra-Orthodox Jews from England flew in from London and Manchester to conduct the Yom Kippur services. I had some interesting conversations with them that became heated. They raised the usual objections: Why do you have three Gods? How can a man be God? Why isn't there world peace? Why do you need a mediator? (Answers; we have one God who makes Himself known in different ways, a man can't be God, but God can indwell the body of a man, there will be world peace when Jesus comes back and even Judaism had a High Priest who was our mediator)

The night of the Yom Kippur service, the Ultra-Orthodox men became challenged by my belief when I said God spoke to me. They persecuted me, but told me I was invited to come back the next day. During a break in the service on Yom Kippur, I shared with the Ultra-Orthodox men, and they were impressed I knew so many Messianic prophecies by heart.

On my last day in Cork, there was a Sukkot service. The Congregational leader demanded to know if I was Jewish because his grandson had seen me distributing Gospel tracts the day before. I assured him that even though I believed in Jesus, I was still Jewish. He made me read the Hebrew during the service and was surprised I knew how. He said I was always welcome at the synagogue. At the same time, he said it was a closed Jewish service and asked all the Gentiles to leave.

After I returned home, some of the people from Cork sent in donations to my ministry which pretty much paid for the whole trip!

When I returned home, I mailed t-shirts and other Gospel materials to people I met in Ireland. I received this note from Ann:

"We were busking [ministering from a bus] in Prince's Street in Cork and I wore one of the T-shirts. People were challenged. My first connection was with a lady at the bus stop. After mentioning the weather, she proceeded to say she liked the writing on the T-shirt. This opened up a short conversation and I was encouraged. Passing a few young men on two occasions (on my way to busking) I could hear one of them reading out loud 'Jesus loves you.' While we were busking, a group of 5 or 6 young foreign (I think Spanish) students asked if they could have a photo with me. I know I was not the attraction. They wanted a photo of the Jesus Tshirt. A woman on the bus who has a drinking problem stood by us and looked so sad. She said something like 'I'm always disappointed and as she was standing beside me I turned to her and pointed to the words on the T-shirt. I spoke to her about asking Jesus into her heart and she said she'd do it. On Tuesday she was on the bus and I asked her if she had done it. Answer: Yes. She looked brighter and a bit happier. Oh, I forgot. Two of the young Israelis merchandising in the city both said they liked my T-shirt. Bless you!"

ITS TIME TO GO TO PERU

After sharing my testimony at a Messianic Congregation during the Jews for Jesus "Behold Your God!" campaign in Cape Town, South Africa, I was approached by a woman who asked me to minister to her Jewish stepson who was arrested for drug smuggling and was in a jail in Lima, Peru, causing him to come to faith in Jesus. At that time, I knew God would be sending me to Peru, but I just didn't know when.

Every time someone made reference to Peru, I tried to determine if they could reach out to the man in jail in Lima. Finally, a Jewish believer in Atlanta called me to say he knew people who make regular mission trips to Lima. I emailed him information about the man in jail. He e-mailed someone and that person contacted three missionaries who not only visited the man in jail, but were asked to preach to 300 other inmates.

During the Jews for Jesus Ft. Lauderdale "Behold Your God!" campaign, they sent me to minister at the Coconut Grove Arts Festival in Miami. Many of the people from Ft. Lauderdale were at this event. As I was distributing Gospel broadsides, a Jewish woman started screaming and came running towards me. Miriam turned out to be a Jewish believer and was excited to see me witnessing there. Miriam introduced me to her husband Mario (a Gentile believer) who was from Lima, Peru. I mentioned my wanting to visit a Jewish believer in Lima, and Miriam begged me to visit Mario's sister (a convert to Judaism) and her Jewish husband as well as Mario's ailing parents who all lived in Lima. Mario was having immigration issues and was not allowed to leave the country, so he couldn't visit them. I had no doubt this was what the Lord was having me wait for and made plans to go to Lima.

The Jewish believer was out of prison and had married. He had met his wife two days after being released from prison and led her to the Lord. He picked me up at the airport and drove me to my hotel. We had several meals together and were able to fellowship a lot.

I distributed 500 Spanish Gospel booklets in the tourist area of Lima where I met a man, who had Jewish roots and was not completely sure of his salvation. I was able to put him and several others in contact with a local pastor. A friend from Atlanta who had gone on a mission trip to Lima had recommended this pastor to me.

Another friend had mentioned that his brother was a missionary in Peru, but I didn't have any more information than that. I went to the church I was referring contacts to and attended the English-speaking Sunday School class. Would you believe the class teacher was my friend's brother?

I took a cab to the Jewish Center in Lima and immediately witnessed to a Jewish man who needed my cab as I pulled up. I walked around the neighborhood distributing Spanish Gospel booklets, but there were few people. As I walked down the street, a woman came running after me. She was a former missionary and most excited to receive a booklet. She told me to turn around and follow her to the main Jewish area. It was as if the hand of God swooped down and redirected my steps. Going from place to place, I distributed almost 400 booklets starting inside Lima's only kosher bakery, then in front of a grocery store and, in general, around the Jewish area. Many Jewish people as well as others were challenged with the Gospel.

The believer who had inspired my visit to Lima and his wife had me over for Shabbat dinner, and I told them I had wanted to find my college roommate who was from Lima. The believer looked in the phone book and found someone outside of Lima with the same last name as my college roommate. He called the number, and it turned out to be my college roommate's father. The father said my college roommate had stayed in Miami after graduation, but just happened to be in Lima on business. He gave us his number, and two hours later my college roommate was at the believer's apartment with his girlfriend. My college roommate knew me before I knew Jesus and was most surprised by my "occupation" and belief.

I went to the Chabad for Shabbat services and was called to the Torah twice because I was a Kohen (from the priestly line) and the only Levi there. I didn't have the right opportunity to share, so I prayed and the Rabbi asked me to put him in touch with my friend "the believer" so the Rabbi could invite him to High Holiday services. The believer later told me it was the same Rabbi who had helped him in jail.

I remembered Mario's request to visit his relatives in Lima. Mario's sister and brother-in-law didn't want to meet with me, but I did visit his parents (who claim to be believers). The believer's wife translated for us. Mario's parents could hardly contain themselves. They were beaming and practically jumping up and down from our visit. I left some Gospel booklets for Mario's sister and brother-in-law. Afterward, Miriam wrote me this note:

Mario and I are so happy that you visited his parents. What a Godsend you are, literally, right? Lol. How true, how true!!! Can you tell me what your impression was of his parents' health? How is Mario's mom? How was she in spirit? Sometimes she cries on the phone with Mario. Thank you again. Can never thank you enough for what you have done.

CLIMB EVERY MOUNTAIN

My friend Shelley invited me to St. Louis, Missouri, for a weekend of outreach. While in St. Louis, we visited a local Chabad during a Friday night Shabbat Service. As we drove up, we noticed a sign saying, "Welcome Western United States Chabad Rabbis." This Chabad usually had only a handful of people, but because of this special event, there were over thirty Chabad Rabbis from all over the western United States.

We went inside. Because this was an Orthodox Synagogue, the men sat on one side and the women sat on the other. Shelley had to go on the other side without me. Before the service started, men were sitting all around reading their prayer books. I sat down and someone asked me who I was. I told him, "I'm Steve Kaplan, from Atlanta, Georgia, and I'm a Christian missionary to the Jewish people." He started laughing and said, "No really, who are you?" I said, "I'm Steve Kaplan, from Atlanta, Georgia, and I'm a Christian missionary to the Jewish people." He kept on laughing and said, "No really, who are you and what do you do?" I said, "Ok, I sell fire insurance to synagogues." He stopped laughing, and realized I really was a missionary.

During our time there, I was able to speak to about seven of the Rabbis and challenged them to read Isaiah 53. After a while, a very tall, big Rabbi came out from the back and started questioning me. We exchanged names. He was from Crown Heights Brooklyn, New York. He said, "I know who you are. You're Steve Kaplan, and you came to my house in Crown Heights and tried to give me a Bible. You have to leave!"

Up until that time, I had never been to Crown Heights, Brooklyn, and had no idea what he was talking about. He still insisted I must leave. I got Shelley, and we left. When we got back to the car, I started to pray that they would all know Jesus, especially the Rabbi from Crown Heights. As I was praying, the Holy Spirit impressed upon me that I must pray for an opportunity to witness to the Rabbi's family. I thought this was rather strange, but we are called to trust and obey.

Several months later, my friend Margie contacted me. She is a sold-out woman for God who goes wherever God leads her. At the time she contacted me, she was ministering in Malaysia. She suggested I go to

Kathmandu, Nepal. I reminded her I was a missionary to the Jewish people. She explained that many Israelis who serve in the army save up their money and then travel around the world before going to college. Many Israelis go to climb Mt. Everest, which is near Kathmandu, and then they meet in Thamel, the tourist area, for the largest Passover Seder in the world!

I decided to go to Kathmandu, Nepal, during Passover. Margie set up a speaking tour for me in Nepal, made arrangements for me to be picked up at the airport, put me in touch with several missionaries and made arrangements for me to visit a ministry in India as well.

I used frequent flyer miles and booked a seat in Business Class, roundtrip from Atlanta to Kathmandu for only $93. I flew from Atlanta to Frankfurt, and the plane was late, so I only had 10 minutes to make my connection to Vienna, Austria. The flight from Vienna to Kathmandu only flies once a week, so if I missed it, I would have a problem. Although I landed in the same terminal I would be leaving from, I still had to clear passport control and security. I'm 6foot2inches tall and weighed about 400 pounds at the time. I threw my carry-on bag on a luggage cart and pushed it very rapidly as I ran through the German airport terminal in my *"Jesus Loves You"* Jewish Star T-shirt. Most stared at me and my shirt as I flew past them. I'm sure it was quite a scene to see. It was close, but I made the flight.

I made my flight to Vienna and had a few minutes before the last leg to Kathmandu. I looked at the next gate to see if there might be Jewish people around and saw the flight was going to Tel Aviv. I gave many people Gospel tracts and shared with some. I looked at the next gate, and they were going to New York. The people on line were all Orthodox Jews!!! None of them would take tracts. Some laughed at me, some stared at me, and the rest looked confused.

Nine hours later, I landed in Kathmandu. While changing money at the airport, I gave Gospel tracts to and shared with many Israelis who were on line. One man asked how I knew he was Israeli, and I smiled. I can usually hear an Israeli accent or just look at their mannerisms and know. He was open, and I was able to share the Gospel with him.

After I cleared passport control, my suitcase was nowhere to be found, and I filed a missing luggage report. When I went outside to find my driver to the hotel or my contact who had helped to organize my itinerary, neither was in view.

A cab driver insisted I go with him because he had the last available cab and there was now a curfew in Nepal. I heard about a strike, but had no idea I was stepping into a civil protest against the King of Nepal. He had seized power from his people, which became a major crisis topping the news worldwide for weeks to come. The Israeli I had met at the airport was in this cab and grateful I was climbing in. He had waited an hour for the driver to fill the cab.

As we left the airport, the streets were filled with debris, and armed police officers stopped our vehicle every 100 yards or so. The reality of being in the middle of a war zone set in. I was in shock, but had the Lord's peace and was reminded of the verse about not getting involved in civilian affairs. Still, I couldn't help but wonder if someone might shoot at us as we drove by.

The cabbie told me he wouldn't take me to my hotel because of the violence and brought me to his friend's hotel where they tried to overcharge me. The next morning I called another contact who insisted I take a cab to his part of town and stay with his family. Some of the protestors tried to attack our cab, but we made sure to let them know I was a tourist, which meant they should not bother us.

I spent three days with my contact's family because of the curfews. (Curfew violators could be shot on sight, and by the time I left Nepal, fourteen people had been killed for violating curfew and hundreds of others had been shot at and injured.) Because of the turmoil, conferences and church services I was supposed to speak at were cancelled. We were trapped in the house and eventually almost ran out of food and toilet paper. Oy!

As the curfews lessened, I went to Thamel, the tourist area. I stayed at the Kathmandu Guest House, which was a gated community with its own restaurant, Internet access, barber shop and various other stores. It is considered a luxury hotel but only cost $90 per week. The entire tourist area is only about five streets long, and my hotel was right in the middle. Each street was an oversized alley-way with many pedestrians, rickshaws, cars, bikes, trucks, goats, dogs, cows, beggars and drug dealers. Many stores have Hebrew letters on their signs to attract Israeli tourists.

Whenever there wasn't a curfew, I would venture out in front of the hotel and hand out Gospel tracts. It was like fishing in a fishbowl because all the tourists, including the thousands of Israelis who came from the surrounding countries for Passover, were stuck in the five-block area around my hotel. When we had curfew, I would hang out in the hotel lobby and watch our situation being televised on CNN. Absolutely unreal!

Whenever I was out and about, people kept asking if I was a WWE (World Wresting Entertainment) wrestler, since that was one of the only TV channels they could get, and at over six feet tall, I towered over people. As people drove by, they saw my shirt and yelled out their windows, "Jesus Loves You!" People who walked by responded in a similar manner. The kids would follow after me calling me "Big So", "Big So" because I was so much taller and bigger than the native population. Japanese tourists at my hotel kept asking if I was a Sumo wrestler.

While in Themal, I distributed 800 Passover tracts, primarily to Israelis, and shared with people from all over the world. Many of the Israelis would pass by over and over because we were trapped there by the political unrest and curfews, and this gave me an opportunity to continue conversations that I wouldn't have had otherwise.

Believers gave me Nepalese Gospel tracts and Bibles to give out, and I left them with seventy *"Jesus Loves You"* T-shirts and 100 Gospel tracts. For years afterwards, our ministry supplied hundreds of T-shirts and Gospel tracts, which I've been told have been used to lead many to the Lord.

One evening, I was distributing tracts, and Shlomo (an Orthodox Israeli) took one and asked what it was about. I told him, and then he threw it on the ground. I prayed for him, and when he walked past me again, he just ignored me, so I prayed even more. Ten minutes later, Shlomo came back. He asked if I was Jewish. I assured him I was. He asked if my mother was Jewish. (Orthodox Jews consider Jewishness through the mother.) I assured him both my parents were Jewish. Shlomo invited me to the Passover Seder. He told me to go to the Chabad to buy a ticket, so the next day I went in plain clothes. I met an Orthodox American Jew, Richard,

216

who was excited to hear I was from Atlanta because his best friend was the son of the Chabad Rabbi who lived in my neighborhood.

When Judah (another Orthodox American) heard I was from Atlanta, he asked if I knew his cousin who was the wife of the Chabad Rabbi in the next town over from where I lived. I told him I did know her, and I was about to send them a postcard. I also told Judah that I met her father (who was Judah's uncle) the year before. Judah was so excited to meet someone who knew his family.

The next day, Shlomo invited me to wrap tefillin, even though I was wearing a *"Jesus Loves You"* Jewish Star T-shirt. You should have seen their faces when I went to the Chabad. Richard was shocked, and Judah couldn't stop shaking, but they didn't rescind my invite to the Seder. Shlomo told me his best friend was marrying the daughter of the Chabad Rabbi in my neighborhood, so he would be in Atlanta in June for the wedding and asked for my e-mail.

On the way to the Seder, I was interviewed by a television news crew and made sure to share the Gospel. Last year's Seder had over two thousand people, but even with all the turmoil, they still had over a thousand people for the current event, which was held in the Raddison Hotel. I sat at an empty table and waited for the Lord to bring people, and shared with them as they sat down. Most had already received tracts from me. One man was open; he let me share. The next day, when I bumped into him on the street, he accepted a Hebrew-English New Testament.

In addition to the main event, the Chabad decided to have a Seder in English in the front lobby, which gave me a whole new table of people to share with. I sat next to an American Jew originally from the town next to mine on Long Island, and he laughed when I told him about my belief. He said, "They (meaning the Chabadnicks), ain't going to get me, and you aren't either."

Judah was conducting the Seder with Richard and told a story about his father. When I realized who Judah's father was, I burst out laughing. Everyone asked what was so funny, and I told them Judah's father threw me out of a synagogue last year in St. Louis. When I prayed for the father after that happened, the Lord told me to pray for an opportunity to share with his family. I never thought that prayer would be answered in Kathmandu, Nepal!

As the evening progressed, I shared with a new age Israeli who told me he had never met a Jewish Believer in Jesus before. Just as our conversation was getting really deep, Richard came over and put an end to it. I began talking with Judah and was able to discuss many questions. We traded e-mails and have kept in touch.

The next day was Thursday and the day my-once-a-week flight was available. I decided I wanted to leave and would try to get on the flight, but I became so sick that a doctor told me I shouldn't travel. Many tourists get sick from something they ate resulting in nausea and diarrhea. The restaurants are very careful to keep their food clean so they don't lose customers. As soon as I took a bite of the food at the Seder, I realized there was no way they properly prepared the food for over 1,000 people!

On Friday, I visited the Chabad to pray for them. I told Richard and Judah I was sick, and an Orthodox Jewish British woman, whom I didn't know, said I was sick because I had Jesus inside of me.

On Saturday, I went to a church, shared my testimony and encouraged the people in the congregation to reach out to the Jewish people in Nepal. After the service, dozens of protestors came down our street. Their arrival meant no cabs would be coming, so we began walking several miles 'til we found a cab. I went to the travel agent to change my flight, but they wouldn't let me. My contact in India understandably never made it to Nepal to pick me up, which meant I had to forego my trip to that part of India.

Because I had thought I would be going to India, I had gotten a visa. I decided to travel there on my own. I asked Israelis for ideas of where in India they would go. They all suggested different destinations but seemed interested to start in Delhi. Many Israelis were booking flights to Pokhara, Nepal (a lake resort with many trekking trails), and I thought that would get me away from the turmoil in Kathmandu. I felt led to book a week in Pokhara and then four days in Delhi. I was at the travel agency for about two hours and shared with many Israelis!

Before going to the airport the next morning, I started distributing tracts until protestors lit boxes on fire and the police chased everyone away.

One Brazilian tourist (with Jewish roots) later e-mailed me this note:

"As soon as I stepped out of the shop, you reached us with that piece of paper and we exchanged a few words while walking. I felt good at that moment we met and smiled at you, which I usually don't do when people hand me papers on the street. As soon as I got to the hotel I read it and wept. I felt happy that another soul had found the atonement of God, and experienced that kind of emotional reward that only thru God we can achieve."

I shared my airport cab with an American who recently quit his job to travel in Asia and "find himself." He had just come from Delhi and his Christian friends, and he felt convicted when I told him why I was in Nepal.

At the airport, an Israeli let me share with him for over an hour. When I arrived in Pokhara, Nepal, the cabs were all on strike. Someone with a bicycle attached to a small flatbed put me on the back and rode me to my hotel. Everyone was laughing and waving. The kids ran after us and again asked if I was a wrestler and called me "Big So.". "Big So."

When I went to distribute Gospel tracts, there was no one around. I asked God, "Why am I here?" Seconds later, a Gentile from Sweden came by, let me share and prayed to receive Jesus. He gave me his address, and I mailed him a Bible when I got home. Four Israelis came by next, and I shared with them. The Orthodox British woman was there with her family, and I made sure they were reminded every day that Jesus loved them.

As I walked down the street looking for an Internet café, I felt led to go into one on the second floor and exerted myself to climb the stairs even though there were so many cafés at street level. I met and shared with a young Canadian woman there named Mary.

Again, we were trapped there in Pokhara due to the ongoing political crisis, so I had longer conversations with many people. I handed out 150 Gospel tracts during the week, primarily to Israelis, and had many divine appointments. My week was extremely unnerving, as the only cars on the road were caravans with soldiers with drawn guns and queues of United Nations Human Rights trucks.

While in Pokhara, I met two believers who asked for *"Jesus Loves You"* Jewish Star T-shirts (which I mailed them when I returned home), and we had a small prayer meeting. We were a former Hindu, former Buddhist and Jew all praying to Jesus. We went out on their roof, which had a beautiful view of the lake. It was so peaceful. As I walked back to my hotel, store owners quickly closed their stores as hundreds of protestors flooded down the street carrying torches. I just wanted to get out of Nepal and away from the unrest!

I flew back to Kathmandu and waited for the flight to Delhi, India. I was happy to leave Nepal, but had no idea what I was going to do in Delhi. I prayed, and God used Mary whom I had met in an Internet Café in Pokhara. She just happened to be on my plane to Delhi and asked to share a cab. She suggested a hotel, which turned out to be a block away from the Chabad and a group of guest houses used by Israelis. I couldn't have planned it better if I'd tried.

In Dehli, it was over 100 degrees every day, and the streets were filthy. I saw more animals and cars than in Kathmandu and even saw a man riding an elephant. I usually stood by the entrance to the guest houses near the Chabad. A Jewish woman said, "You're in the wrong place. Everyone here is Jewish!" I said, "That means I'm in the right place!" I distributed about 150 Gospel tracts, primarily to Israelis. I had lots of conversations with people from all over the world, especially with those who had seen me in Kathmandu.

Even though I was wearing a *"Jesus Loves You"* Jewish Star T-shirt, I was invited to wrap tefillin at the Chabad House. They videotaped me and tried to trick me into saying Rabbi Schneerson is the Messiah, but I changed it to Jesus. They showed me a video of a Jewish believer witnessing to Rabbi Schneerson in which he called the man ill. They called me ill. I told them that was *lashon hara* (that is, speaking badly of someone which is something they are not supposed to do). So they stopped. They invited me to a prayer meeting with about twenty-five people. Again, you should have seen their faces when I walked in with a *"Jesus Loves You"* Jewish Star T-shirt.

On my last day in Delhi, a cab driver took me to his Sikh Temple where I showed off my T-shirt and prayed everywhere. He took me by the Capitol buildings, and I prayed for all of India.

The conflict in Nepal escalated so much, the US Embassy in Nepal finally told Americans to get out, so the airline would allow me to fly from Delhi to Vienna instead of to Kathmandu for the return trip, but only if I left a day early. I was so happy!

I flew to Vienna, and I found a hotel room in the tourist area and showed off my *"Jesus Loves You"* Jewish Star T-shirt to the thousands of people from all over the world. I had various encounters and could sense anti-Semitism in some exchanges. I shared with several Jewish people, including a Russian Jewish woman who wanted to sell me a discounted ticket to a classical concert. I had no personal interest in going to but felt led to attend.

Before the concert started, I shared with an 18-year-old Bosnian Muslim and a Bulgarian from the Orthodox Church who had a life-changing experience and really wanted to believe in Jesus.

At the concert in Vienna, I met a believer from Johannesburg, South Africa, who just happened to attend a home fellowship group hosted there by one of my friends, Natalie a Jewish believer. On the way home from the concert, I met an American Orthodox Rabbi who teaches Talmud in Montreal, Canada. We stood in the middle of the sidewalk and spoke for well over an hour. He was dressed in full, black Orthodox garb, and I was wearing my *"Jesus Loves You"* Jewish Star T-shirt. We had some heated discussions, and Israeli passers-by were most amused by our intensity and the contrast in our appearances.

I prayed over Vienna before catching my flight to Frankfurt and then home. I don't remember ever being happier to go home.

A few months later, I went to minister in Las Vegas, Nevada. While distributing Gospel tracts, an Israeli, walked by and stopped. He was most surprised to see me and said, "I saw you in Nepal, I saw you in India, and now I see you in Las Vegas!" I ran into him several more times in the mall and told him, "God is trying to get your attention!" He finally accepted a Hebrew New Testament and promised to read it.

A year or so later I was ministering in Tacoma, Washington. I stayed at a friend's house in Tacoma. He told me he really didn't know any Jewish people to share with. I prayed that he would be able to share with Jewish people. I came home one night, and my friend said, "You aren't going to believe this. The doorbell rang and it was two Israelis selling oil paintings!"

While I was in Tacoma, I visited the local Chabad one day. It was located in the Rabbi's house. The wife answered the door and did her best to completely ignore my *"Jesus Loves You"* Jewish Star Tshirt and quickly sent me downstairs to talk with her husband the Rabbi.

The Rabbi had me wrap tefillin because it is a mitzvah (good deed) for him. We had a long conversation, and I made sure to tell him all about my beliefs. I ended the conversation by saying, "I guess I'm not invited to Shabbat dinner?" He said, "You are more than welcome to come, but just don't wear that shirt or tell anyone what you do for a living!"

I came back later for dinner. We went around the room and told where we were from and what we did for a living. When it was my turn, I said, "I'm Steve Kaplan. I'm from Atlanta, Georgia, and I fly around the world." Everyone laughed and they just went on to the next person. When they got to the Rabbi's wife, she said she was from Crown Heights, Brooklyn. I had to ask if she was related to the Rabbi I met in St. Louis. It turns out she wasn't, but the Rabbi's family lived right across the street from her family!

The Rabbi in Tacoma told me he had just been at the big and tall Rabbi's house in Crown Heights the week before, and this Rabbi was responsible for setting up Chabad outposts all over the world in places like Kathmandu, Nepal, and Tacoma, Washington. The Rabbi was dumbfounded and excited that I knew the Rabbi from Crown Heights, and his son Judah. I was dumbfounded that God used me to witness to the modern day "Paul" of the Chabad movement.

ISRAEL

MALL OUTREACHES TO ISRAELIS

Every Hanukkah, we try to do an outreach to the 40-80 or more Israelis working at the malls around town. We usually give them some kind of Gospel material wrapped in Hanukkah paper with chocolate Hanukkah candies. We've given them a Hebrew translation of Stan Telchin's book *Betrayed!* (Ada, MI: Chosen Books, a division of Baker Publishing Group, 2007), Isaiah 53 on a scroll as well as other booklets in Hebrew, as that seems to really get their attention. We even gave them *"Jesus Loves You"* T-shirts one year! Two Israelis saw my T-shirt and immediately pulled out a camera to take my picture as many others have done. One Israeli told me I had given her a T-shirt two years ago, and she wears it to bed every night.

I usually wear an "I Love Israel" T-shirt when I deliver the Hanukkah gifts. The Israelis absolutely light up and often tell me they were expecting me again that year. When I stop by, they often ask questions about Messiah!

ISRAELI OWNED RESTAURANTS

Several restaurants in my neighborhood are owned by Israelis. I love to eat there wearing a *"Jesus Loves You"* T-shirt, as many other Jewish people usually eat there as well. I have had numerous conversations with people while dining. One of the Israeli owners complained to me that his Christian waitress was always telling him about Jesus. I just laughed and told him he should listen to her. She was most happy when I was able to give her boss Gospel materials in Hebrew.

DON'T BE AFRAID

Several years after my first trip to Israel, I booked a ticket to Israel with a group; but they canceled the outreach. I went there anyway. The Jewish believer I went with the first time happened to be there with a group, so I volunteered with them the first week and ministered on my own in Jerusalem for a week.

I went to a church there and ran into someone I knew. She was in Israel on a special visa that precluded her from sharing the Gospel. She told people it was illegal to share the Gospel, but that is not true. Unfortunately, I believed her.

Later, I found out it was only illegal for her and anyone else in Israel on a humanitarian aid visa who signed a paper saying they were not going to share the Gospel. Because I believed her, I was absolutely dumbfounded and upset. How could I be in Israel and not share?

A few minutes later, I was walking down the street and saw this elderly woman with very high, blond, cotton-candy hair and a big, "I love Jesus" broach on her lapel. Her name was Jerry, and she was handing out Bibles and witnessing the love of Jesus to everyone she came in contact with.

What a blessing she was, and literally a God-send. She assured me it was perfectly legal to witness in Israel as long as you do not witness to minors (unless you are a minor) and as long as you do not pay someone to change their religion. Of course, she was absolutely right.

Jerry was from the Dallas, Texas, area and said she would take me to lunch any time I was in Dallas. She was in her eighties and had been to Israel some 34 times. So don't you dare say you are too old! We met one time and did an outreach in front of the Knesset. Jerry passed away, but will always be remembered fondly and lovingly!

HERE AM I, SEND ME

I received an e-mail from a woman in Israel who wrote about Eddie and Lura Beckford and their Chess Club/Bible Shop in Arad. Apparently, the Ultra-Orthodox Jews in Arad took issue with the Beckford's ministry and would constantly harass them and persecute them. The Ultra-Orthodox actually blew up their Bible Shop. The woman who wrote the e-mail was asking people to help the Beckfords.

> *"Then I heard the voice of ADONAI saying:*
> *"Whom shall I send?*
> *And who will go for Us?"*
> *So I said, "Hineni [Here am I]. Send me."*
> *-Isaiah 6:8*

Eddie and Lura are bold witnesses for the Lord. They are a very bright light in a very spiritually dark place! The elderly men in Arad had been playing chess and dominoes in the park with no bathroom facilities. Since Eddie loves to play chess and used to organize chess tournaments, they got the idea to open a chess club. They also ministered to the dozens of Holocaust survivors living in Arad as well as anyone else they could help. I started volunteering with the Beckfords sometime in the mid-2000s.

On one of my trips to work with the Beckfords, I walked through the customs doors at Ben Gurion airport wearing a *"Jesus Loves You"* Jewish Star Tshirt. I felt like a celebrity! Hundreds of people on the other side of the doors were waiting and watching for their loved ones to walk through and got to see my Tshirt! Their faces had a range of expressions, with many people laughing in amazement.

On our trips over the years, when my friends and I would come to work with the Beckfords, we would bring reading glasses and ethnically Black dolls. The reading glasses were used to minister to the elderly, and the Black dolls were used to build relationships with Arabs, Ethiopians, Sudanese and Black Israelites.

The Chess Club was located at the shuq, an Israeli marketplace, near the center of town. It had a bathroom, a water cooler, a coffee maker and a wall with hooks for people to hang their coffee cups on. Of course, the Chess Club doubled as a Bible shop with a wall of Bibles and books in various languages. The Beckfords received these for free from a printer in Jerusalem who has since passed away. He got funding from believers around the world and printed all the Bibles and books in various languages and gave them away to people doing the Lord's work!

The Beckfords also used the Chess Club/Bible Shop to give away clothes and soup and to have evangelistic concerts. The Orthodox would come around and persecute whoever volunteered there. The Orthodox would question, "Why do you have to come here and do good?" The Orthodox would contact Eddie and Lura's landlords and get them evicted from their home. Because of that, they have moved many times over the years.

Eddie and I would go to public places and distribute Gospel materials. There are almost no Orthodox at the beach, so no one really bothers you if you hand out materials there. I went to the Dead Sea one time, and the first four tracts I gave out were Arabic, Hebrew, Russian and English. You usually meet people from all over the world.

When we would go to public squares, the Orthodox would start harassing us, and the police would come. The Orthodox would lie, and we would have to spend time giving reports at the police station, but it gave us an opportunity to share with many we would never had met otherwise. Eddie has been falsely accused many times and has spent a lot of time in jail simply for sharing the love of Messiah. I actually had to fly over to Israel one time to testify on Eddie's behalf.

Over the years I have been to Israel more than 20 times, primarily to visit the Beckfords. We've had many interactions with Israelis and others, and some of them are described below:

"We went to Tel Aviv and distributed Gospel materials at bus stops, picnic areas, rest areas or anywhere people frequent. At one large bus stop waiting area, I gave an Orthodox soldier (with a gun) a book which he ripped up. As he began ripping up other people's books, I walked up to him (gun or no gun), looked him in the eye and said, "If you want to burn in hell then go right ahead, but don't you dare prevent other people from having an opportunity to meet their Messiah, Jesus, who died for sin and rose from the dead!" He stopped ripping up books! What I did is called, "Holy Chutzpah!""

As I walked around Jerusalem with a couple of my friends, I decided to just walk up to people and asked them who they thought Jesus was. The very first person I spoke to was Mikah. He was somewhat open and came to my friend's congregation that Friday night. Two years later, Mikah moved to Atlanta and called me. I took him out to dinner and shared again. There was a believer at the next table who teaches the Old Testament, and he reinforced everything I shared with Mikah! Mikah was surprised the Virgin Birth was in the Old Testament and was most receptive to receive all the Gospel materials I gave him.

One Friday night (Shabbat), Eddie and I went to the main square in Arad to distribute books. A hostile storekeeper shouted obscenities at us. The Orthodox came and grabbed our books from people and ripped them up. We jumped in the van and drove around. Since it was Shabbat, the Orthodox chased us on foot; and people were just sitting around. We stopped wherever there were people and gave out more books and Bibles. When we drove back later, people were still sitting there reading the books and Bibles we gave them. If the Orthodox hadn't come, these people would not have received these materials, because we would not have been on the run. Because we were motorized and the Orthodox were on foot, they were bewildered because they couldn't find us.

We distributed many Gospel tracts in front of the bus terminal in Beer Sheva. I offered one to a man named Eli, but he didn't want it. Eli said he was already a believer, and I asked him why. Eli said he had gone to a festival two months ago and met some Jews for Jesus who prayed he would know the Messiah, and that night he had a dream and met Jesus. He said he started reading books and is now trying to bring his family to his local Messianic Congregation!

Another time I went to the same bus terminal, and an Orthodox man jumped on my back. The security guard thought it was funny, but I was not amused. The police came, and we all had to leave.

I distributed tracts in an Orthodox neighborhood in Jerusalem and was harassed by anti-missionaries. They tried to get the tracts from people, but the people wouldn't give them up. After I gave out all my Hebrew tracts, I walked away and was stopped by the police who made me come to the police station because the one harassing me complained to them. The police asked if I gave tracts to minors, and I hadn't, and if the tract was derogatory, and it wasn't. The police let me go with a warning. I didn't know it at the time, but the anti-missionaries were called Yad L'Achim. They put my picture on their website, and someone from Israel recognized me and sent me an irreparable computer virus that my email provider thankfully blocked.

We drove down to Eilat, at the southern tip of Israel, and distributed Gospel materials along the way. We gave out materials near the mall, on the beach and throughout the shopping area. As I walked by the police station, with five police officers standing outside, I just cringed because I didn't want to witness to them. The Lord convicted me and I gave each one a tract. When one realized what it was and made a derogatory comment, they all handed them back. One started arguing with me, so it gave an opportunity to further share the Gospel, which resulted in someone else taking the tract again!

I went with Eddie to open the Chess Club/Bible Shop one day. I filled a bag with Hebrew and Russian Gospel booklets and went to the center of town to distribute them. I was surrounded by six Orthodox Jews. They shouted, "Missionary, Missionary!" and told people not to take my booklets. They asked people for their booklets and ripped them up. They taunted me with, "You stupid idiot, go home!" When they blocked me from distributing, I yelled over and over, "I'm Jewish, and I believe in Jesus, and I'm being persecuted for my faith! Somebody call the police!" A crowd formed, and people took Gospel booklets out of curiosity. The police came but didn't do anything. It was midday, and Lura came by and took me to lunch. As we went to the car, a mob of Orthodox followed us. I turned around and said, "Whoever loves Jesus, follow us!" They stopped dead in their tracks. Lura and I laughed so hard!

Another time we were distributing Gospel tracts in the Arad town square. The Orthodox started harassing us. Then they followed us wherever we went. They followed us into a store and went up to a woman. They told her we were missionaries and asked her what she thought of that. She said, "I think it's wonderful. I believe in Jesus, too."

Ruth (an Israeli on my plane) was excited to see my *"Jesus Loves You"* T-shirt because she remembered seeing it a few months ago while she was visiting her daughter who lived in my apartment complex. Ruth insisted her son-in-law Ezra drive me home from the airport when I returned home. I was never so happy to be stuck in traffic for over an hour because Ezra kept asking me questions about my belief in Jesus.

We drove to Sderot, a small Israeli city near Gaza that has been bombed thousands of times. We went to Sderot to minister to the people who are shell-shocked. We didn't know that Israel had proclaimed a national "Love Sderot Day" the same day we went. Eight of us wore *"Jesus Loves You"* T-shirts in both English and Russian. We sat at a café playing Gospel songs and distributed Gospel newspapers. We were interviewed by a local newspaper reporter. The locals were happy to have us, and a number of people took our pictures. We got the chance to share with many interested people during our stay.

Twenty Yeshiva students in Sderot harassed us. The police came, and I continued to distribute Gospel materials despite their interference. The police asked for my information but allowed me to continue. We stayed for hours and shared with many of the locals.

Eddie and Lura have been so effective in proclaiming Jesus that the local Orthodox place false articles in the Arad newspaper about them. This gave Eddie and Lura an opportunity to write an article about their ministry for the newspaper, which told the truth and shared the Gospel message. Eventually, the Orthodox got to the newspaper owners and had Eddie and Lura banned from writing articles. As a result, Eddie and Lura created their own newspaper with all the articles being about Jesus, in both Hebrew and Russian.

Later, when I was distributing the Beckfords' newspapers in the center of Arad, I was surrounded by several Orthodox and was prevented from distributing them. They started yelling, and the police came. The police chief told me I had to leave. I reminded the chief it was legal for me to be there, but he told me I was causing a disturbance. I said, "I'm not causing the disturbance, they are. What if I was to get twenty of my friends, walk down the street, meet an Orthodox Jew wearing a black hat and decide we didn't like black hats. Would that mean everyone wearing a black hat must take it off? Would that be right?"

I told the chief to think long and hard about what he was saying to me. The chief scratched his head, told me to wait and disappeared for 30 minutes. While I waited, the Orthodox continued to harass me and lit the newspapers on fire.

The chief finally came back and told me he would allow me to continue, but to hurry up and finish. Lura came to get me and filmed the "scene." The head Rabbi pushed the camera into Lura's head. The Chief was standing right there and asked Lura why she hit the Rabbi's hand with her head!

Eddie and Lura told me after I left, people started coming to the Chess Club/Bible Shop for weeks afterwards. They wanted to get a copy of the newspaper that caused so much trouble and took several copies for their neighbors as well. An Arab man wanted to know why Jews were fighting Jews. Eddie and Lura shared with him, and he prayed to receive Jesus.

Eddie and Lura put the video of the confrontation on YouTube (This is why people hate the Jews part 5) and it had been viewed over one million times until YouTube took it down. Jews for Jesus produced a movie called *Flowers of the Son* and used footage from the video in the movie.

On July 1, 2009, Eddie and Lura Beckford joined the staff of our ministry,Jewish Outreach International (www.savethejews.org). A new parking garage was being dedicated in Jerusalem. The Orthodox were giving the owners a lot of grief because the parking lot was open on Shabbat.

The *Jerusalem Post* wrote a negative article about the Orthodox and their behavior. They used the way the Beckford's had been treated by the Orthodox as an example, and on July 2, 2009, they put the Beckfords' picture in the *Jerusalem Post.* Eddie's *"Jesus Loves You"* Jewish Star Tshirt was prominently displayed.

Over the years, the Beckfords led many people to the Lord. Their house served as a Messianic Community Center. They discipled many and equipped other ministries and ministers with evangelistic t-shirts and Gospel materials. A Korean film company made a movie, *Restoration*, about the persecuted believers in Israel, and included the Beckfords. It is estimated the Beckfords gave out over one million Gospel books, Bibles and other materials while in Israel!

T-SHIRT TESTIMONIES

From Israel: I wore my "JESUS LOVES YOU" T-shirt on the last day in israel, when we drove to the Ahava Factory, the Dead Sea, Arad and Beersheva. To tell you the truth, I was reluctant to wear it in Israel, but I won't be anymore – I had so many opportunities to witness while wearing it. The first Jewish man said, (after seeing my shirt) "Jesus Loves Me Too?" I Said he sure does and he hugged me, kissing me on the cheek and taking a new covenant. Religious people even took the new covenant in Beersheva but the point is, I told them I loved them in Hebrew first – I am convinced the key to witnessing and sowing to the Jewish people is to love them and they see it – never, ever have I heard so many Jewish people tell me they loved me too. Oh the joy In serving Jesus. I gave out more bibles here, than on any other trip – Hallelujah. – Looking forward to next year in Jerusalem, the Lord willing. Blessings, Psalm 122:6

From Israel: We gave a stack of about 20 shirts, in Russian, to our friend. He is a home group leader and an evangelist with our fellowship. A few days later, at the big annual forest gathering of northern congregations, we saw several people wearing these shirts. Love your newsletters, and your work, and you. Much Shalom, b'Shem Yeshua, and Hag Simeach.

Eddie & Lura from Israel: Thought you would like to know – [One of the Israeli men] asked for a sweat shirt with *Jesus Loves You* in Russian. He is wearing it everywhere! Here is a miracle There is a little old Jewish lady (unbeliever) who sells socks at the shuq. When she first met us, she was very hostile, but over the years she has softened and now she wants one of your shirts for her (grown-up) son to wear. [She was] asked if he realizes what the words mean and did she know he would get a little trouble from the orthodox wearing it. She said it was understood and she wanted the shirt. We never met her son, but just the fact she asked for the shirt for him is a major step in the right direction! Eddie wears his shirt every time we go to court, which is fairly often! Actually he wears it every time we go anywhere. We also gave some of the T-shirts to a tour group from Norway and they wore them on their tour through Israel and then back in Norway!

Eddie & Lura from Israel: We just had two young girls from California stay with us for almost a month. They wore the Jesus loves you T-shirts all over town. Eddie wears one almost every day. He wore one to the police station this morning.

Eddie & Lura from Israel: Sudanese refugees in Arad were so happy to see 'Jesus loves you' T-shirts, they wanted some and are wearing them!

Eddie & Lura from Israel: Hi Steve! A tour group (55 people) from Norway and Denmark also visited us and we passed out T-shirts. They put them on immediately and are going through Israel with them and praying for opportunities to share the gospel! Below is a letter from a pastor who just visited us. We gave him one of your T-shirts. I thought you would like to know what he did with it! He wants to meet with the Russian churches in his area of Virginia and get some more T-shirts from you, both English and Russian. *From Virginia Pastor:* "I wore the Jesus loves you T-shirt you all gave me, all the way home. Walked through the airport with the T-shirt on. The plane to London was full of Hasidim and Orthodox Jews going home from the holidays. Nonetheless, they got the witness they needed through the T-shirt I wore, and I got no flack from them."

My friend told me while he was in Israel, he wore a Hebrew "Jesus Loves You" T-shirt and it caught the attention of an Israeli man who said he was curious about Jesus. My friend shared the Gospel with him and the Israeli man prayed to receive Jesus!

MISCELLANEOUS GOD STORIES

EXPECT THE UNEXPECTED

Hundreds of thousands attend the annual Gasparilla Festival in Tampa, Florida. My friend Alan, from Apple of His Eye Ministries, and I got together for this event, and we ate at a deli with Jewish people who were challenged by our T-shirts. We distributed hundreds of Gospel tracts and shared with many!

A *Tampa Tribune* reporter asked me questions and actually printed the following story:

> "Save Our Souls" - Describing himself as a Jewish Believer in Jesus, Steve Kaplan of Atlanta handed out pamphlets asking, "Do you know the Messiah?" Kaplan, 45, an ordained Baptist Minister [actually, I'm only licensed] said he has passed out such tracts at past Gasparillas, as well as at Mardi Gras in New Orleans and several Olympic Cities. Most people walked by without taking the pamphlets from Kaplan, who wore a white T-shirt emblazoned with the Star of David and the words, "Jesus Loves You." Others accepted a pamphlet, gave it a quick look and let it flutter to the ground. "The believers love that we are here," he said. "The non-believers say they hate Jesus, or Jesus doesn't love them."

My father once asked me if I was going to spend my whole life passing out pamphlets on street corners? Street evangelism is so fruitful especially when God multiplies your outreach by getting it highlighted in a newspaper. I never thought I would be doing street evangelism on a Saturday **and then showing my father the newspaper article on Sunday.**

DO HOMOSEXUALS GO TO HELL?

My friend Brenda, a Jewish believer, asked me to minister to her homosexual friend who had some Jewish roots. I had dinner with him and his friend (a homosexual college professor), and we ate at a restaurant where he knew the homosexual waiter. They asked lots of questions and gave me lots of opportunities to share. The waiter sat with us, too, (three for one, such a deal) and asked if I was a homosexual, and I told him I wasn't. He asked if all homosexuals go to hell, and I told him just the ones who reject Jesus!

THE REVEREND JESSE JACKSON

My friend Bill Adams with Sports Fan Outreach International invited me to his event at the Super Bowl. There were over 120 street preachers from all over the United States at our outreach retreat center. We had one of the ministry tables at the center and equipped people with T-shirts and tracts. We gave out thousands of tracts and challenged many!

The Reverend Jesse Jackson walked by with his entourage. I offered them Gospel tracts, but they didn't want them? I wanted to yell out, "Hey Jesse, it's me Hymie, from Hymie Town!" (Derogatory terms Jackson once used towards Jewish people), but that wouldn't have been Christ like. It is beyond my understanding how so called followers of the Jewish Messiah could be anti-Semitic?

My desire is to bless those who bless you,
but whoever curses you I will curse,
and in you all the families of the earth will be blessed.
-Genesis 12:3

PEPSI'S BIRTHPLACE

My friend Keith invited me to speak at his church in New Bern, North Carolina. Before the 500+ mile journey to the eastern shore of North Carolina, my friend from Augusta, Georgia, called. He attends a prayer meeting for Israel the first Wednesday of the month and invited me as I happened to be passing through at the time.

Along the way, I shared with Israelis at malls in Lithonia and Augusta, Georgia, and Columbia, South Carolina. When I gave an Israeli a Gospel tract about Moshiach, she yelled "Moshiach," grabbed my arm and made me dance and chant "Moshiach, Moshiach, Moshiach!" in the mall.

Stopping by Myrtle Beach, South Carolina, I distributed Gospel tracts in a *"Jesus Loves You"* Jewish Star T-shirt. Israelis own many of the stores there, and I went from store to store sharing with Israelis and anyone else who came across my path. There were so many Israelis in Myrtle Beach, they actually had a kosher restaurant for a while. I was able to go and show off my T-shirt! I had intended to stay there for three days, but had an overwhelming inkling to drive on to New Bern (Jewish population=100).

I prayed about where to eat in New Bern and the Lord sent me to IHOP. I overheard the couple at the next table and asked where in New York they were from. They were Jewish, laughed at my shirt, asked me why I believed and then invited me to their synagogue. At the synagogue, they wanted to know who I was and kept introducing me as a "Jew for Jesus." I shared with several people and was invited back!

The next day I rented a table at a Women's Expo I heard advertised on the radio. The vendors had give-away items, and I was one of the only vendors with bags. Many people came to me for free *"Jesus Loves You"* Jewish Star bags, and then walked around with them. We equipped several believers with *"Jesus Loves You"* T-shirts and Gospel tracts, and many Jewish people and others spoke to me about Jesus!

I spoke and had a ministry table at my friend's church, shared with 36 Awana children and equipped a team going to Honduras with Spanish *"Jesus Loves You"* T-shirts!

On the way home, I visited Era, an elderly widow who once mistakenly called me because she thought I was the Steven Kaplan who owned a local strip club. She actually called me twice, and I asked what she wanted the second time. It turned out she was trying to witness to Steven Kaplan the strip club owner about Jesus.

DON'T MISS AN OPPORTUNITY

While on an outreach in South Florida with Rock of Israel, we were supposed to go to the beach but it was too windy. We went to the Adventura Mall instead. We were able to share with Israelis working at kiosks. They actually had a Judaica store in the mall, so we walked in. The Jewish people working there said they liked our "Rock of Israel" T-shirts! I asked, "Do you like what's on the back?" I turned around and the T-shirt said, "Jesus is the Rock!" They were somewhat surprised.

As we left the Judaica store, there were some Orthodox men from the local Chabad asking people to wrap tefillin, the straps with little Scripture-filled boxes on them that devout Orthodox men wear when they pray. They consider it a mitzvah (good deed) to have Jewish people wrap Tefillin. They asked me, and I made sure to witness as they wrapped me up with the leather straps so that I looked very Orthodox.

I met a pastor and his wife who then gave me an opportunity to witness to a Jewish woman they had just met. When I ran into this same couple in the food court several minutes later, they asked about my conversation with the Jewish woman and invited me to share my testimony, which I did at their crowded table!

I asked if they wanted to receive the Rock of Israel newsletter, and they gave me a post office box number in Surfside, which is on Miami Beach. I told them my grandfather used to live in Surfside. They asked where, but I couldn't remember. I asked what street they lived on, and they said, "Hawthorne Avenue." I said, "That was the street he lived on!" They asked what the cross streets were, but I couldn't remember. I asked what their cross streets were and realized it was the same cross streets as my grandfather! They asked who my grandfather was, and it turned out that's who they bought their house from! He told me my grandfather held their mortgage for 15 years. I asked if they ever witnessed to him? The pastor put his hand on his forehead, looked down and apologized for not witnessing to my grandfather. Don't miss an opportunity!

GOD ANSWERS PRAYERS

During the Jews for Jesus "Behold Your God!" campaign in Montreal, Canada, we had a lot of opposition from an anti-missionary group called "Jews for Judaism." They followed us around and tried to intimidate us and distributed literature to people who took our Gospel tracts to try to counteract our message.

Jews for Judaism sometimes had someone distributing literature right behind where we were assigned. I did my best to walk up and down the street to position myself in a shady location while the anti-missionary would be forced to stand out in a sunny spot dressed in his woolen suit. Devious, yes, but I watched them squint and sweat, making them less effective. Scripture says:

> **"Behold, I am sending you out as sheep in the midst of wolves,**
> **so be wise as serpents and innocent as doves."**
> **-Matthew 10:16**

During the campaign we rented a hotel conference room and hosted a debate between Shmuley Boteach (Orthodox Rabbi I had been praying for ever since seeing him on Larry King Live) and Dr. Michael Brown (Jewish Believer Apologist with an awesome website: www.realmessiah.org). These two debate frequently, and I believe Dr. Brown clearly wins the debate every time. Many Scriptures and Talmudic passages are discussed, and the many non-believers who attend are challenged.

After the debate, I went up to Rabbi Shmuley's book table. Several people were hanging around, but I was the only obvious Jewish person. Rabbi Shmuley picked me out of the crowd and asked, "How could Jesus be the Messiah? He didn't fulfill all the Messianic prophecies!" I looked him right in the eye and said, "He fulfilled all the Messianic prophecies pertaining to His First Coming!" For a split second, I felt as though the light bulb went on in Shmuley's head.

Cyril Gordon and I were visiting Jewish people in the Beverly Hills area. As I drove up Rodeo Drive, Cyril said, "There's Larry King! I stopped the car, jumped out and ran over to him and the other obviously Jewish man he was with. Because we were going on visits, I was wearing a plain shirt. I told Larry King I had been praying for him for years and that I loved his show. Larry thanked me, and he and his friend each took Gospel tracts before I ran back to the car to move it out of the middle of the street. I had been praying for Larry King and Shmuley Boteach ever since I saw the debate with David Brickner.

JUST SHOW UP, LET GO & LET GOD

I went to Long Island for my nephew's Bar Mitzvah. I was alone in my hotel room watching Ben Hur, and there was a knock on the door. It was my two nephews, their cousin and their friend wanting to hide in my room from hotel security (Don't ask). All four of them are Jewish and they came in during the part of the movie when Jesus was being led to the cross. They asked me all kinds of questions. The next day, an Orthodox group invaded the hotel for Yom Kippur, and needless to say they, as well as people at airports in Long Island, Philadelphia, New York and Charlotte, were quite challenged by my Tshirt!

I KNOW YOU

During the Jews for Jesus "Behold Your God!" campaign in Miami, Florida, our team was assigned to pass out Gospel broadsides at a basketball game. As we walked over to the field, (From our downtown hotel which was literally within one block of my cousin's office) we found out there was no game that night. Instead, we met and shared with a Jewish homeless man. We asked where he was from, and he said, "Atlanta!" That's when I realized someone from my church had once brought him to my apartment for one of our Bible study fellowships! I believe the Lord really convicted him after that!

HELP POLICE

While distributing Gospel tracts with my friend Robert from Rock of Israel in Brookline (a Jewish area of Boston), an Orthodox Jewish man told me I tried to get him in trouble with the police in New York City. I didn't remember him until he started cursing me with the same words I remembered from a New York subway when I started shouting for the police. In training, they told us to shout, "I'm Jewish, and I believe in

Jesus, and I'm being persecuted for my faith! Someone call the police." if someone starts persecuting us.

HERE'S LOOKING AT YOU KID

While distributing Gospel tracts in a Boston subway, a Muslim vendor from Casablanca, Morocco, asked me for one. I watched (and prayed) as he read the tract. Later, I walked over and shared with him. He had grown up on a street with many Jewish people and was curious about what we were doing. He gave me his contact information, and I gave him a book to read, and he started reading it. Several minutes later, he walked over to me and prayed to receive Jesus.

I'M SO BORED

While distributing Gospel Tracts in front of a Boston train station early in the morning, I felt bored. I prayed that God would give me an open Jewish person to share with. A few minutes later, I noticed a man wearing a Jewish star standing near me. I asked him, "Who do you think Jesus is?" He said, "That's what I'm trying to figure out! I've been reading the Bible, and I'm up to the Book of Revelation. Can you explain it to me?" He let me share my testimony, answer many questions and take his contact information for follow-up. I kept in touch with him for many years, and he eventually came to faith.

GET OUT OF HERE

I volunteered to go with Robert Specter and his Rock of Israel ministry to the streets of New York City, primarily Brooklyn and Queens. While on the outreach, we stopped off in Crown Heights, which is the headquarters for the Chabad movement. We walked around the neighborhood wearing T-shirts with a big Jewish Star that said, *"Jesus is the Rock of Israel."*

Orthodox people were completely dumbfounded by our presence and insisted we leave their neighborhood. We walked into several stores, but the store owners didn't throw us out because they were hoping we would buy stuff, which we did!

As we walked past some kind of headquarters building, we were stopped by a Rabbi. He asked me to put on tefillin. I shared the love of Messiah with him as he put the tefillin on me, and a crowd formed around us. We found out later, someone had taken a picture of the Rabbi putting the tefillin on me. The picture ended up in the Chabad newspaper on-line with the heading: "Pic of the Day, Missionary Puts on Tefillin!" There I was, wrapping tefillin while wearing a "*Jesus is the Rock of Israel*" Jewish Star T-shirt for all the Chabad followers worldwide to see! Over 50 people wrote in with mostly negative comments. Several said they knew me from Atlanta! My prayer and heart's desire is that they would all know their Jewish Messiah.

GOD IS IN CONTROL

We were in New York City to finish the last Jews for Jesus "Behold Your God!" campaign outside of Israel. There were 60 similar outreaches in all, and I had participated in 25 of them. They recognized me for participating the most. During the New York event, I was on the team that focused primarily on the various Orthodox Jews and went to New Jersey, Westchester and Brooklyn as well as New York City. I encountered a lot of verbal abuse, and we actually had our tire slashed while stopped at a red light. Needless to say, we spent a lot of time escaping hostile situations and filing police reports. We shared with many people, and some did actually listen.

> *"...so My word will be that goes out from My mouth.*
> *It will not return to Me in vain,*
> *but will accomplish what I intend,*
> *and will succeed in what I sent it for."*
>
> *-Isaiah 55:11*

Afterwards, I sat on the plane going home completely exhausted. I was squished against the window with almost no room to move. The seat next to meet was empty until a 14 year-old-girl who weighed at least 200 pounds sat down next to me. Now I was even more squished, as I am a sizable man as well. I thought, *Lord, thank You that it is only a two-hour flight to Atlanta, but I just sacrificed five weeks of my life dealing with hostile Orthodox Jews!* Seconds later, there was an announcement over the intercom asking for Steven Kaplan to identify himself to the flight attendant! They upgraded me to First Class!

DO YOU KNOW MY BROTHER

While distributing Gospel broadsides in front of the Great Synagogue of Sydney, Australia during the Jews for Jesus "Behold Your God!" campaign, a Jewish man walked up to me. He was from New Zealand and wanted to know if I knew his brother. It turned out his brother is the world-famous evangelist, Ray Comfort. I tried sharing with the man, but he wasn't really interested. Later on, in 2009, Ray Comfort spoke at my church and thanked me for trying to share with his brother.

YOU ARE NOT WELCOME HERE

During the Jews for Jesus "Behold Your God!" campaign in Sao Paulo, Brazil, our team had been assigned to the neighborhood around the local Jewish Center. The Sao Paulo Jewish Center has 30,000 members and is one of the largest in the world. There are many swimming pools, dining halls, playgrounds, walkways, and so on. It is like a miniature city. There was practically no pedestrian traffic around the Jewish Center, but a whole city of Jewish people lived just a few feet away.

We went to the main entrance of the Jewish Center and prayed they would let us in. There were many guards, and we asked if we could have a tour, but no one seemed to be interested in helping us. A Jewish man and his family walked out of the Jewish Center, saw our T-shirts and burst out laughing. We asked him if he would like to give us a tour. Since he was leaving, he said "No," but signed us in as his guests and gave us his contact for follow-up.

The looks on people's faces as we walked around were priceless. We got into many conversations, and several Jewish people gave contact information for follow-up. After about 30 minutes, one man started yelling at us and told us he found our T-shirts offensive. I asked him why he was at the center on Shabbat. We just ignored him and hung out at the juice bar talking with people. The hostile man rallied a group of about eight and got security to talk to us.

As my teammates spoke with security, I spoke with the angry mob. I asked why they were all out on Shabbat, and one man answered it was because he wasn't that religious. I made sure to share the Gospel with all of them, and then our team was escorted to the front gate and asked to leave. I gave our security guard a Gospel tract as he walked us out. Praise God, we were able to be in there for about one hour!

The next day (Sunday, our day off), we went to a museum which happened to be hosting a Dead Sea Scrolls exhibit. Later that night, the Jewish man who signed us in as his guests picked some of us up, showed us around and we all went to dinner together where we shared Jesus with him.

While distributing Gospel broadsides, we stopped at a café where several young men were drinking at a table outside. While sharing with them, I noticed some men walking down the street wearing yarmulkes. I offered them Gospel broadsides, and one man took one. One of the young men at the table asked if I knew who that was, and, of course, I didn't. It was Henry Sopel, Brazil's head Rabbi, who is constantly on television and is pretty much the voice of Judaism for Brazil.

While distributing Gospel broadsides, I stopped to buy water and a man walked by. When I looked at him, the Holy Spirit told me he was Jewish, and I should talk to him. He was Jewish, spoke little English and I determined he wasn't a believer in Jesus. I got his contact information, gave him a decision card and called over my teammates who shared with him. Then he recited the prayer on the card. After that, I explained the responsibilities of being a follower of Jesus (my teammate translated) and he asked if we could recommend a Messianic Congregation.

AROUND THE WORLD

Since the JFJ BYG Melbourne, Australia campaign was the week before my friend Glen's wedding in Johannesburg, South Africa, I decided to literally fly around the world to attend both events. I flew from Atlanta to California to Australia to South Africa to England to Atlanta. What an adventure!

The JFJ BYG Melbourne, Australia campaign coincided with the Grand Prix, which attracted many people from all over Australia, Western Europe and other places. We distributed Gospel tracts on street corners and subway entrances, organized billboards, had "Psalm Reading" tables, radio interviews and evangelistic marches throughout the Orthodox neighborhood.

Our team of almost 30, distributed about 120,000 Gospel tracts, prayed with about 100 people to receive the Lord (including three Jews), received contact information from hundreds of other people (including Jews, Gentiles, believers and seekers) who wanted more information. We had conversations with hundreds of others while displaying our evangelistic T-shirts to hundreds of thousands.

Before going to Johannesburg, South Africa for Glen's wedding, I tried to find the nicest accommodations at the lowest price in Sandton (the area I stayed in before). Sandton is considered the financial capital of South Africa. I placed a bid for a room in Sandton on a website similar to

Priceline, and prayed God would put me where I needed to be! The Lord gave me a beautiful hotel at a great price that was also walking distance from the gym I used to work out at during my previous stay in South Africa.

The day after I arrived, I walked out of the hotel to go to the gym. I just stopped and looked at the apartment building across the street as it seemed familiar. I realized I had gone to visit a Jewish family there previously. The grandmother is a believer, but she wanted prayer and witnessing for her daughter who wasn't a believer, so we went there to minister to them. I also remembered praying for the daughter's son Stephen. I tried remembering her name, but couldn't and prayed God would give it to me.

I continued to the gym and purchased a membership for the week that I would be there. I worked out and went into the sauna. As I was about to leave the sauna, two young men walked in. One young man was wearing a Star of David necklace, so I immediately sat down and prayed for an opportunity to share.

As I began to witness to the two young men, the one with the Star of David told me his grandmother was Jewish and believed in Jesus. He told me his name was Stephen, and, of course, he turned out to be the one we had prayed for years ago. I told him how I had just passed his grandmother's apartment building and remembered praying for him and wanted so much to visit her again. Stephen gave me her name, telephone number and apartment number.

Glen is a Jewish believer. He asked me to wear a *"Jesus Loves You"* T-shirt to his wedding (that was definitely a first). The ceremony was attended by several of his Jewish friends and relatives, and I was asked to say a few words. I visited my friends' congregation and met with most of the leaders as well as several congregants for fellowship, Bible study, encouragement and evangelism.

I called several Jewish people I keep in touch with by e-mail and tried to set up meetings. I spoke to Richard, whom I met during the Cape Town outreach. He had told me he was coming to Johannesburg, so I invited him to my friends' wedding, and he was touched. Unfortunately, he wasn't coming to Johannesburg (to move his Jewish fiancée to Cape Town) until the day I was leaving.

The plumber I had witnessed to on the prior outreach invited me to synagogue and dinner with his family. His wife is a convert to Judaism, but claims to know Jesus and asked me to share my beliefs in front of their family!

I wore a *"Jesus Loves You"* T-shirt to the South African opening weekend of *The Fockers,* a comedy that attracted a Jewish crowd. I also wore it to malls, the gym and kosher restaurants. A woman told me I was bold for wearing my T-shirt to the kosher restaurant. She was Jewish, believed in Jesus but her family was Orthodox. I was thrown out of one store because someone complained about my Tshirt. I also wore it while distributing 1,500 Gospel tracts at the University, where I shared with many Jewish people. Some remembered me from 2001, including a Jewish lady and many Muslims. Several believers asked for prayer.

I tried to meet with two Jewish sisters who seemed to have fallen away from Jesus. Neither one came to our agreed upon meetings. My friend took me to a bakery, which we realized was right next door to where one of the fallen sisters worked. We went in to say "Hello," but she was on a lunch break. We waited for her, and as she walked up, she did a double-take when she saw us. She had renounced Jesus, married an Orthodox Jewish man and become Orthodox. She was shocked to see us but was friendly toward us.

Stephen's grandmother couldn't meet with me until right before I was leaving. I went to visit her and had a wonderful time. She introduced me to one of her Jewish neighbors who also believed in Jesus, and the neighbor told me she remembered taking a Gospel broadside from me while on vacation with her family in Cape Town during our Campaign there.I remembered meeting her, too. She couldn't really talk in front of her family as they are quite hostile to her beliefs.

The neighbor told me she had a Jewish friend in the building and asked if I wanted to meet her and share with her. Of course, I said "Yes." She said, "We have to hurry though because she is packing right now to move to Cape Town." Would you believe the lady busy packing turned out to be Richard's fiancée! When we arrived at her apartment, she was on the phone with Richard. I told her I knew Richard, and she gave me the phone. Needless to say, Richard and all of us were completely shocked.

T-SHIRTS IN MINISTRY

Because the *"Jesus Loves You"* T-shirts proved to be great evangelism tools, I tried to equip as many people as I could. I would go to Promise Keepers conferences as well as churches and local festivals and give them away for donations. We gave away many at the Sandy Springs Festival as well as the Southern Baptist Convention.

We had a booth at the "Taste of Alpharetta" north of Atlanta one year. I set everything up, and it began to rain. It poured and poured. We had a canopy, but it really wasn't waterproof. As I sat there getting wet and holding things from blowing away, *I wondered why I was there?*

The festival was only open from 4 to 11 PM. Around 8 PM, the weather let up a little, and a friend showed up to help. It was still raining, but there were people walking around. Hundreds of teenagers were out in the rain, and they were soaking wet. They discovered we were giving away dry T-shirts and started coming to our booth. They came in groups of three or four, and there was almost always a Jewish youth among them. We spent the rest of the night witnessing to dozens of Jewish youth and others who gladly came to get dry T-shirts. It was one of the most amazing outreaches we ever had.

The leadership at my church changed, and the majority of our church members left for other churches. This became challenging to our church Missions program, so my Missions pastor suggested I start a separate 501(c)(3) non-profit ministry. We were recognized by the IRS and officially started ministering through Jewish Outreach International on January 1, 2008. Although my church gave me the money to start this new organization, they no longer had the funds to help support it.

Once we started Jewish Outreach International, we also built a website: www.savethejews.org. We actually gave away free T-shirts on our website, and I figured we could do that until it got out of control.

Although I had been with Mount Vernon Baptist Church for over 10 years, I believed it was time to find a new church. I prayed about joining Johnson Ferry Baptist Church. I believe the Lord told me I could, but I would only be there for a short time. Two significant things happened while at Johnson

Ferry. I met an Israeli that I still minister to years later, and I had a witnessing opportunity that I often use as an example when people ask how to witness to Jewish people.

Johnson Ferry was having a sample sale to raise money for their youth. We had a table there with our *"Jesus Loves You"* T-shirts. One of the Jewish vendors cursed me out because of my T-shirts. The next day, another Jewish vendor walked over and asked, "Why do you believe this crap?" I could have quoted Scriptures, but prayed and told the vendor I used to have a drinking problem, but Jesus took the desire of alcohol away from me. The vendor confessed she just found out her daughter was an alcoholic and admitted that's what she was struggling with. I spent the next 30 minutes sharing about Jesus.

> ***"'Not by might, nor by power, but by my Ruach!'***
> ***says AdonaiTzva'ot."***
> ***-Zechariah 4:6b***

Thanks to the suggestion of Norman Hunt, Lee Veal's pastor, I was invited to give away T-shirts at the Bailey Smith Real Evangelism Conference at First Baptist Woodstock. Our tables were across from their World Impact Center. I couldn't help but notice the poster they had on the wall with the different countries where they minister. Because of my burden for Ireland, I looked at the information they had regarding it. The ministry was headed up by Steve Hyland who had an e-mail address from The Coca-Cola Company!

I thought, *I really need to meet this man!* I learned that he was friends with a friend of mine and knew all about my ministry from our mutual friend. He invited me to a prayer meeting one Wednesday night, and I came to his church (First Baptist Church of Woodstock) the following Sunday. That morning, he invited me to a prayer time led by Dr. Johnny Hunt, the pastor of First Baptist Woodstock, and he introduced me to the deacons and church staff at that meeting.

I had heard so many wonderful things about Woodstock over the years and had often thought about joining. Steve prayed with me that if it was God's will, that I would join. Dr. Hunt preached, "Be strong and be bold for the

Lord! Many Jewish people have given up a lot to follow Jesus." I knew God was speaking to me, and I joined First Baptist Woodstock on March 15, 2009.

Every now and then we would get T-shirt requests from people in the United States, and then we started getting requests from people in Russia. We would get more and more. I could tell by their postal codes (zip codes) it was from regions and cities all over Russia.

I looked on a map at the Baltic States: Estonia, Lithuania and Latvia, and wondered why we didn't receive requests from there. A month later, we started receiving requests from all three of these Baltic States.

More and more requests came from Russia. People told me they wanted shirts to wear to an Israeli consulate or to Jewish day schools in their area. Others told me they wanted to send T-shirts to relatives in Israel. Word of mouth about the free T-shirts spread like wildfire. Someone told me they started advertising the free T-shirts on a Christian television program that went all over Russia.

Unfortunately, the ministry was now in debt, and I was, too. I was using my credit cards to fund the free T-shirts. I didn't have the money to pay the mortgage. I had to take steps to get control of my finances. I stopped spending and put all my credit cards into a debt reduction program at a lower interest rate. I stopped giving away free T-shirts and started selling them at various conferences. I also applied for a loan modification on my mortgage.

Just as I was about to complete my loan modification on my mortgage, I discovered two of my roommates were smoking pot in and around the house in front of my Jewish neighbor I was trying to witness to. As much as I desperately needed their rent money, I had to honor God and ask them to leave.

This negated my loan modification because my income was lower, and I had to start all over. The bank holding my second mortgage didn't want to wait any longer because I was expected to modify the first mortgage before doing the second mortgage. The bank holding the second mortgage informed me they were going to just cancel the debt. Praise God!

When I started selling my T-shirts at various conferences, I also started buying other items to sell to help pay for the conference expenses. I began buying items at different trade shows, which opened up a whole new avenue of witnessing as many of the vendors and other buyers are Jewish.

I was stopped five times by Jewish people at the Atlanta Gift Show one year as they were curious about my *"Jesus Loves You"* T-shirt and wanted me to share my testimony. Another time at the Atlanta Gift show, I was stopped three times by Jewish people to have a picture taken of me in my *"Jesus Loves You"* T-shirt. They also wanted me to explain in front of all the onlookers.

I went to trade shows in Las Vegas that were so Jewish, they set up kosher eateries at the trade shows. I actually ran into a friend who is a Jewish believer. He was selling at that trade show, and his Israeli boss saw my *"Jesus Loves You"* T-shirt in the morning. When I stopped by their booth in the afternoon, his boss was most surprised his employee knew me, and we shared with him.

I also started buying Judaica from vendors in Israel, and have started to build relationships with several of them. There are two brothers in Tel Aviv that I buy from, but I had never met the one brother because he was always working somewhere else. I pray for both of them.

When I was leaving Israel one time, a man came up to me at the airport and asked if I had purchased something from his brother in Tel Aviv. His brother told him about a man buying items wearing a *"Jesus Loves You"* Jewish Star T-shirt. Of course, it was the brother I had been praying for and hadn't met. He told me he was actually at the wrong terminal and knew it was a divine appointment. I told him I had been praying for him, and he reluctantly took a tract.

I started selling our ministry items at various denominational, national and international conferences. What a blessing it is to equip hundreds and thousands of believers from literally all over the world with *"Jesus Loves You"* Jewish Star T-shirts and Gospel materials.

I contacted the Messianic Jewish Alliance of America (MJAA) about selling items at their conferences. My first contact with them was at their Southeast Regional Conference in Orlando, Florida, which has the strictest marketplace rules of all their conferences. The woman in charge of the market place told me, "No Jesus, No Christ, No Crosses!" I thought, "NO WAY!" God said, "YES WAY! YOU ARE GOING!"

"To the Jewish people I identified as a Jew, so that I might win over the Jewish people. To those under Torah I became like one under Torah (though not myself being under Torah), so that I might win over those under Torah."
-1 Corinthians 9:20

Different people minister in different ways, but we must all be obedient to what God calls us to do. I adjusted and started selling *"I Love Israel"* T-shirts and later added *"Yeshua Loves You," "I Love Yeshua"* and eventually *"Yeshua Loves You"* Jewish Star T-shirts in Hebrew letters.

One of the Messianic Rabbis bought a Hebrew T-shirt from me. Several months later, the Rabbi's wife called me to say her husband said the T-shirt was the best evangelistic T-shirt he had ever worn. Jewish people constantly came up to him and asked what it said, giving him opportunity to share. They and some of the other congregations in Florida have now ordered hundreds of the Hebrew T-shirts for their various outreaches.

One summer, I came home from the annual MJAA Messiah Conference near Harrisburg, Pennsylvania, and my car air-conditioning died. The car had well over 200,000 miles on it, but I didn't want to get a new car until all the debts were paid off. The debt was finally paid off. I prayed about buying a van so I could put the *"Jesus Loves You"* logo on it as well as our ministry contact information.

The Lord led me to a dealership not too far from my house. As I pulled up, there was a Black salesman outside waiting for the next customer! It turned out he was an Ethiopian Jewish pastor and praying to make a sale. I left the dealership that night with a new van and a loan for $30,000. I didn't want to go into debt again, but needed the van. I had the logos put on it, and have received numerous phone calls, talked to people looking at it in parking lots and have seen many people take pictures of it.

We had some fundraisers and really focused on paying off the van. Praise God, the entire van loan was retired in less than one year.

Initially, I would visit my parents in Florida and make T-shirts using their equipment. Eventually, one of our supporters donated enough money for us to buy a machine to make them in my garage. We paid some of the Jewish believers who had prayed with me to receive the Lord, to make T-shirts. As of the writing of this book, we have produced well over 35,000 evangelistic T-shirts in four languages that have gone out to at least 94 countries we are aware of. The following are but a few of the many responses we've received from around the world:

From Australia: "Hi, Steven. writing to thank you for the T-shirts. i have put them to use already. it sparked a discussion by itself with someone i walked by. i hope these shirts will assist in some way to glorify our Wonderful Saviour. Jesus is so lovely. i am just about to move into a house with some brothers in Jesus Christ. it has been so blessed so far. i hope to see the Holy Spirit burn through the neighborhood and Our Mighty King Glorified through us all being together in that place. Thanks again brother. 'Love your enemy'"

From a Belarus Orphanage: "One boy prayed to receive Jesus the day I gave him one of your shirts. He is Jewish, and from Uzbekistan. He came to the orphanage with no clothing whatsoever. That day, we left him with your shirt, a Bible and some money to let the orphanage get him some additional clothing...but most importantly, we introduced him to Jesus. He had only just arrived like two days prior to our visit. God is in the details for sure!!"

From a Bolivian Orphanage: "The boys loved the shirts. I wish you could have been there to see their faces and hear them when they asked if they could keep them forever. Most of them put them on right away. The older boys were all about to do their chores so they did not put them on because they did not want to get them dirty. We have a new little dwarf boy in the home. He is five and even though it was so big on him he wanted one. I put it on him and it looked like a dress. Everybody got a laugh out of it. He keeps saying over and over in Spanish "Is it mine? Can I keep it forever?" All the boys said to tell you, "Thank you very much." I gave the girls their T-shirts today and they were excited to be receiving a new shirt. I let them know who had sent them down and I had someone translate for me the meaning of the star... Thank you so much from all the girls. I also want to thank you for thinking of all these boys and girls and sending all those shirts down. I know that was not an easy task and I know you must have a big heart to do something like this. Thank you so much and God bless."

From the Dominican Republic: "We just got back from Santo Domingo, and the Jesus Loves You T-shirts were a blessing to the school children and the merchants, hotel manager, cleaning lady for our room, and the drivers that carry us back and forth to school. The materials you sent [were passed] out at the airport in Miami because our plane was delayed in D.R., so we missed our flight out from Miami, and American Airlines put us up at a hotel in Miami, and she gave out the materials at the airport and the hotel."

From England: Someone ordered a *"Jesus Loves You"* T-shirt from England because his wife saw someone wearing it on TV and then did a Google search to find us! Then she ordered one.

From Germany: "I wore your T-shirt for the first time yesterday. It did get looks from people."

From Budapest, Hungary: "We went on an outreach in Budapest, Hungary. We were stopped 9 times to have our *"Jesus Loves You"* T-shirts photographed!"

From a Mexican cruise: "We had a fantastic time on our Mexican cruise. Thanks to your T-shirts and hats we met a lot of believers on the ship. Gave a Hebrew tract to an Israeli woman and her Jewish Argentinian friend. [We] had two great conversations witnessing to [two] unsaved Russian Jews that live in LA. She is somewhat open and is meeting with someone for Bible studies once a week. I gave her David Hocking's "Who is the Messiah?" booklet. Please pray for them. Anyways while walking through Puerto Vallarta we met a believer who ... loved your hat and begged me for it. So I gave it to him. He runs a shop in the flea market by the ship. He asked me if I think that his Jewish customers will be angry with him and he will lose them as customers. I told him "Yes, he will lose some business," and he replied with, "I don't care - I'm going to wear it anyways.""

From Norway: "All of the shirts are gone, taken of Ywam Rovanemi Findland and some of Ywam Borgen! My sister is using hers whenever possible. she is one of the few Norwegians really trying to evangelise in any way possible! she was walking in Tromso, the biggest city in the north of Norway, and a woman came running over to her and was really happy that "someone" was making a statement like in the old times....it's kind of over in Norway to make a stand like this or in any kind of way, outside the churches... she was at a meeting and heard a woman called the Israeli embassy to find out where to get these clothes! There is a big need for this according to my sister, where she is living and doing, so she asked for more. Myself, I was at the doctor for pain in my chest with my shirt on, and she was looking really at "Jesus Loves You." in the end, she said I had to see a shrink and nothing was wrong in my chest! Didn't occur to me that seeing I was wearing this shirt, that made a lot of her decision. I do not know! Some have been asking, "Are you a Christian?" Shirts have been going to the base leader's mother and father-in-law... they are Finnish and travel to St. Peterburg to evangelise Jewish people in there! They have a congregation that are travelling with a bus often into Russia to evangelise..."

From Pakistan: "We have received the box. Many, many thanks for sending us these kind of T-shirts that have a message of unity and Jesus' love. We want to distribute among our youth by organizing a small Bible study seminar. Thanks for your nice cooperation. God bless you and your vision through T-shirts."

Glorious from Tanzania: "Our outreach team has made your T-shirts their outreach uniform."

A Ukrainian Pastor (who was in Atlanta for our church Missions conference) told me he saw a group of five people wearing *"Jesus*

Loves You" T-shirts sharing with Ultra-Orthodox Jews in Kiev, Ukraine!

From LA: We went to the Los Angeles Jewelry District in our *"Jesus Loves You"* T-shirts and distributed Gospel tracts and witnessed to many Jewish Jewelry vendors! A Jewish Man saw our T-shirts and approached us. He went on and on about how much he loved his Messianic Congregation. He never mentioned the Lord, but just how much he loved his congregation. I asked if he had ever asked Yeshua to forgive his sins and did he know for sure that Yeshua forgave him? He didn't know for sure and prayed to receive his Messiah! An Orthodox Jewish man ran after us and begged us to come to a prayer meeting because they needed us for a Minion (10 Jewish men are needed to pray)! We went and shared with everyone at the prayer meeting!

From California: "The Lord continues to use these precious T-shirts...even on children. Yesterday, a woman waved me down after we left Jamba Juice to ask me the meaning of the T-shirts. I shared the Good News."

From Colorado: "Shalom Steve, I am mailing out a check for you today for the additional T- shirt you sent. We did receive it, thank you very much. I will try to send an additional donation next month. The elder Rabbi that I wrote you about, Eliezer Urbach (he had the Russian ministry and food bank), passed away recently. On the 1st day of Sukkot, the Lord called him home. Today will be the first week to have the Russian service without him. I am so glad that you got the T-shirt to me in time because the day he wore it to service was only 3 days before he passed, and he was thrilled to have it and wear it that day. Thanks again and G*d Bless"

From Florida: "Hello Steven, ... I met you briefly at Promise Keepers in Sunrise, Florida. I have had a very ignorant opinion about Jews all of my life. I grew up in a suburb of Chicago in a very antiSemitic environment, then I moved to Florida and lived in a very heavy Jewish populated area of Ft. Lauderdale. My opinion never changed until I experienced complete brokenness about 2 years ago and was given salvation and grace by Jesus! In my hunger for the Word I have learned a lot about the Jews. Needless to say my thoughts are a lot different. I am learning every day. I have the pamphlet that you had given me. I have not made the opportunity to witness to a Jew yet, but I will work on it. I also must commend you. I respect what you are doing in your mission work. God bless you...PS Please send me a large T-shirt."

From Florida: "Just wanted to let you know, _____ and _____ wore the shirts (star of David with JESUS) to the University of Florida Thursday all day. They came back with story after story of what God did. They were rejoicing because they knew it would be real tough or real wonderful...and God would use it. Just wanted to encourage your heart...Come on down and go on campus sometime with them. Love in Christ."

From Florida: "I am so happy and excited with the arrival of your box at work. It was a message to everyone around me! When I showed them the contents, the message came out "JESUS LOVES YOU"! An Israeli non-believer thanked me for the Hebrew Bible inside, and she promised to read it!"

From Florida: "Thank you Steven. We were overwhelmed and could not stop rejoicing when your package came yesterday. It is such a blessing. We will use these tracts, and we will use every one of them. Thank you for the "T" shirts as well. They were totally unexpected. It is such confirmation. We want to win souls to the Lord and this will be a great help. The outreach "Festival of Ingathering" will be on Oct. 16 this Saturday, so your sending these to us is very timely. Please pray all that the Lord wants to do will come to pass on this day. Shalom, Love in Yeshua"

From Georgia: "I wore my shirt on Saturday to go running and to Kroger, and I did not get any pies in the face! God bless you, and thank you!"

From the Atlanta Airport: "Steve, I was standing behind 3 guys from Israel in the security line at the airport. One of them mentioned my shirt so I had an opportunity to witness to them. Praise GOD!!!!"

From Georgia: Someone said she bought a *"Jesus Loves You"* Tshirt at a thrift store for her son's mission trip to WV!

From Georgia: "I was thumbing through the pages of your website and saw the T-shirt offer. I'd like to order one. I am Rabbi of a growing congregation of Messianic believers. This would be a great tool to put out the message of Yeshua!"

From Georgia: "Steve, While driving up my street I saw neighborhood kids playing basketball. I waved at them and then did a quick double-take when I saw what I thought was a kid wearing a T-shirt with a Magen David. Of course I stopped and sure enough it was a Magen David that said *"Jesus Loves You"* in it. ... I asked him if he got it from Steve and he said yes and that he met you online. Anyway, he said he wears it to school and I could tell he was very proud of it. He was glad to hear that we know each other. Funny, huh. I loved it."

From Georgia: "Hi Steve! Sorry this took so long. You were speedy getting my T-shirt out to me and I was slow on the return. I love it and have already worn it to exercise class and received lots of comments. You remain in my prayers. Love in Y'Shua"

From Georgia: "If you could have only seen the faces of the children when the shirts were handed out. Thank you. God Bless you, my brother. Director of Family Services."

From Georgia: "Steven...we met at Lion of Judah MC / Macon Ga ... The reason I'm writing you is that for the first time ever as I was coming out a restaurant this pm after synagogue this young gentleman came up to me as I was getting into my car and said "Can I buy your shirt?" I said, excuse me? You see I've just never had anyone say that to me or even ask me that before. I was

257

wearing one of your T-shirts. So I asked him why he liked it and he said he liked the message and the 6-point star on it. He asked me where I got it. Anyway, had I had another shirt with me (any shirt at all) I would have just given him the one I had on and left knowing that I had spread the Gospel if you will. So...how much would it cost me to buy maybe 5 shirts and have them shipped over to me via USPS? I guess firstly I should ask do you even ship them? If this is going to become a part of my ministry then I suppose I ought to have a few shirts in the car, apparently. One never knows when someone is going to want to wear the Good News. You just never know how G-d is going to use the simplest things, do you? If so let me know. I guess what I'd want are 5 large shirts either white on blue or blue on white, it don't matter. Thanks."

From Milledgeville, Georgia. "[A friend] told me she had worn one of your *"Jesus Loves You"* T-shirts to a thrift store, and while she was there, the local prison brought in a group of prisoners to go shopping. [My friend] said one of the prisoners turned out to be Jewish and she was able to share with him!"

From Indiana: "A woman had gone to a conference in Seattle, Washington, and was able to share with many people along the way both flying out to Seattle and coming back home to Indiana. She gave out several of the *"Jesus Loves You"* T-shirts to people from all around the United States but was most excited to be able to give a *"Jesus Loves You"* T-shirt to a woman from American Samoa!"

From Massachusetts: "I prayed for a divine appointment, and a girl with a Jewish grandparent at Autozone asked about my shirt. Why the star of David with Jesus Loves You? I said Jesus came for the lost sheep of Israel, He/disciples were Jewish and Scripture told of Him coming. I gave her your tract."

From Missouri: "The St. Patrick's Day outreach was FUN; as usual! My most memorable story of the day was talking to a group of three guys and girl who were all about my age. Let me introduce you: [One] was pretty drunk and so was [a second one]. The conversation started because I overheard [them] begin to make fun of their friend ____ because he was Jewish. Obviously they were doing this because I was walking by in the "Jesus Loves You" Star of David T-shirt. I stopped and asked them what they thought about Jesus. [One] said he had never really thought about it and for sure he had never thought about the connection between Jesus and being Jewish. [Another] said life was [x#x%] and so was religion so party while you can! [The first one] said he grew up Catholic and used to kind of be interested in religion, but the older he got the less it seemed to relate to his life so he pretty much gave up going to church or anything. At this point the guys kind of started making gross comments, so I was like, you know what, if they are going to be like that I am going to move on to people who aren't drunk and who do want to listen. So I just said "Well it was nice to meet you guys, thanks for answering my question. You guys be careful today," and started to walk away. But [one of them] said "Hey wait! You asked us our opinion, but we didn't hear yours." The other guys joined in "Yeah, can you explain to us why you even are asking that question, because you could be here partying too so if it is important enough for you to ask, we want to know what you think." I wanted to make sure they REALLY were going to listen so I said "You guys really want to hear what I think?" ;-) They said they really wanted to hear. So I gave the gospel short and sweet with a little bit of a Jewish flair for [the Jewish guy] and a little bit of a Catholic flair for the other guys.

Right at this point one of their girlfriends came up and she said she also grew up Catholic. She said the point of Jesus was to show us how to be good people. She had an interesting story to illustrate this. She said "Remember the story about the feeding of the 5,000? Well, come on, who really goes on a day trip and doesn't bring anything to eat? I think those people really had packed food for themselves but they were too lazy or selfish to get it out during meal time. They wanted to see if they were going to be provided a free meal. But since Jesus was such a good person and a good communicator, He convinced the people to eat the food that they brought along. Thus, Jesus brings out the best in us.

Before I could even respond to what she said, [the Jewish guy], who had heard the Gospel for the first time 5 seconds earlier, said "Or, it could be that Jesus was the Son of God and preformed a miracle." OUT OF THE MOUTHS OF BABES! I am not saying that he fully understands or believes, but he sure was open! I am PRAYING!!!"

More from Missouri: "We were in Wal Mart yesterday picking up some stuff for my Grandpa. [My brother] was wearing his Jesus Loves You Star of David T-shirt. The woman checking us out said "Jesus loves you??? I have never heard that before! Are you Jewish? Because I am, that's why I ask." [My brother] shared with her all on his own! I was very proud of him."

From Missouri: "We went to a Jewish mall. I walked the mall wearing a Jesus Loves You T-shirt. A woman was selling Dead Sea products. She pointed to my shirt. She is from Israel. She told me Jesus walked on the Sea of Galilee. I asked her how she knew that. She said it was something she learned to help sell. I gave her the Gospel. Her co-worker came to talk. He was OPEN and wanted to hear the Gospel and has been researching different religions. He asked many questions and soaked in the answers from Scripture. I asked if I gave him a Bible, would he read it. He was excited and had tears in his eyes as I gave it to him! He said he will read it. I'm praying his Israeli roommate will also. I asked [the Israeli] how she will recognize Messiah. She said she'll know. I asked if she reads Tenach; it speaks of how to recognize Messiah. She didn't seem interested, but was a little curious. I gave her tracts dealing with Messianic claims. She was receptive to taking them. MANY people saw our shirts and discussed among themselves. We got many comments, too! The shirts ARE a witness!"

More from Missouri: "I wanted to tell you, do you remember the _____ family? I believe they have 9 kids in their family. Anyway I work with [the dad]. A few weeks ago we had a work picnic. I was surprised when his clan arrived wearing the Jesus Loves You T-shirts! Some of my family were there and recognized the shirts because they saw you wear it. I [said] that you designed them and the [family] got the shirts from you! It's a small world! My entire company and family members and retirees and even the Mayor of Chesterfield all saw your witness wear! You never know how God will use you and the shirts!"

From Nevada: "We recently returned to the mall—what a great day it was! On this particular day, I wore a shirt that said, "Jesus loves you" inside a Star of David. God used this shirt to open many conversations, and it made me wonder why I'm not wearing this shirt more often—especially in malls. I will in the future. I had great conversations with three young Israelis, and shared the Gospel."

From Nevada: "A friend says she wears her *"Jesus Loves You"* Tshirt to clean her Jewish non-believing boss's house."

A man from Nevada writes: "I had a run-in at a restaurant w/ a very large Jewish man over the Star of David shirt I was wearing. He was very angry and offended at the message that "Jesus Loves You." He made a commotion and many people heard his frantic argument that Jewish people don't believe in Jesus. I was able to share the Good News of Yeshua with him. He tried to make the Gentile managers understand why he was upset at my shirt. I'm sure it must have seemed to be a funny snapshot. Here is this not-yet-saved Jewish man explaining to 2 goyim that Jews do not believe in Jesus and they just want him to quiet down! It was like a scene out of a Woody Allen movie, where Woody just had to get his point across no matter what was happening around him. Anyway, this Jewish man has yet to meet me he keeps putting it off. But he did say he was sorry for coming across so rough! I forgave him, but will not let him off the hook in getting together with him. Thanks and God bless."

From Nevada: "I wanted to tell you I had an awesome day at the UNLV campus. I had many great conversations. I spoke with a Jewish girl who is very open. She walked up to me as I was wearing your T-shirt and cap. After campus I stopped quickly at Trader Joes. A woman walked up to me to tell me that she loved my shirt and where did I get it. She is a Jewish believer whose entire family is saved! Blessings."

More from Nevada: "I headed over to an art fair in Summerlin which has a large Jewish population. I decided to call my friend to see if she could meet us. She lives next to the art fair and is a Jewish unbeliever that I have been praying for [over] a long time. Anyways when I called her she had just left the fair to walk home and said that she was just thinking about me as a man in a white T-shirt with a Star of David just walked by her. I said "That is so funny as he is my friend from Atlanta that I am going to meet.""

From New York: "We have a young friend, (9th grader), who is a fabulous witness in the local high school. I gave him one of your shirts because I knew he would use/wear it. Yesterday he told me that last year he wore your shirt every day he had chorus because the chorus teacher was Jewish and he was trying to get her attention. The family is involved in 4H and spends a week in August at the county fair showing animals and participating in activities. His stepsister told me that some man at the fair offered him $50.00 for his, (YOUR), shirt. He refused to sell it!!! PTL."

From Ohio: "I wore Steve Kaplan's sweatshirt, and a Jewish girl loved it and thanked me for wearing it. She just gave her heart to Jesus a year ago. THANKS!!!!! Jesus is our JOY!"

From Ohio: "I wore your *"Jesus Loves You"* shirt on casual Friday. Management received one complaint about the shirt out of dozens of people. Don't worry; my job is not in jeopardy and there was no disciplinary action. I don't want you to feel discouragement about this. Jesus is bigger than the problem!!"

From Oregon: "How about a testimony? We met one guy who already had one of your shirts and we asked him where he got it. He replied that he bought it at the Good Will in Portland, about a year and a half ago, just after our last visit to the area! Someone must have donated it after not wanting to wear it anymore, but God made sure that the shirt got back into play!"

From Pennsylvania: "At PANERA bread by University of Pittsburgh, the person who made my meal asked, "What is Jews for Jesus? We were talking about them this morning." I answered, "Why were you talking about Jews for Jesus?" She said she was Jewish and her friend was Christian and it "just came up." I guess she figured I knew something in a Jesus Loves You Star of David shirt. I shared dad's testimony (Orthodox Jew coming to faith) and Messianic Scriptures. Panera had no customers, so there were several minutes of uninterrupted witness!"

More from Pennsylvania: "I just thought I'd check in and let you know that today was the first chance I had to wear the T-shirt. I wore it to school and was approached by many students and teachers. I had the opportunity to attest to my faith more than 30 times today! I'm not sure if any of them were Jewish, but regardless, if I helped nudge ANYBODY just a little closer to salvation, Jewish or not, I am very happy. And I tell you now, I am thrilled. It could not have gone better. Thank You and Best Wishes."

From Pennsylvania: "One lady in her 40s was pushing a baby stroller with twins in it (her children) and she said, "YOU'VE GOTTA BE KIDDIN' ME!!" It started a good conversation. She was raised Orthodox and left it during college, married late, had twins after age 40 and she said, "Just last night I was wondering if we missed it and if He really IS the Messiah? and now I see you here with this shirt! What can you tell me that will show me that He IS our Messiah?" So I took out my ministry card, and wrote down Psalm 22, Isaiah 53, Daniel 9:26, Zechariah 12:10 and gave her a 3 minute synopsis of the verses and why those verses point to Him. As she left me, she said, "When I get the twins in bed for their nap I will get my Tanakh down and read these!" That's just ONE story I could tell you about what happened while wearing that shirt!"

More from Pennsylvania: "I wore a Jesus Loves You T-shirt to a Beth Moore Bible Study and the ladies really liked it. It gave opportunity to tell about the need to share the gospel with Jews."

From Texas: "THE LORD BLESSED ME AT THE CHRISTIANS UNITED FOR ISRAEL MEETINGS IN WASHINGTON DC - ALL THE JEWISH PEOPLE I MET TOOK THE WORD OF GOD. I WORE THE JESUS LOVES YOU T-SHIRT AT THE BURGER KING AND A DEAR YOUNG FELLOW CALLED ACROSS THE ROOM - "I LIKE YOUR T-SHIRT". - I LOOKED AT HIM AND SAID, ARE YOU JEWISH" AND HE SAID YES, I HUGGED HIM AND HIS TWO FRIENDS - HIS NAME IS ... AND I GAVE GOSPEL TRACTS. THEY THANKED ME AND WERE SO SWEET. PSALM 122:6"

From Washington: "THANK YOU once again for your STAR of DAVID shirt with JESUS LOVES YOU. It is the best witnessing shirt that I have ever had!!! First, it is a "SILENT WITNESS" to everyone that can read ENGLISH & tells them that "JESUS LOVES THEM" which is something everybody needs to know!!! The great thing is that it is on the front and the back so more people get to read it!!! The STAR of DAVID is a witness about ISRAEL!!! Many people have made positive comments about the shirt as I stood in line 1 day, the man behind me told me that he was a JEW. TODAH RABAH for thinking of such a neat way to witness and making it available!!!"

From Washington: "I was in church and [a man] from Israel spoke about his life. I am grateful for people who go to nations full-

264

hearted and strong for God to share the message of a wonderful loving God. He shared with our congregation the Jesus loves you T-shirts, and I might not have money to fly everywhere and share God's Word and love, but I would love to wear a shirt that expresses Jesus' love and my faith in God."

From Washington, DC: "We the Divine Exchange Ministry, Inc. (DEMI) Women of Exchange would like to once again thank you for your great support in the giving of the T-shirts and your prayers for the Retreat Experience. The women were tremendously blessed and the power of God delivered healing to the abused, disadvantaged and under-served women. Steven, this was the very first time in the District of Columbia that a retreat of this concept was ever presented and we are so grateful to the Father. Fifteen women received Christ!"

We are called to proclaim Jesus (Yeshua) and trust God for the results. An Arab man from the West Bank became a Christian. Someone gave him one of our *"Yeshua Loves You"* Jewish Star T-shirts. He wore that T-shirt to a pro-Israel rally in New York City and held up a sign saying, "I am a Palestinian Christian who loves Israel!" His picture was on various news websites, Israeli television and in the *Jerusalem Post.* Numerous friends contacted me from Israel to tell me they saw the T-shirt. Millions of people probably saw this man's powerful proclamation as well as our T-shirt telling them Yeshua loves them!

POSTSCRIPT

Green Velvet

I was Bar Mitzvahed in a green velvet suit. My only sibling who married had bridesmaids wearing green velvet dresses at his wedding. My sister combined both events with her green velvet gag-gift. God gave me a green velvet couch to teach me about Jesus and the shedding of His blood for the atonement of sin.

God had me pray for a green velvet bow and answered that prayer with a poster of Scarlett O'Hara wearing a dress with green velvet bows on it. God used that same poster to show me his promise of a job at The Coca-Cola Company had been fulfilled, and then confirmed it with a video of Scarlett in that same dress with the green velvet bows on it.

In my life, green velvet represents the blood Jesus shed to atone for the sin of the world. Amazingly, I worked right across the street from the Margaret Mitchell House where *Gone With The Wind* was written. In the movie *Gone With The Wind*, green velvet curtains were made into a dress for sinful Scarlett to wear to the jail to visit Rhett, and you might say she chose death. Will you choose life or will you choose death?

Get Out Of The Boat

Do you know what the hardest part about outreach is? It's actually doing it! How can you walk on water if you never get out of the boat? If you do get out of the boat but take your eyes off Messiah, you will drown! Get out of the boat, keep your eyes focused on Messiah and you will walk on water!!!

No one knows the exact number of Jewish people in the world. Many debate about even who is Jewish. The world Jewish population is estimated at about 14 million. There are about 6 or 7 million in Israel and 6 million in the United States, close to 500,000 in France, about 400,000 in Canada and 300,000 in the

United Kingdom, with close to 200,000 each in Russia and Argentina, followed by 100,000 each in Germany, Australia and Brazil.

Jews are coming to faith in Jesus all over the world. Messianic congregations are popping up all over. There are thought to be over 500 Messianic congregations in the United States and over 100 in Israel. It is thought there are over 300,000 Jewish believers worldwide, although it's impossible to know for sure.

My advice to those wishing to spread the Gospel message but wondering how to get started it this: Get out of the boat and be a PAL!

Pray-for opportunities to share and for the people you are sharing with

Available-Be in the right place at the right time and be available to share your testimony and to answer questions. (Dr. Michael L. Brown wrote a series of books on *Answering Jewish Objections to Jesus* (Ada, MI: Baker Books, a division of Baker Publishing Group). Jews for Jesus, Rock of Israel, Christian Jew Foundation, Jewish Voice Ministries and Chosen People Ministries International are some organizations that will train you and take you out to share with people.

Love-Be a true friend to the people you are sharing with. Show them love and respect.

Do you know how many times I wanted to quit? Do you know what a struggle it is to depend solely on God for your money? I remember being at a Good Friday service and crying out to the Lord for finances. I told the Lord I would be more than happy to work a temporary job, but deep down I knew the Lord wanted me ministering full time. As I got ready to drive off, I adjusted the rear view mirror and it fell off. I went back into the church office to see if I could find some glue and happened to glance at my ministry mailbox. Inside the mailbox was an envelope containing $3,000 from an anonymous donor! I was absolutely dumbfounded and knew God was providing for all my needs and I only needed to trust Him!

Imagine watching David Brickner debate Shmuley Boteach on Larry King Live. I prayed for both Larry and Shmuley. In my wildest dreams did I ever think I would get to witness to both of them in person? I got to witness to Larry King while driving down Rodeo Drive in Beverly Hills and Shmuley Boteach during a Jews for Jesus campaign in Montreal, Canada. Keep your eyes on Messiah and you will walk on water.

It is my hope that this book inspires you to get out of the boat and reach out to the Jew first and also to Gentiles. If you keep your eyes on Messiah, you will walk on water.

SUPPORT US

Please pray for our ministry.

If you would like to receive our monthly prayer newsletter by e-mail, sign-up on our website:

www.savethejews.org/newsletters

If you would like to support us financially, donations can be made through our website, www.savethejews.org/donations, or you can mail donations to:

**Jewish Outreach International
P.O. Box 720375
Atlanta, GA 30328**

Download: InSpire U App
and unlock free resources

Available July 2020

(Available on both Google Play and Apple Store)

Let us know you've read this book

What you'll find:
Witnessing Pamphlets
Workshop Training Guidebook
Daily Inspirationals
and more...

ABOUT THE AUTHOR

Steven Barry Kaplan is an extraordinary man.

As a Messianic Jew, he's dedicated the past 25 years of his life to witnessing to Jews, conducting mission trips world-wide.vAlthough he is now a Jewish believer in Yeshua, (Jesus)...he wasn't always.

He'll tell you he came to faith because of the witnessing of a Gentile co-worker, that he's been healed of alcoholism, bitterness, anger, unforgiveness and the love of money.
He is passionate about his love of Christ, and lives his passion. He shares his passion, and his stories through presentations world-wide.

His primary ministry and outreach is conducted as President and founder of **Jewish Outreach International, a 50I (c) 3 organization,** organized to provide support and Gospel materials to other Jewish evangelists world-wide.

He leads mission trips, and is welcomed as a featured speaker world-wide. Contact him for your next event, if you're seeking to motivate your audience and bring change to this world.

His education and background is diversified. He is:
- A Licensed Southern Baptist Minister, *(Certified by the North American Mission Board of the Southern Baptist Convention as an Interfaith Evangelism Specialist on Judaism),*
- Holds a diploma from the Bible Training Centre for Pastors. -Bachelor of Arts Degree from the University of Miami active in the Sigma Phi Epsilon Fraternity.
- Holds a diploma in computer technology from New York University

You can contact him at: https://SaveTheJews.org
Read more at https://SaveTheJews.org.

ABOUT THE PUBLISHER

Founded in 2014, by Diane K. Bell, Legacy Lane Publishing focuses on helping new and emerging writers. Ideal clients are heart-centered Christian- principled authors with a God-driven message.

Don't get caught in the self-publishing maze. Take advantage of professional guidance, and marketing expertise. Our clients delight in becoming #1 Best Selling Authors, and learning today's most effective book marketing techniques.

For more information contact:
https://LegacyLanePublishing.com
Phone: 303-242-4461